Trade Issues in the Caribbean

CARIBBEAN STUDIES

A series of books edited by Roberta Marx Delson, Humanities Department, US Merchant Marine Academy, Kingspoint, New York 11024-1699, USA

Editorial Board

Laennec Hurbon, Centre National de la Recherche Scientifique, Paris, France; *Frank Moya Pons*, Fondo para el Avance de las Ciencias Sociales, Santo Domingo, Dominican Republic; *J. Edward Greene*, Institute of Social and Economic Research, University of the West Indies, Kingston, Jamaica; *Betty Sedoc-Dahlberg*, Center for Latin American Studies, University of Florida, Gainesville, USA

TRADE ISSUES
IN THE CARIBBEAN

Edited by

Irma Tirado de Alonso
Florida International University
Miami, USA

Gordon and Breach
Philadelphia • Reading • Paris • Montreux • Tokyo • Melbourne

Gordon and Breach Science Publishers

5301 Tacony Street, Drawer 330
Philadelphia, Pennsylvania 19137
United States of America

Post Office Box 161
1820 Montreux 2
Switzerland

Post Office Box 90
Reading, Berkshire RG1 8JL
United Kingdom

3-14-9, Okubo
Shinjuku-ku, Tokyo 169
Japan

58, rue Lhomond
75005 Paris
France

Private Bag 8
Camberwell, Victoria 3124
Australia

"Trade Flows and Economic Integration among the LDCs of the Caribbean Basin" by Francisco Thoumi originally appeared in *Social and Economic Studies* 38:2 (1989). It is reprinted here with the permission of the Institute of Social and Economic Research.

"Economic Policy, Free Zones and Export Assembly Manufacturing in the Dominican Republic" by Francisco Thoumi is reprinted from *Small Country Development and International Labor Flows: Experiences in the Caribbean*, Anthony P. Maingot, ed., 1991, by permission of Westview Press, Boulder, Colorado.

Library of Congress Cataloging-in-Publication Data

Trade issues in the Caribbean / edited by Irma Tirado de Alonso.
     p.   cm. -- (Caribbean studies : v. 7)
    Includes index.
    ISBN 2-88124-550-1. -- ISBN 2-88124-555-2 (pbk.)
    1. Caribbean Area--Commerce. 2. Exports--Caribbean Area.
3. Caribbean Area--Economic policy.   I. Tirado de Alonso, Irma.
II. Series.
HF3312.3.T7   1992
382'.09729--dc20

92-15396
CIP

CONTENTS

INTRODUCTION TO THE SERIES

The purpose of this series is to provide a forum in which the major themes and trends affecting the entire Caribbean region will be explored in depth. Thus, while the island-specific approach is not eschewed, the aim is to develop perspectives on problem-solving in the area as an entirety, both on the local level and in the international context. Hence the emphasis is on the qualitative and quantitative interpretation of the economic and political culture in which the modern Caribbean operates. Historical, demographical and sociological issues, when relevant to the central focus of the series, will also be examined.

Caribbean Studies publishes the research of academic scholars working within the region, as well as Caribbeanists working internationally. Simultaneously, it is hoped that the volumes function as a reference data source for libraries, foundations and government agencies with an interest in the Caribbean, either exclusively or peripherally.

It is the editors' hope that the series will increase comprehensive Caribbean studies internationally, and will similarly stimulate innovative research and development of methodology suitable to comparative perspectives. Only when the Caribbean is evaluated in its broadest panorama can the true global importance of the region be appreciated.

ACKNOWLEDGEMENTS

The preparation of the manuscript for this book was facilitated by a grant I received from the National Science Foundation (Grant No. INT-8512276) to study the trade of manufactured goods in the Caribbean Basin. Through many seminars sponsored by the Institutes of Economic and Social Research of the Caribbean Basin (IESCARIBE), I had the opportunity to thoroughly familiarize myself with the Caribbean Basin and to cooperate and share knowledge with many economists engaged in the research of international trade in the area.

A number of colleagues provided me with valuable experience. I am very grateful to both Dr. Jorge Salazar-Carrillo and Dr. Raul Moncarz for their encouragement while they were respectively chairmen of the Department of Economics at Florida International University. Secondly, I want to recognize the contributions made to this volume by Dr. Francisco Thoumi and thank him for his recommendation to contact Dr. Gregory Schoepfle at the US Department of Labor. Dr. Schoepfle was very supportive in making time to contribute two chapters to this volume, one in collaboration with Dr. Jorge F. Pérez-López and one with Dr. Joseph Pelzman. Dr. Angel Ruiz and Dr. Juan Castañer, my ex-colleagues at the University of Puerto Rico, were also very cooperative in adding Puerto Rico's trade experience to the book. I likewise received valuable and constructive comments from Dr. David R. Hicks of Auburn University during the preparation of this book.

I am grateful to Dr. Suphan Andic for all of her encouragement. I started this publication while she was a visiting professor in the Department of Economics at FIU, and she provided me with all the assistance I needed to advance this venture.

I am particularly indebted to Dr. Roberta Delson, editor of the Caribbean Studies series, who was instrumental in the publication of this volume.

I am thankful for the services I received from some of my students at FIU, in particular Yuna Chen, Jose Lacal, Ima Pazos, Kim Riley and Bernadette West. Last, but not least, I am grateful to Ivan, Kevin and Nadeshka for giving me the motivation needed to complete this undertaking.

Irma T. de Alonso

CONTRIBUTORS

IRMA T. DE ALONSO is an associate professor and graduate program coordinator in the Department of Economics, Florida International University, Miami. Dr. Alonso received her PhD degree (1969) from the University of York, England, and her MA (1965) and BA (1963) degrees from the University of Puerto Rico.

JUAN A. CASTAÑER is the area director for export promotion at the Puerto Rico Economic Development Administration. Mr. Castañer received his BA degree (1973) in economics from the University of Puerto Rico and his MA degree (1977) in economics from the New School for Social Research in New York.

JOSEPH PELZMAN is a professor of economics at George Washington University, Washington, DC, where he has taught since 1980. Dr. Pelzman earned his BA (1971) and PhD (1976) degrees in economics from Boston College.

JORGE F. PÉREZ-LÓPEZ has been the director of the Office of International Economic Affairs in the Bureau of International Labor since January 1987. Dr. Pérez-López earned his PhD (1974) and MA (1972) degrees in economics from the State University of New York at Albany. His BA (1968) in economics is from State University of New York at Buffalo.

ANGEL L. RUIZ is a professor of economics at the University of Puerto Rico, Rio Piedras Campus, and a consultant to the Puerto Rico Planning Board, Office of the Governor. Dr. Ruiz graduated with a BA degree (1959) from the University of Puerto Rico and earned his MA (1962) at the University of California, Berkeley. He earned his PhD in economics from the University of Wales, Aberystwyth.

GREGORY K. SCHOEPFLE has been the director of Foreign Economic Research in the Office of International Economic Affairs, US Department of Labor, Washington, DC, since 1984. Dr. Schoepfle graduated with a BA degree (1966) from Oberlin College. His MS (1968) and PhD (1969) degrees in economics were earned at Purdue University.

FRANCISCO THOUMI is a research associate with the United Nations Research Institute for Social Development in Geneva. He holds a BA degree (1962) from the Universidad de los Andes in Colombia and a PhD degree (1973) in economics from the University of Minnesota.

TABLES

GRAPHS

PART 1

Introduction

CHAPTER 1

Trade Trends in the Caribbean

Irma T. de Alonso

Sir W. Arthur Lewis, the only Caribbean economist to date to receive the Nobel Prize, expressed in his prize winning acceptance speech that the more developed countries (MDCs) affect the growth of the less developed countries (LDCs) via their trade relationships.[1] When the MDCs experience economic growth, they increase imports from the LDCs which helps the LDCs to achieve economic growth via export growth. The question he posed in the speech was what happens if the rate of growth in the MDCs is decreased, and as a result the rate at which MDCs import from the LDCs is reduced as well. Given that eventuality, his recommendation was for the LDCs to trade among themselves in order to compensate for the decreased demand from the MDCs.

The purpose of this book is to explore the existing trade relations of the Caribbean islands. What products do they trade? With whom do they trade? In what ways has their industrialization efforts changed their patterns of trade? Are they able to trade among themselves, as suggested by Lewis?

The Caribbean islands are small heterogeneous nations in terms of cultural, political, social, and economic features. They differ in land mass, population, and output, as Table 1.1 manifests. By their colonial heritage they speak different languages, they are very diverse ethnically, and have independent political systems. Each nation has a distinct currency, each expressed differently in terms of the U.S. dollar.

Nevertheless, they share some similarities, as well. They are all small trading nations, highly dependent on foreign trade for subsistence. All the nations are predominantly agricultural, and their main exports are primary products. They also have a common industrialization strategy, which has consisted of attracting foreign investment by way of offering tax holidays

3

Table 1.1. The Caribbean: Area, Population and Per Capita GDP, 1989

Country	Area Sq.Km.	Population (000)	Per Capita GDP (U.S.$)
Anguilla	91	8.0	2,413
Antigua & Barbuda	442	82.4	2,570
Aruba	193	60.9	10,100
Bahamas	13,942	247.2	8,562
Barbados	431	253.8	5,250
Bermuda	54	58.6	18,000
British Virgin Islands	153	12.1	7,260
Cayman Islands	260	25.9	14,954
Cuba	114,478	10,587.0	2,272
Dominica	248	81.3	1,162
Dominican Republic	48,442	6,900.0	759
Grenada	344	99.2	1,295
Guadeloupe	1,705	339.7	4,396
Haiti	27,749	5,700.0	355
Jamaica	10,962	2,484.0	1,348
Martinique	1,110	330.0	5,970
Montserrat	102	11.9	4,500
Netherland Antilles	800	176.0	6,390
Puerto Rico	8,897	3,297.0	4,600
St.Kitts-Nevis	269	43.4	2,027
St. Lucia	616	143.0	1,370
St. Vincent & the Grenadines	386	104.9	1,000
Trinidad & Tobago	5,128	1,279.9	3,099
Turks & Caicos Islands	430	13.0	3,300
U.S. Virgin Islands	342	109.1	19,030

Source: Caribbean/Central American Action, C/CAA's 1990 Caribbean and Central American Databook.

and allowing the repatriation of profits, among other subsidies and incentives.

The Caribbean represents an important geopolitical area which has attracted the attention of developed nations. The mother countries have often extended various favorable investment and export incentives. A case in point are the agreements under the Lomé Convention, which offers duty free entry to the European Economic Community (EEC) for products originating in their ex-African, Pacific and Caribbean (ACP) colonies. The

United States through the Caribbean Basin Economic Recovery Act
(CBERA), better known as the Caribbean Basin Initiative (CBI), also offers duty free treatment to a series of products from the area. Canada,
although not possessing territories in the Caribbean, is also proposing export incentives to English Speaking Caribbean countries through the instruments of CARIBCAN.

The first part of the book serves to introduce the reader to the prevalent
conditions of trade in the Caribbean. Chapter 2 analyzes the structure of
trade in the Caribbean Basin. With that intention, the chapter explores the
value, the rate of growth, the origin, the destination, and the composition
of the imports and exports of the countries of the Caribbean Basin. The
result is that trade is an important component of economic activity in the
region, where the volume of trade (exports plus imports of goods and
services) as a proportion of the Gross Domestic Product is in the vicinity
of 60 percent, although in some countries it can be much higher. With few
exceptions, the rate of growth of trade has decreased in the decade of the
1980s as compared to the 1970s, mainly as a response to the difficult
external debt situation faced by most of the countries of the area. Most of
the foreign trade takes place with the United States and with the countries
of the European Community. A negligible fraction of trade takes place
among the Caribbean islands themselves, and when it does happen, it
occurs among countries which have been linked by integration
mechanisms. Most of the goods exported by Caribbean countries are
primary goods (some agricultural products, and some mining products),
while their principal imports consists of capital goods and raw materials.

Chapter 3 analyzes trade flows and economic integration among the
LDCs of the Caribbean Basin. A gravity equation is utilized to analyze the
pattern of Caribbean Basin trade flows. The equation is used to explore the
structure of trade and to identify some of its characteristics. The equation
is applied to four categories of trade: total, total except fuels, manufactures, and natural resource based products except fuels. The estimation is
for the decade of the 1970s, when trade demonstrated significant growth
rates, and it was undertaken for three years: 1971, 1975, and 1979.
Bilateral exports of the Caribbean Basin show many empty cells, indicating non-existent trade relations among countries. Trade is more active
among the integration schemes in the zone: the Caribbean Common
Market (CARICOM) and the Central American Common Market
(CACM). The smaller countries tend to have very weak linkages with
other countries, particularly outside their common markets. The larger
countries in the Basin, like Colombia and Mexico appear to export to the
Basin, but to import very little while Venezuela has a different perfor-

mance since it has imported from most of the countries of the Caribbean Basin.

One of the important characteristics of intra-Basin trade is that it has been determined more by total income of the exporting country than of the total income of the importing country. In general, bigger countries have succeeded in exporting more than smaller countries, generating a bilateral surpluses and deficits pattern, which has diminished the promotion of economic integration. Another important determinant of trade is distance. It appears that decreasing the distance between countries through improved communications and transportation systems could be one of the best ways of promoting integration in the region.

Part 2 of the book is devoted to examining industrialization and trade in the Caribbean. The experience of the following six countries is considered: the Dominican Republic and Haiti, which share the Island of Hispaniola, in Chapter 4; Barbados, Jamaica, and Trinidad & Tobago, representing the English Speaking Caribbean, in Chapter 5; and Puerto Rico in Chapter 6.

The Dominican Republic and Haiti have followed different industrialization strategies. Both nations have attracted foreign investment by offering generous tax holidays and by offering high ceilings of profit repatriation, along other incentives and subsidies. Both countries have banked on assembly operations to strengthen their export of manufactures. However, the Dominican Republic has maintained a predominant import substitution strategy, while Haiti has tended to promote exports of manufactures. This feature is reflected in their composition of exports: while in the Dominican Republic, the share of manufactured goods constitute 25 percent of the total, in Haiti the share is a strong 85 percent.

In the Dominican Republic, there is a dual manufacturing sector: one geared to the production for the local market, and another for exports, located in tax free zones. The inward development of the industrial sector was mainly the result of the approval of the Industrial Incentive Law in 1968, which was instrumental in the production of consumer goods which were previously imported. In order to discourage imports, high tariffs were imposed on imported consumer goods, while exemptions were provided for imports of raw material, intermediate goods, and capital goods. The local manufacturing sector thus became capital intensive, and relied heavily on imported inputs. On many counts the sector has been found inefficient.

In Haiti, most of the manufacturing activity, which consists mainly of assembly operations, is destined for export. With the low level of income prevailing in Haiti, the inward orientation of manufacturing activity did not succeed. In contrast to the Dominican Republic, there are no free trade zones in Haiti, but industrial estate facilities are offered. These are devoted to assembly operations.

Both the Dominican Republic and Haiti participate in trading arrangements with the United States, such as the provisions of the Generalized System of Preferences (GSP), the United States Tariff Scheme (USTS), previous sections 806.30 and 807, the CBERA, the Multifiber Arrangement (MFA), and the sugar quotas. As such there is a high concentration of trading partners: the United States is the main one, with the European Community, which also offer some additional provisions, as a distant second.

The purpose of Chapter 5 is to determine the trade experience of manufactured goods of three of the most developed countries of the CARICOM, namely, Barbados, Jamaica, and Trinidad & Tobago. These three are the largest exporters of manufactured goods within the CARICOM.

The principal feature of the development of the manufacturing sector in the English Speaking Caribbean was the encouragement of foreign investment to carry out production for both local and export markets. Industrial production was targeted at domestic and regional markets in response to the conditions of import substitution created by each country and by integration arrangements. Incentives were provided in terms of high tariff protective barriers, duty free import of raw material and of intermediate and capital goods, tax holidays, and liberal profit repatriation, among other government inducements.

Despite the incentives offered, the manufacturing sector is relatively small in the English Speaking countries: less than 10 percent of GDP in Barbados, and the same in Trinidad & Tobago, with the highest of 16 percent corresponding to Jamaica. The sector is composed of two parts: one segment producing for the local market, and another characterized as operating in enclave-type free zones, intended for assembling component parts of goods, which are re-exported back to the United States. Industrial production of food and agricultural output has been the dominant activity for these countries. For exports, assembly of electronic components and textiles and apparel have been the major activities.

The English Speaking Caribbean countries have been able to increase their exports of manufactured goods, but at high concentration levels. Barbados has concentrated in the export of electronic components, Jamaica in miscellaneous manufactures, and Trinidad & Tobago in the export of chemicals. Their structure of imports show heavy reliance on industrial supplies and capital goods; plus food and other consumer goods. This structure reflects the constraint faced by these nations in their objective to reduce their dependence on imported goods.

There is also a high concentration in the trading partners. The U.S. is the main partner, regarding exports and imports, followed distantly by the EEC and Canada. Some trade takes place among the CARICOM countries, but it is mainly among the MDCs.

The purpose of Chapter 6 is to analyze the impact on the Puerto Rican economy of its exports of merchandise to the Caribbean, using input-output analysis. Puerto Rico has commercial links with the countries of the Caribbean through the twin-plant scheme and "936" financing. The twin-plant concept has been developed by the Government of Puerto Rico, as production-sharing mechanisms with other Caribbean countries. The "936" financing refers to the U.S. Internal Tax Revenue Code Section 936 by which profits from U.S. subsidiaries located in Puerto Rico can avoid U.S. taxes provided that those profits are deposited in Puerto Rican banks. The Government Development Bank then lends part of those funds to eligible Caribbean countries to finance manufacturing activities, at subsidized rates.

Puerto Rico's external sector is concentrated in the production and export of goods destined mainly to the United States, of which 88.9 percent of total exports are destined to the U.S. Intra-Caribbean trade is insignificant as a proportion of total exports, and it comprises only 4.7 percent of total exports. It has been found that Puerto Rico's main trading partner in the Caribbean is the Dominican Republic, to whom Puerto Rico sends 40.8 percent of its intra-Caribbean exports. With respect to Puerto Rican imports from the region, it has been shown that 41 percent enters under the CBERA, and roughly half of these correspond to products from the pharmaceutical industry. There is a close correspondence between imports from the Caribbean and twin-plant operations.

Manufactures are Puerto Rico's main exports, but the composition is different, depending on the country of destination. Exports to the U.S. are characterized by capital-intensive and technology-intensive types of manufactures, like pharmaceuticals and chemicals. However, the exports to the Caribbean, and to the Dominican Republic in particular, are characterized by labor-intensive manufacture, like textiles and apparel, electrical machinery, and agricultural products. Thus, trade with the Caribbean provides greater employment and output effects for Puerto Rico, per dollar of exports, than trade with the U.S. This is an important finding to take into consideration when promoting intra-regional trade.

Part 3 of the book considers export assembly manufacturing in the Caribbean: Chapter 7 is concerned with this topic in general and Chapter 8 presents the specific case of the Dominican Republic. The Dominican Republic is a leading assembly location in the Caribbean.

Export processing zones (EPZs) has emerged as a result of the dual need of developing countries of increasing export earnings and the need of manufacturers in developed countries to reduce their costs of production. The Caribbean, with a demand for foreign exchange earnings, its proximity to the U.S., and cheaper labor costs than in the U.S., has offered an ideal location for U.S. manufacturers. The U.S. government, as well, has offered incentives for the evolution of these EPZs.

The U.S. government through the Generalized System of Preferences (GSP) and the CBERA offers duty free entry to specific products manufactured in the area. In addition, reduced duties are offered through the United States Tariff Scheme (USTS), previous section 807, which assesses duty only on the worth done abroad when domestic components are shipped abroad for assembly and then re-entered in U.S. The extended 807 program also grants special access to the U.S. market for textile and apparel assembled imports that use American fabrics that are cut in the U.S.

The countries of the Caribbean compete with each other in attracting foreign investment by offering incentives. These incentives range from duty free import of capital goods and components used in the assembly operations, in addition to tax holidays, exclusion from local and consumer taxes, subsidized rental space, infrastructure improvements, and allowance of profit repatriation, among others. The main inducement, however, is the labor cost differential, as average hour labor costs, which at the most, fluctuates from about one-half to one-third of the cost for similar work performed in the U.S.

In the Caribbean most of the EPZs are characterized by their proximity to urban areas, or near to international ports and/or airports. Most of these export oriented facilities consist primarily of assembly plants. The broad majority assemble apparel products and, to a lesser extent, electronic products. The export assembly operations have been one of the most dynamic sectors in these nations, in terms of their rate of growth of exports to the U.S. Assembly operations in developing countries tend to employ primarily unskilled or semi-skilled production workers. The labor force of assembly operations is comprised predominantly by women, within the 16-25 age range.

Assembled products from the Caribbean destined to the U.S. constituted 18 percent of all Caribbean Basin exports to that country in 1987. In cases like Haiti, St. Lucia, Antigua, and Montserrat, assembled products accounted for 50 percent or more of exports to the U.S., for the same year. As such, the exports of assembled products are a significant source of foreign earnings for developing countries.

Assembly operations also generate indirect employment from the purchase of local inputs, the so-called backward linkages, and from local expenditures by assembly workers, through the macroeconomic or multi-plier effects. However, in some cases these assembly operations have replaced other products, such as sugar, in particular, which generates higher local value-added activities, and have greater influence within the local economy.

Chapter 8, which unfolds the development of export assembly opera-tions in the Dominican Republic, concludes that in spite of the recent success, the subsector development has been limited by financial, institu-tional, legal, and infrastructural constraints, and more generally by a lack of an effective promotion policy by the government.

In the last few years, assembly manufacturing in the Dominican Republic has become more attractive than in the past. In particular, the political instability in Haiti, the U.S. limits on apparel imports from the Far East, and increases in labor cost in that area, have conspired to affect producers to choose the Dominican Republic as an alternative location. In addition to the incentives provided by the U.S. government, the wage costs in this nation have fallen substantially relative to alternative Caribbean markets, due to fluctuations in the exchange rate.

The last section of the book analyzes the special economic relations between the U.S. and the Caribbean. In particular, Chapter 9 questions the need to continue U.S. trade preferences and development assistance to the region. The U.S. has two trade programs, the basic policy objective being that of providing the necessary stimulus for growth and development through the promotion of exports of manufactured products from develop-ing countries. The first is the Generalized System of Preferences (GSP), which has been extended to most developing areas, and the second is the Caribbean Basin Economic Recovery Act (CBERA), which applies only to the Caribbean Basin.

The GSP applies to approximately 4,000 products, subject to certain rules-of-origin, from 140 developing countries. It has been modified on various occasions, but the main constraints for a country to be excluded from the preferential treatment are: (1) if the value of the exports exceed an absolute dollar value limit; (2) if it accounts for 50 percent or more of the value of U.S. imports; and (3) if the country has graduated from the program. At the inception of the program, the exclusion was based on a product graduation scheme, and then it was modified to encompass a country graduation scheme. A given country with a per capita GNP in excess of a certain specified amount, for a period of two years, is no longer eligible to receive preferential treatment. Overall, the preferential treat-ment of GSP-eligible products has provided a small number of more ad-vanced beneficiary developing countries (BDC), primarily in Asia, (the so-called new industrialized countries (NICs): South Korea, Hong Kong,

Taiwan, and Singapore) gaining the majority of the economic trade advantages of the GSP program. Following the modifications in 1988 the four NICs were removed from GSP beneficiary status.

Although the countries of the Caribbean Basin are eligible to the GSP, few countries in the area account for most of the benefits, in particular Mexico and the Dominican Republic. In order to provide additional benefits to the area, the CBERA provided the elimination of U.S. import duties on most products imported, with certain exceptions, from those countries designated as beneficiary countries. To be eligible, products must meet certain rules of origin requirements. In many aspects the two programs are similar, but the main differences are, first, that the list of products under CBERA is wider than under GSP, and, second, that there is no graduation from CBERA, so that the U.S. market is assured.

The evaluations undertaken for the benefits of the CBERA indicate that there has been a change in the export commodity structure for the countries of the Caribbean. By 1986, U.S. imports of agricultural products exceeded those of crude and refined petroleum, and by 1989 U.S. imports of apparel had become the major item imported from the region. However, the short-term impact of the CBERA on products eligible for CBERA, not including the GSP, has been limited and has tended to favor few of the beneficiaries: the Dominican Republic, Haiti, and Jamaica, in the Caribbean, plus the Bahamas, and Costa Rica, Honduras, and Guatemala in Central America.

Why are only some countries receiving the benefits of the preferential treatment? The authors conclude that the degree of utilization of the programs depends in large part on the stage of development of the beneficiary's economy. The countries of the Caribbean Basin reflect the lower phase of development in that manufacturing production is concentrated in some basic classifications, like food products and miscellaneous manufactures, rather than the wider manufactures classifications. There is also concentration on both exports and imports; in which exports are dominated by agricultural products, while imports are dominated by machinery, transportation equipment, and other manufactures. At the same time the area is not characterized by an industrial labor force.

Overall the less-advanced BDCs in the Americas have concentrated on a narrower set of products than NICs or the resulting average for all LDCs. This leads into the hypothesis that any advantages afforded by the preferences offered by the GSP and CBERA programs have not substantially improved the trade or development prospects for many of the less-advanced BDCs in the Americas and the Caribbean. In addition, their domestic infrastructure, the structure of domestic output and trade are not sufficiently developed and diversified enough to attract direct foreign investment from the more-advanced LDCs in Asia.

The questions to pose are: 1) is there a need for U.S preference programs to be left as they currently are or should they be modified?, and 2) how should they be modified? The authors are of the opinion that it is in the interest of the less-advanced economies of the Americas and the Caribbean to encourage the gradual elimination of preferences to the most-advanced LDCs. The U.S. should begin to examine which most-advanced developing country exports have proven to be successful in the U.S. market, thus requiring no further differential treatment. The graduation should be used to move industries up the development ladder and out of preferential programs, once competitiveness has been achieved.

It is evident from this volume that the countries of the Caribbean have a long way to go before they can start trading among themselves, as suggested by Lewis. There is a basic need of infrastructure, training of workers, and the establishment of internal markets before they can succeed at increased integration. In the interim the U.S. and other developed countries are offering some incentives which may help these countries develop their manufacturing structure. But if the benefits are going to accrue to all nations, then the incentives cannot be uniform, but rather would have to be based on the need of those which are least-developed among the beneficiary developing countries.

NOTES

1. W. Arthur Lewis, "The Slowing Down of the Engine of Growth," *American Economic Review*, Vol. 70, No. 4, (1980), pp. 555-564.

CHAPTER 2

The Structure of Trade in the Caribbean Basin

Irma T. de Alonso

1. INTRODUCTION

This chapter contains a detailed analysis of trade within the Caribbean Basin in recent years. With that intention, the value, rates of growth, origin, destination, and composition of imports and exports of the area will be examined. The sources of information for the analysis have been statistics from the Interamerican Development Bank[1] and the United Nations.[2]

The Caribbean Basin is a composite entity within which several homogeneous zones, based on geography, culture, and/or language, are easily distinguished. For purposes of this study, fourteen countries, representative of the Caribbean Basin and members of the Interamerican Development Bank, have been divided into the following four regions:

Region 1: Central America: Costa Rica, El Salvador, Guatemala, Honduras, Nicaragua, and Panama

Region 2: Dominican Republic and Haiti

Region 3: Barbados, Jamaica and Trinidad-Tobago, representing the English Speaking Caribbean

Region 4: Colombia, Mexico, and Venezuela

The rest of the countries of the Caribbean Basin, not included in this study for lack of analogous statistical data, comprises many islands of varying sizes. Among them, the following can be mentioned: Cuba, Puerto Rico, The Bahamas, Netherlands Antilles, Martinique, Guadeloupe, U.S.

Virgin Islands, British Virgin Islands, St. Christopher-Nevis, St. Lucia, Dominica, and many other smaller islands.

The countries of the Caribbean Basin possess unsuspected strength. By 1987 the population of the four regions under study was about 175 million people, who generated a Gross Domestic Product of approximately $380 billion, and a per capita income close to $1,900 in real 1986 dollars (Table 2.1). In population and output these nations exceeded one single country in South America, namely Brazil, which in 1987 had a population of 141 million and a GDP of $343 billion.[3]

The population of the fourteen countries was divided as follows: seventy-five percent resided in Region 4 of the mainland nations of Colombia, Mexico, and Venezuela; fifteen percent in Region 1 of Central America; seven percent in Region 2 of the Dominican Republic and Haiti; and the remaining two percent in Region 3 representing the English Speaking Caribbean. Colombia, Mexico, and Venezuela accounted for nearly 85 percent of the total regional GDP, Central America had nearly ten percent, while the remaining five percent was divided into Regions 2 and 3. In 1987 per capita GDP varied from a low of $300 in Haiti to a high of $4,108 in Venezuela (Table 2.1).

2. VALUE AND RELATIVE IMPORTANCE OF TOTAL TRADE

Figures for GDP, and exports and imports of goods and services by country, in real 1986 dollars, for 1970, 1980, and 1987 are shown in Table 2.2. The volume of international trade, measured by exports plus imports of goods and services, grew less rapidly between 1970 and 1980 than the regional GDP. While trade increased by an annual rate of 4.21 percent, GDP grew at an annual rate of 5.72 percent. From 1980 to 1987, however, the rates of growth decreased substantially. While GDP grew at 1.07 percent, the volume of exports and imports of goods and services increased slightly by an average annual rate of 0.30 percent.

The volume of trade as a proportion of GDP reflects the importance of international trade in an economy. This trade depends on the economic size of the country and the nature of its industries. For the region as a whole, the ratio between the volume of trade and total GDP grew from 0.62 in 1970 to 0.68 in 1980, and then, by 1987, it decreased to 0.61. This was the result of deliberate efforts to lower the value of imports in order to improve the deteriorating situation of their trade balance as well as their critical external debt condition.

The ratio of total trade to GDP increased for all nations from 1970 to 1980 except for Honduras in Region 1 and Venezuela in Region 4. By 1987 it is found that the ratio had decreased in comparison to both 1970

Table 2.1. Characteristics of the Countries of the Caribbean Basin, 1987

Country	Population (thousands)	% of Region	% of Total	GDP (Million 1986 dollars)*	% of Region	% of Total	Per Capita GDP (1986 dollars)*
Region 1:							
Costa Rica	23,613	11.8	15.3	34,188	16.4	9.1	2,011
El Salvador	2,791	21.0	1.6	5,611	13.0	1.5	900
Guatemala	4,934	35.7	2.8	4,440	33.9	1.2	1,376
Honduras	8,434	19.8	4.8	11,604	10.7	3.1	782
Nicaragua	4,679	14.8	2.7	3,657	9.0	1.0	879
Panama	3,501	9.6	2.0	3,079	17.0	0.8	2,549
	2,274		1.3	5,797		1.5	
Region 2:							
Dominican Republic	12,863	52.2	7.4	11,252	83.6	3.0	1,401
Haiti	6,716	47.8	3.9	9,408	16.4	2.5	300
	6,147		3.5	1,844		0.5	
Region 3:							
Barbados	3,805	7.1	2.2	8,345	11.4	2.2	3,532
Jamaica	270	62.8	0.2	954	48.8	0.3	1,704
Trinidad-Tobago	2,391	30.1	1.4	4,073	39.8	1.1	2,900
	1,144		0.7	3,318		0.9	
Region 4:							
Colombia	131,253	22.8	75.2	323,627	14.6	85.7	1,581
Mexico	29,942	63.3	17.2	47,342	62.2	12.5	2,423
Venezuela	83,039	13.9	47.6	201,244	23.2	53.3	4,107
	18,272		10.5	75,041		19.9	
Totals	174,534		100.0	377,412	100.0	100.0	

Source: Interamerican Development Bank, Economic and Social Progress in Latin America, 1988 Report.
*Preliminary estimates.

Table 2.2. GDP and Import and Exports of Goods and Services, by Country, 1970, 1980, 1987 (million 1986 dollars)

Country	GDP			Exports			Imports		
	1970	1980	1987	1970	1980	1987	1970	1980	1987
Region 1:									
Costa Rica	2,932	5,075	5,611	1,002	1,771	2,421	1,161	2,097	2,170
El Salvador	3,437	4,723	4,440	732	1,203	892	803	1,261	991
Guatemala	6,911	11,978	11,604	1,334	2,510	1,584	1,131	1,701	1,128
Honduras	1,905	3,243	3,657	762	1,216	1,339	801	1,355	1,201
Nicaragua	2,849	2,950	3,079	650	715	487	636	1,277	870
Panama	2,784	4,759	5,797	1,058	2,084	2,269	1,152	1,820	1,683
Region 2:									
Dominican Republic	4,050	7,917	9,408	698	1,527	1,513	994	2,363	2,174
Haiti	1,221	1,941	1,844	199	521	437	217	792	653
Region 3:									
Barbados	783	922	954	441	646	546	665	664	481
Jamaica	4,102	3,788	4,073	1,367	1,343	1,923	1,539	1,440	2,168
Trinidad-Tobago	2,644	4,420	3,318	1,131	1,349	1,060	1,102	3,829	2,707
Region 4:									
Colombia	22,329	38,179	47,342	3,343	6,132	8,136	3,890	7,342	7,210
Mexico	99,049	187,689	201,244	9,014	20,093	35,849	8,678	24,317	13,965
Venezuela	48,627	72,850	75,041	31,121	19,968	23,313	6,964	17,893	12,783
Totals	200,839	350,434	377,412	55,852	61,078	81,769	29,733	68,185	50,184

Source: Ibid.

Table 2.3. Ratio of Exports and Imports of Goods and Services to GDP, by Country, 1970, 1980, 1987

Country	1970	1980	1987
Region 1:			
Costa Rica	0.74	0.76	0.82
El Salvador	0.45	0.52	0.42
Guatemala	0.36	0.35	0.23
Honduras	0.82	0.79	0.69
Nicaragua	0.45	0.68	0.44
Panama	0.79	0.82	0.68
Region 2:			
Dominican Republic	0.42	0.49	0.39
Haiti	0.34	0.68	0.59
Region 3:			
Barbados	1.41	1.42	1.08
Jamaica	0.71	0.73	1.00
Trinidad-Tobago	0.84	1.17	1.14
Region 4:			
Colombia	0.32	0.35	0.32
Mexico	0.18	0.24	0.25
Venezuela	0.78	0.52	0.48

Source: Table 2.2.

and 1980, except in the following few cases: Costa Rica, Jamaica, and Mexico. In the larger countries, international trade represents a smaller proportion of GDP than in smaller ones. This is due in part because they have a sizeable domestic market, and larger factor endowment. For Colombia, Mexico, and Venezuela the ratio was around 0.25, while for Barbados, Jamaica, and Trinidad-Tobago, which are small open economies, it was above 1.00 in many instances (Table 2.3).

The growth rates of exports and imports for the period 1975-1985 are given in Table 2.4. Rates in excess of 5 percent for exports are found in half of the fourteen countries: Costa Rica, Guatemala, Honduras, Haiti, Barbados, Colombia, and Mexico. The cases of Costa Rica, Honduras, Barbados, and Mexico, have been remarkable, not only because of their high value, but also because it has exceeded the rate of growth of imports.

Table 2.4. Caribbean Basin: External Trade Indicators, 1985

	Growth Rates (1975–85)		Ratio of Exports to		Balance of Trade
	Imports	Exports	Imports	GDP	(mill U.S.$)
Region 1:					
Costa Rica	4.7	7.2	90.1	22.0	−109
El Salvador	4.9	2.8	70.7	12.1	−282
Guatemala	4.8	5.5	90.7	9.6	−109
Honduras	8.2	10.3	87.6	23.2	−110
Nicaragua	na	na	na	na	na
Panama	4.5	0.5	na	21.8	−1082
Region 2:					
Dominican Republic	4.9	−1.6	59.2	na	−509
Haiti	12.0	7.9	39.4	9.0	−268
Region 3:					
Barbados	10.9	14.9	57.9	28.6	−255
Jamaica	−0.1	−3.1	50.8	na	−546
Trinidad-Tobago	0.3	1.9	140.3	28.9	616
Region 4:					
Colombia	10.7	9.3	86.0	12.0	−579
Mexico	7.9	22.0	155.7	na	na
Venezuela	2.5	3.2	165.4	24.6	4854

Source: U.N. International Trade Statistics Yearbook, 1986.

*na = not available.

The ratio of exports of goods to imports of goods show that the three oil producing nations of the Basin (Trinidad-Tobago, Mexico, and Venezuela) had ratios in excess of 100 percent. They were also the only nations with positive trade balances. The rest of the nations had varying ratios, depending on whether their exports consist of the assembly of imported materials or they export mainly agricultural products and other goods based on natural resources. The lowest value was found in Haiti, while the highest values were found in the Central American nations. The ratio of exports to GDP show that in six of the fourteen nations (Costa Rica, Honduras, Panama, Barbados, Trinidad-Tobago, and Venezuela) about one-fifth of the output is exported. Haiti and Guatemala exported less than 10 percent of their GDP (Table 2.4).

Table 2.5. Distribution of Total Exports and Imports by Region 1985

Regions	Imports		Exports	
	Value (mill U.S.$)	Pctg. Dist.	Value (mill U.S.$)	Pctg. Dist.
Region 1: Central America and Panama	6,341	13%	4,160	7%
Region 2: Dominican Republic and Haiti	1,689	3	924	2
Region 3: Barbados, Jamaica and Trinidad-Tobago	3,240	6	2,977	5
Region 4: Colombia, Mexico and Venezuela	25,564	51	40,876	70
Region 5: Other Caribbean Islands	13,672	27	9,603	16
Total	50,505	100	58,540	100

Source: Ibid.

*Puerto Rico is excluded.

3. EXPORTS AND IMPORTS BY REGION

The total value of exports of the Caribbean nations, in 1985, was approximately $58.5 billion, whereas the total value of imports was $50.5 billion. The percentage distribution of total exports and total imports by region is presented in Table 2.5. It should be noted that most of the exports (70%) came from Region 4 of the continental nations. The region "rest of the Caribbean," comprised by all the other Caribbean islands, had an important share (16%) led by Cuba and the Bahamas.[4] The Dominican Republic and Haiti exported a minor 2 percent, while Barbados, Jamaica, and Trinidad-Tobago exported 5 percent, notwithstanding the oil exports from Trinidad-Tobago. The countries comprising Region 1 (Central America) had a higher proportion (7%) than the CARICOM, due mainly to trade within the region.

In 1985, Colombia, Mexico, and Venezuela were the area's main importers (50.6%), with the rest of the Caribbean islands occupying second place (27.1%). Central America and Panama imported much more than the other two regions, 12.6 percent as compared to 3.3 percent by the Dominican Republic and Haiti, and 6.4 percent by Barbados, Jamaica, and Trinidad-Tobago.

4. DESTINATION OF EXPORTS AND SOURCES OF IMPORTS

Most of the Caribbean nations export mainly to the United States and Europe. In 1985, an average of 48 percent of the region's exports were destined to the USA, and 23 percent to Europe. Only about 4 percent was traded with another Caribbean nations, with the exception of the three countries representing the CARICOM (Table 2.6).

Honduras, the Dominican Republic, Haiti, Barbados, Trinidad-Tobago, and Mexico sent more than half of their exports to the United States in 1985; however, Europe was the main destination for Nicaraguan and Colombian exports. The Central American nations traded more among themselves than was the case among the more developed countries of the English Speaking Caribbean comprising the Caribbean Community (CARICOM). Few of the exports were sent either to Canada or to the countries of Latin America. The only exception has been Jamaica where Canadian firms extract and ship bauxite to Canada.

In 1985 the USA was the main source of imports, with the few exceptions of Nicaragua and the Dominican Republic (Table 2.7). Europe supplied more than one-fifth of the imports of Nicaragua, Trinidad-Tobago, Colombia, and Venezuela, while the countries of South America provided more than one-fifth in the cases of Costa Rica, Nicaragua, Panama, the Dominican Republic, and Colombia. The rest of the Caribbean islands were relatively important suppliers to Haiti, Barbados, and Jamaica.

Utilizing data published by the Interamerican Development Bank in their 1984 Report,[5] it is possible to analyze the trade of these Caribbean Basin nations within the intra-regional Latin American trade category, although as mentioned, this trade is small in size, relative to their total trade (Table 2.8). It was found that the countries comprising Central America, traded more than 95 percent of their goods among themselves, due to the Central American Common Market (CACM). In cases such as Guatemala, 99.7 percent of the intra-regional Latin American trade was with the Caribbean Basin countries and only 0.3 percent with the rest of Latin America. In the extreme case of El Salvador, 97.5 percent of its commerce was intra-Latin American trade, all of which was with Costa Rica, Guatemala, and Nicaragua. After abandoning the CACM in 1969, Honduras became

Table 2.6. Destination of Final Exports, 1985 (percentages)

Country	USA	Eur	Can	LAIA	CACM & Pan	Carib	Rest of the World
Region 1:							
Costa Rica	34	30	1	1	27	2	4
El Salvador	38	24	2	–	25	1	10
Guatemala	36	18	1	4	29	2	10
Honduras	53	26	–	–	8	3	10
Nicaragua	25	36	–	4	14	–	22
Panama	64	18	–	2	9	4	2
Region 2:							
Dominican Republic	76	16	2	–	–	2	3
Haiti	73	23	1	1	–	1	1
Region 3:							
Barbados	53	8	2	–	–	17	20
Jamaica	48	18	14	2	1	8	9
Trinidad-Tobago	61	14	1	2	1	11	10
Region 4:							
Colombia	33	43	1	8	2	4	9
Mexico	58	19	2	3	2	1	14
Venezuela	33	23	4	7	2	4	28

Source: Ibid.

the least integrated country in the region. Honduras traded only 75 percent of its goods with the rest of Central America, mainly through bilateral trade agreements. However, within Latin America's intra-regional trade, Honduras traded 99.5 percent with other nations in the Caribbean Basin.

In the case of Region 2, as part of intra-Latin American trade, the Dominican Republic traded mainly with Venezuela (85.5%) and Haiti (7.7%). For Haiti, the Dominican Republic and Venezuela were also the main trade partners. Forty-one percent of Haiti's exports were destined to the Dominican Republic and 26 percent to Venezuela.

For Barbados in Region 3, trade was concentrated with other CARICOM nations: 76 percent of the total was traded with Trinidad-Tobago and close to 10 percent with Jamaica. The main trade partners of Jamaica, within the context of intra-Latin American trade, were Trinidad-

Table 2.7. Imports by Country of Origin, 1985 (percentages)

Country	USA	Eur	Can	LAIA	CACM & Pan	Carib	Rest of the World
Region 1:							
Costa Rica	41	13	2	22	14	3	5
El Salvador	32	13	2	18	29	–	6
Guatemala	35	15	2	14	20	7	7
Honduras	40	18	3	13	15	2	9
Nicaragua	19	21	2	28	16	5	9
Panama	32	11	1	24	4	1	27
Region 2:							
Dominican Republic	35	11	1	40	2	1	10
Haiti	52	13	6	2	1	16	10
Region 3:							
Barbados	48	14	6	5	1	18	8
Jamaica	45	12	5	13	1	17	7
Trinidad-Tobago	40	21	7	6	1	6	19
Region 4:							
Colombia	35	24	4	21	2	1	13
Mexico	66	16	2	4	–	–	12
Venezuela	46	25	5	11	1	2	10

Source: Ibid.

Tobago (37.5%) and Venezuela (21.5%). Eighty percent of Jamaica's intra-Latin American trade was with other Caribbean Basin nations and 20 percent with the rest of Latin America.

Trinidad-Tobago traded in equal proportions with Regions 1 and 3: 20 percent with Central America and 21 percent with the CARICOM nations. Trinidad-Tobago is the least integrated nation with respect to the remaining Caribbean Basin nations. Illustrative of this, is the fact that 49.2 percent of the country's intra-Latin American trade was destined for the rest of Latin America, and the remaining 50.8 percent for the Caribbean Basin nations.

Colombia's intra-regional exports have been concentrated in Venezuela (59.1%), while Venezuela's main trade partners were Jamaica (10.5%), Colombia (10.4%) and Mexico (9%) in almost equal shares. Both Colom-

Table 2.8. Percentage Distribution of Intra-Regional Exports of the Caribbean Basin Countries with Latin America, 1979

Country	Region 1						Region 2		Region 3			Region 4		
	CR	ES	G	H	N	P	DR	Ha	B	J	TT	C	M	V
Region 1:														
CR	–	24.7	22.2	16.8	39.3	36.3	0.3	–	–	0.1	0.4	0.9	6.6	3.0
ES	20.3	–	47.2	–	18.8	9.2	–	–	–	0.4	–	0.6	4.3	7.0
G	26.1	64.2	–	37.9	22.5	4.1	0.1	6.1	–	0.6	10.0	1.8	9.0	6.0
H	11.0	–	15.4	–	14.0	3.4	0.4	–	–	0.4	7.4	0.7	3.2	4.0
N	16.6	8.6	9.6	16.9	–	11.2	–	–	–	0.1	–	0.1	0.6	5.1
P	14.9	–	0.6	3.2	1.0	–	0.5	–	–	4.2	3.1	6.1	3.4	5.2
Region 2:														
DR	2.2	0.2	1.4	4.8	0.4	7.7	–	41.3	–	1.9	3.9	0.8	2.2	8.2
Ha	0.2	–	0.1	–	0.2	0.6	7.7	–	0.6	1.3	0.1	0.2	0.1	
Region 3:														
B	0.1	–	–	2.1	–	–	–	0.6	–	12.1	12.4	0.1	–	1.7
J	1.6	–	0.1	3.9	–	0.1	0.4	14.1	9.8	–	8.6	0.7	0.5	10.5
TT	0.3	0.2	–	5.3	0.2	0.3	0.2	2.3	76.0	37.5	–	1.1	0.1	0.5
Region 4:														
C	0.9	–	–	1.7	0.3	8.5	0.7	0.1	–	–	0.2	–	7.6	10.4
M	0.2	–	3.0	1.2	0.6	7.3	–	0.1	–	0.1	4.0	1.8	–	9.0
V	0.6	–	0.1	5.7	1.3	7.9	85.5	26.4	4.6	21.5	0.7	59.1	16.1	–
Rest of LA	5.0	2.1	0.3	0.5	1.4	3.4	4.2	9.0	9.0	19.8	49.2	26.0	46.3	29.4

Source: Interamerican Development Bank, Economic and Social Progress in Latin America, 1984 Report, Page 113.

CR = Costa Rica; ES = El Salvador; GR = Guatemala; H = Honduras; N = Nicaragua; P = Panama; DR = Dominican Republic; Ha = Haiti; B = Barbados; J = Jamaica; TT = Trinidad-Tobago; C = Colombia; M = Mexico; V = Venezuela.

Table 2.9. Commodity Composition of Trade, 1985 (percentages)

	Exports		Imports	
Country	Primary Goods	Manuf. Goods	Primary Goods	Manuf. Goods
Region 1:				
Costa Rica	66	28	26	70
El Salvador	63	37	38	62
Guatemala	71	29	34	65
Honduras	87	12	27	73
Nicaragua	85	15	36	64
Panama	86	13	34	64
Region 2:				
Dominican Republic	45	19	49	51
Haiti	61	36	43	57
Region 3:				
Barbados	10	52	35	63
Jamaica	37	63	59	40
Trinidad-Tobago	82	18	30	70
Region 4:				
Colombia	83	17	26	70
Mexico	85	12	18	58
Venezuela	96	4	19	80

Source: U.N. International Trade Statistics Yearbook, 1986.

bia and Venezuela traded more with other Caribbean Basin nations than with Mexico, while Venezuela was Mexico's main trade partner.

5. COMMODITY COMPOSITION OF EXPORTS AND IMPORTS

In 1985, most of the Caribbean nations exported primary goods and imported manufactured goods, as can be seen in Table 2.9. The only exception was Barbados where the agricultural sector is small. The only country in the region where imports were almost equally divided among both types of goods was the Dominican Republic. The only country that imported more primary goods than manufactured goods was Jamaica, which showed a heavy dependence on imported food items.

The commodity composition of exports and imports by Standard Industrial Trade Classification (SITC) for 1985, at the one-digit level are given in Table 2.10. It shows that in the cases of Central America, the Dominican Republic, and Colombia, most of the exports were in Classifications 0 and 1 (food and live animals, and beverages and tobacco). Jamaica's most important exports are under Classifications 2 and 4 (crude materials, excluding fuels, and animal and vegetable fats and oils), while Classification 3 (mineral fuels) were the main exports of Trinidad-Tobago, Mexico, and Venezuela. Manufactured goods (Classifications 6 and 8) are the main exports only for Haiti. In 1985, chemicals (SITC 5) were important component of exports for Trinidad-Tobago, while machines and transportation equipment (SITC 7) were Barbados' main exports. Barbados' economy has been mainly dedicated to electronic component assembly plants and they are included within this classification.

The commodity composition of imports by SITC shows that manufactured goods (SITC 6 and 8) have been prominent imports for the region as a whole. In general, SITC 5 and SITC 7 are notable components as well. Mineral fuels (SITC 3) are the main imports for the Dominican Republic and for Jamaica. The highest share of food imported (SITC 0 and 1) corresponded to Haiti.

Utilizing the United Nations International Trade Tapes, a study undertaken by the Institutes of Economic and Social Research in the Caribbean Basin (IESCARIBE) for the Interamerican Development Bank, concluded that around 175 different commodities, at the three digit SITC classification level were exported from the Caribbean Basin.[6] However, most of the exports were concentrated in a small set of sixteen goods as shown in Table 2.11. The set of sixteen commodities represented 89.2 percent of the trade if oil is included, and 83.4 percent when oil is excluded. Almost all the commodities exported belong to the classification of goods derived from natural resources, excluding paper and paperboard, furskins, and clothing. Although the data in Table 2.11 refer to 1979, the same pattern was repeated for each year for which information was available.

6. CONCLUSIONS

The principal findings of the analysis are:

1. The volume of international trade for the Caribbean Basin region grew less rapidly between 1970 and 1980 (4.21%) than the regional GDP (5.72%). From 1980 to 1987, however, there was a slight increase in GDP (1.07%), while the volume of

Table 2.10. Percentage Distribution of Trade by Industrial Classifications, by Country, 1985

Countries	SITC Classifications					
	0 + 1	2 + 4	3	5	7	6 + 8
Exports						
Region 1:						
Costa Rica	69.0	1.5	0.9	7.2	4.2	13.8
El Salvador	42.9	12.5	2.9	6.6	2.9	31.6
Guatemala	59.1	9.9	6.0	10.4	1.1	13.5
Honduras	78.8	13.9	0.7	2.0	–	4.3
Nicaragua	65.7	24.8	1.2	5.1	0.2	2.6
Panama	76.0	3.3	7.3	3.3	–	10.0
Region 2:						
Dominican Republic	75.3	0.6	–	4.0	4.4	17.0
Haiti	29.0	11.7	–	3.1	–	40.0
Region 3:						
Barbados	12.5	–	23.9	4.5	45.4	12.8
Jamaica	19.1	66.0	2.4	2.4	2.0	7.9
Tobago	4.2	0.5	70.7	15.4	1.9	7.1
Region 4:						
Colombia	59.3	5.6	16.3	3.6	1.1	12.6
Mexico	7.9	3.2	68.1	3.9	7.7	7.3
Venezuela	0.6	–	95.4	0.4	–	3.2
Imports						
Region 1:						
Costa Rica	8.2	3.0	20.0	20.8	14.6	24.4
El Salvador	15.9	4.4	0.3	19.3	12.1	23.8
Guatemala	6.7	4.6	16.9	24.6	17.9	29.3
Honduras	10.1	2.1	12.4	20.3	24.8	30.4
Nicaragua	9.4	3.5	23.2	15.9	23.2	24.9
Panama	10.8	2.0	21.2	12.3	23.5	28.5
Region 2:						
Dominican Republic	6.7	7.4	35.2	11.7	23.2	15.9
Haiti	23.7	9.8	14.4	9.3	17.0	25.0
Region 3:						
Barbados	13.8	3.1	18.1	8.1	31.8	22.9
Jamaica	17.3	4.8	30.7	9.7	16.0	20.4
Trinidad-Tobago	16.6	4.9	2.8	10.6	36.7	28.2
Region 4:						
Colombia	6.6	7.7	11.7	20.8	28.2	22.6
Mexico	11.6	12.7	4.3	14.3	14.9	15.6
Venezuela	9.8	9.2	2.4	14.2	42.3	21.5

Source: Ibid.

Table 2.11. Caribbean Exports by Category of Goods, 1979*

SITC	Commodities	Percentage of Total	Percentage Without Oil
011	Meat, fresh, chilled, frozen	1.5	2.3
031	Fish, fresh, simply preserved	1.4	2.2
051	Fruits and vegetables	3.7	5.7
061	Sugar and honey	25.8	39.8
071	Coffee and substitutes	10.6	16.3
072	Cocoa	0.8	1.2
121	Tobacco, unmanufactured	0.6	1.0
212	Furskins, raw	0.5	0.7
263	Cotton	2.4	3.8
283	Minerals	2.7	4.2
292	Crude vegetables, materials, nec	0.5	0.7
331	Petroleum	6.5	–
332	Petroleum products	28.7	–
513	Carboxylic acid	2.2	3.5
641	Paper and paperboard	0.7	1.0
841	Clothing	0.6	1.0
	Others (159 products)	10.8	16.6
	Total	100.0	100.0

Source: *IESCARIBE estimates utilizing U.N. International Trade Tapes.*

*Colombia, Mexico, and Venezuela are excluded, but the rest of the Caribbean islands are included.

exports and imports almost stagnated increasing by an average annual rate of only 0.30 percent.

2. The average of the volume of trade (exports plus imports) as a proportion of GDP has been around 0.60 for the region as a whole. In the cases of the smaller island countries the ratio has been higher than in the case of the larger continental nations of Colombia, Mexico, and Venezuela.

3. Half of the 14 nations under study had export growth rates in excess of five percent, while imports grew at even faster rates in the cases of Costa Rica, Honduras, Barbados, and Mexico.

4. By 1985, 70 percent of the exports of the Caribbean Basin originated from the continental nations of Colombia, Mexico,

and Venezuela. The remaining 30 percent was distributed approximately as follows: seven percent from Central America and Panama, two percent from the Dominican Republic and Haiti, five percent from the English Speaking Caribbean, and 16 percent from the remaining Caribbean islands. Imports were distributed as follows: half of them by the continental nations, one-fourth from the other Caribbean islands, and the remaining imports were 13 percent by Central America, three percent by the Dominican Republic and Haiti, and six percent by the islands representing the CARICOM.

5. Most exports of the Caribbean nations are destined for the United States and Europe. Most imports also come from these two world areas.

6. Most of the goods traded within the Caribbean Basin are commodities belonging to the classification of goods derived from natural resources. Most of the exports consist of a range of small-scale transactions, where sixteen commodities have been identified. Manufactured goods constitute the foremost imported commodities, with few exceptions.

NOTES

1. Interamerican Development Bank, *Economic and Social Progress in Latin America, 1988 Report* (Washington, D.C.: Interamerican Development Bank, 1988).
2. United Nations, *International Trade Statistics Yearbook, 1986* (New York: United Nations, 1988).
3. Interamerican Development Bank, *1988 Report*.
4. Puerto Rico is excluded.
5. Interamerican Development Bank, *Economic and Social Progress in Latin America, 1984 Report* (Washington,D.C.: Interamerican Development Bank, 1984).
6. Adalberto Garcia Rocha and Manuel Gollas, "Flujo de Comercio en el Caribe," an IESCARIBE study (mimeo), 1987; Rafael Trejos and Manuel Gollas, eds., *Industrialization and Trade in the Caribbean Basin* (San Jose, Costa Rica: IESCARIBE, 1988).

CHAPTER 3

Trade Flows and Economic Integration among the LDCs of the Caribbean Basin[1]

Francisco E. Thoumi

1. INTRODUCTION

The international economic relations of the LDCs of the Caribbean Basin have been conditioned by their comparative advantage relative to the developed countries as most of their exports have historically been made up of primary products exported to the United States and Europe. The large size of their exports relative to their GNP makes them very vulnerable to the vicissitudes of the world economy, and the small size of most of their markets limits their possible development strategies.

Economic integration in the Caribbean Basin has been viewed as a way to enlarge the domestic markets, and to diversify the productive base of the countries, and thus lower their vulnerability to the fluctuations of primary product prices.

The integration systems of the region reflect its colonial history. The CARICOM countries are all former British colonies, while the Central American Common Market was founded by countries which had been part of the vice royalty of New Spain and which had formed a unified country during a short period in the nineteenth century.

Physical obstacles to trade in the Caribbean are not as great as in other parts of Latin America, particularly after medical advances eliminated some of the problems posed by the unhealthy Caribbean coast of Central America. However, by the time these advances took place, those countries had already grown into the highlands turning their backs on the Caribbean, so to speak — a fact that contributes to the weak links among the Basin's countries, and which has been difficult to overcome.

Current obstacles to trade include the differences in languages and cultures of the region and very undeveloped communications and transportation system, which are both causes and effects of the weak economic links within the Basin.

In this essay, a 'gravity equation' is used to analyze the pattern of the Caribbean Basin trade flows.[2] The study of intra-Basin trade is interesting because it provides insights about the characteristics of the Basin's integration, about further possibilities and of obstacles to economic integration, and on the possibilities of success of policies such as those proposed by the United States in its Caribbean Basin Initiative, which includes recommendations to increase exports of the smaller Basin countries to Colombia, Mexico and Venezuela.

2. THE MODEL USED

The gravity model has been frequently used to analyze bilateral trade flows.[3] The equation used is similar in all the studies and has the following general specification:

$$PX_{ij} = b_0 (Y_i)^{b1} (Y_j)^{b2} (D_{ij})^{b3} (A_{ij})^{b4} U_{ij} \qquad (1)$$

where PX_{ij} is the US dollar value of the trade flow from country i to county j; Y_i and Y_j are the US dollar values of nominal GDP in i and j; D_{ij} is the physical distance from the economic center of country i to the one of country j; A_{ij} is any other factor(s) either aiding or resisting trade between i and j; and U_{ij} is a log-normally distributed error term with $E(\ln U_{ij}) = 0$.

In these studies the GDP of the exporting country measures productive capacity while that of the importing country measures absorptive capacity. These two variables are expected to be positively related to trade. Physical distance and country adjacency dummies are proxies for transportation costs. Among the other variables affecting trade, the most frequently used have been dummies for the integration systems in which countries participate; total population figures of importing and exporting countries as well as their income per capita levels. Total population figures are a measure of country size, and since large countries have a more diversified production and tend to be more self-sufficient, these variables have normally been expected to be negatively related to trade. As pointed out by Prewo[4] and Bergstrand,[5] there is an inconsistency in this argument as larger populations allow for economies of scale which would translate in higher exports; therefore, the sign of the coefficient of the exporting country would be indeterminate.

The ratio of income per capita of the exporting to that of the importing country has been used by Brada and Mendez,[6] as a measure of the relative development of the export infrastructure in a study of the LDC trade. They expected higher per capita income countries to have fewer bottlenecks and, thus, to export relatively more than low income countries.

While the gravity equation has been very successful as a tool to 'explain' trade flows, it was frequently criticized because of a lack of formal theoretical foundations. However, recent works by Anderson[7] and Bergstrand[8] have produced increasingly more complete derivations of gravity type equations from traditional neoclassical theory. In these works, other explanatory variables such as exporter and importer prices and the bilateral exchange rate are included. Furthermore, while the signs for the coefficients of some variables such as importer income, transport cost and exchange rates are ambiguous, these works justify the inclusion of income per capita variables, which are considered a proxy for the income share distribution and thus, the capital and labor intensity of each country.

In this study there is no attempt to develop a model from which the gravity equation is derived. The aim is more modest: to use the gravity equation to explore the structure of intra-regional trade among the LDCs of the Caribbean Basin and to identify some of its characteristics which made certain types of economic integration more likely to succeed than others. Thus, the gravity equation used in this study reflects the nature of the data available and some of the structural characteristics of the countries studied. In this case the specification used was:

$$\ln PX_{ij} = b_0 + b_1 \ln Y_i + b_2 \ln Y_j + b_3 \ln Y_i/N_i + b_4 \ln Y_j/N_j$$
$$+ b_5 \ln ER + b_6 \ln D_{ij} + a_1 V + a_2 LAFTA + a_3 CARICOM + a_4 CACM \quad (2)$$

where Y_i/N_i are income per capita variables, ER measures the degree of under and over valuation of the bilateral exchange rate, V is a dummy variable for countries with adjacent land borders in which there is common infrastructure and communications that facilitate trade, and the last four variables are dummies for the LAFTA,[9] CARICOM and the CACM.[10]

A difference with other studies is the exclusion of population as an independent variable since within the Caribbean Basin it is highly correlated with GNP. Furthermore, income per capita variables cannot be included if both GNP and Population are also explanatory variables. Thus, in this study GNP captures the impact of both income size and the diversity of economic resources which, as pointed out above, would lead to an ambiguous coefficient sign. However, within the Caribbean context, this indeterminacy is not likely to arise. The overall comparative advantage of the region's countries is determined in relation to the developed countries, and intra-regional trade is a relatively small share of the total, and has a commodity composition substantially different from that of their exports to the rest of the world. In this context, the countries more diversified production are likely to have more items to trade intra-regionally than those which are highly specialized, therefore it can be expected that the countries with a more diversified economy export more intra-regionally, even though they are more closed economies overall.

Income per capita in the Caribbean context measures several things. The richest countries are those with the greatest amount of capital, natural resources and human skills per capita. They are also the ones with the most diversified consumer demand. Therefore, high income per capita countries should have a comparative advantage in the production of a different bundle of goods than low income countries. However, this bundle could be natural resource based, or based on capital or labor skills. A priori, it is not obvious what will be the relationship between intra-regional trade and income per capita of the exporting country. The higher income of the importer country should be associated with higher imports as a more diversified demand opens up more trade opportunities.

The adjacency dummy has proven an important determinant of trade flows (Linnemann,[11] Bergstrand[12]). However, given the geographical characteristics of the Caribbean Basin, this variable is not meaningful when taken literally since some adjacent regions are uninhabited, unexploited and are obstacles to rather than promoters of trade. Thus, the dummy used here considers as neighbors only countries which have border regions which are developed.

The dummies for the three integration systems considered are self-explanatory. The CACM dummy was used for trade among the five original CACM members, except for the bilateral trade between Honduras and El Salvador, since the official data used in this study shows no trade between them for the period after the 1969 'soccer' war.

The bilateral exchange rate is the only variable used in this study that reflects the impact of relative prices on exports and imports. It is also the only variable that is affected by non-structural policy changes of the governments. This is important since short term policies are more likely to have an impact on intra-Basin than on extra-Basin exports which are more dependent on the natural resource based comparative advantage of the Basin relative to the developed countries.

The gravity equation has normally been applied to total trade. In this study, it was considered useful to estimate the equation for four categories of products:[13] total goods traded (TOT), total goods traded except fuels (TEF), manufactures (MAN) and natural resource based products except fuels (NRB).

The gravity equation was estimated for 3 years: 1971, 1975 and 1979. These cover a period of very fast growth in intra-regional trade[14] and include the last year prior to the current great LAC depression. The period under study is one of very fast growth in intra-Basin trade. According to the data used in this study, the value of total intra-Basin exports grew annually at 20.6 percent between 1971 and 1979, while MAN exports grew at 20.3 percent and NRB exports at 17.8 percent.

3. EMPIRICAL RESULTS

Table 3.1 summarizes the results of the 12 estimations made.

The $\bar{R}^2$ coefficients which range between 0.515 and 0.721 are at satisfactory levels for cross section analysis, though they are somewhat lower than those obtained in most of the gravity equation applications to international trade which produced $\bar{R}^2$ coefficients between 0.65 and 0.85. These lower coefficients could be the result of the relatively small share of intraregional trade among several of the Basin's countries, and of the fact that the region's exports are highly influenced by the developed countries' markets.

The $\bar{R}^2$ coefficients were lower in 1979 — a year in which there was political turmoil in Central America, an oil price shock, and the first signs of the crisis began to appear.

In three years studied, the $\bar{R}^2$ rankings for the four goods' categories used as a dependent variables were constant descending from MAN to TEF to TOT and to NRB. The $\bar{R}^2$ for MAN exports were substantially higher than those of NRB exports, which did not exceed 0.56. These rankings are expected as the gravity equation is less likely to give good fittings for NRB products whose trade depends on natural resource availability, a variable not included in it. However, the low $\bar{R}^2$ for NRB exports indicate that the gravity equation used does not do a good job explaining this type of trade.

The exporter country income and the distance between countries are the only non-dummy variables that have statistically significant coefficients in all 12 equations.

The elasticity of intra-Basin total exports with respect to exporting country income is around 1.0 in all three years, while the elasticity of MAN exports is around 1.3 to 1.4, and that of NRB exports ranges between 0.6 and 0.8. Interestingly, as countries increase in size, their tendency to export to the Basin increases proportionally, but the MAN exports increase about twice as fast as NRB exports.

The income of the importing country was not statistically significant in any of the 1971 equations, but was significant in all the others except for 1975 NRB exports. However, the response of intra-Basin exports to the income of the importing country is much lower than it is to that of the exporting country. The statistically significant elasticities of exports rela-

Table 3.1. Gravity Equation Estimates

Variables	Total Trade			Total Trade Except Fuels			Manufactures			Natural Resource Based		
	1971	1975	1979	1971	1975	1979	1971	1975	1979	1971	1975	1979
$\bar{R}^2$	0.618	0.632	0.58	0.63	0.654	0.588	0.721	0.725	0.654	0.559	0.536	0.515
St. Error of Equation	1.798	1.879	2.034	1.706	1.773	1.911	1.756	1.857	2.157	2.015	2.330	2.465
Constant	-24.065 (2.34)	-40.404 (6.59)	-28.250 (3.48)	-3.734 (.38)	-30.000 (5.18)	-12.502 (1.64)	-26.800 (2.67)	-37.544 (6.19)	-17.028 (1.97)	6.928 (.60)	-21.611 (2.84)	-6.275 (.64)
$\ln Y_i$	1.009 (9.48)	1.031 (9.43)	0.965 (8.20)	0.954 (9.45)	1.037 (10.05)	0.864 (7.81)	1.293 (12.44)	1.379 (12.76)	1.278 (10.24)	0.644 (5.57)	0.793 (5.85)	0.616 (4.32)
$\ln Y_j$	0.241 (2.25)	0.382 (3.47)	0.335 (3.10)	0.186 (1.84)	0.453 (4.36)	0.387 (3.81)	0.207 (1.98)	0.493 (4.54)	0.290 (2.53)	0.195 (1.63)	0.322 (2.36)	0.437 (3.61)
$\ln Y_i/N_i$	0.468 (2.03)	1.029 (4.15)	0.820 (3.49)	-0.307 (1.40)	0.008 (.04)	0.000 (.04)	0.426 (1.89)	0.593 (2.42)	0.245 (.98)	-0.387 (1.50)	-0.382 (1.24)	-0.437 (1.53)
$\ln Y_j/N_j$	0.218 (0.95)	0.348 (1.40)	0.523 (2.29)	0.459 (2.11)	0.327 (1.40)	692 (3.22)	0.199 (.89)	0.165 (.67)	0.68 (2.81)	0.442 (1.72)	0.729 (2.38)	0.727 (2.63)
ln of Exchange Rate	1.574 (1.15)	2.870 (4.20)	1.285 (1.29)	-0.546 (.42)	2.086 (3.24)	-0.302 (.32)	1.589 (.94)	-0.571 (2.36)	-0.571 (.54)	-1.128 (.73)	2.103 (2.49)	-0.042 (.03)
ln of Distance	-0.898 (3.96)	-0.904 (3.81)	-0.869 (3.38)	-0.986 (4.58)	-0.997 (4.46)	-0.823 (3.41)	-1.170 (5.28)	-1.156 (4.94)	-1.334 (4.90)	-1.291 (5.08)	-1.388 (4.72)	-1.449 (4.66)
Adjacency Dummy	0.249 (.40)	0.457 (.71)	0.865 (1.24)	0.466 (.80)	0.753 (1.24)	1.073 (1.64)	0.346 (.57)	0.649 (1.02)	0.744 (1.00)	1.154 (1.67)	0.992 (1.24)	1.577 (1.86)
LAFTA Dummy	1.044 (1.21)	0.718 (.00)	1.152 (1.19)	1.904 (2.32)	0.988 (1.17)	1.555 (1.71)	1.947 (2.31)	0.854 (.96)	2.059 (2.01)	1.344 (1.39)	1.540 (1.38)	1.410 (1.20)
CARICOM Dummy	4.261 (6.80)	4.641 (7.08)	4.014 (5.70)	4.823 (5.70)	5.490 (8.11)	4.417 (8.87)	5.373 (6.68)	6.257 (8.78)	5.188 (9.65)	5.225 (6.95)	5.944 (7.31)	5.522 (6.47)
CACM Dummy	3.805 (7.07)	3.935 (7.00)	3.834 (6.31)	4.091 (8.01)	4.213 (7.94)	4.142 (7.26)	4.904 (9.33)	5.132 (9.24)	4.837 (7.51)	4.011 (6.65)	4.016 (5.76)	4.048 (5.50)

tive to importing country income are around .35 for total exports, between 0.3 and 0.5 for MAN exports and 0.5 for NRB exports.

The response of exports to total country income is such that export surpluses are generated in favor of the larger countries and, the surpluses in MAN trade are, in relative terms, much bigger than in any of the other goods' categories.

The income per capita variables yield statistically poor results. The exporting country income per capita is statistically significant only in the total export equations of 1975 and 1979. The fact that it is not significant for any of the other export categories, indicates that the significance is due to the exports of oil from Mexico, Trinidad and Tobago, and Venezuela, all relatively high income per capita countries. The importing country income is a significant variable only in the 1979 TEF, MAN, and NRB equations, an event related also to the oil boom of the relatively high income oil-exporting countries which made it very easy to export to them.

The physical distance between countries is the other variable which is significant in all equations. The distance coefficients show values in the range of 0.87 to 1.45. They are lower for total and TEF exports than for MAN and NRB export. Distance is not an important obstacle for trade in fuels, while it is more important in the last two categories in which market knowledge and fast communications are more relevant. The distance coefficients do not show declines through time, which would have been expected if infrastructural development and technological change had lowered trade barriers, a phenomenon that can be due to rising energy and, consequently, rising transportation prices during the period covered.

The results for the exchange rate variable are weak as they are significant only for total and TEF exports of 1975. Those results are not surprising, as the export response to exchange rates is likely to be slow. The constant terms are relatively large, indicating that variables not included in the gravity equation, such as the natural resource endowment and short and long term policies, also affect intra-Basin exports. This is reinforced by the fact that the values of the constant term for NRB exports, which are less likely to be affected by short term policies, are the lowest among the four merchandise categories, and between 42 and 74 percent lower than those of MAN exports.

The adjacency dummy is not significant in any equation. This is due to the fact that most of the adjacent countries are in Central America, where trade in the CACM is very active among all countries, not only among neighbors. The dummies for CARICOM and the CACM are very significant and have relatively high coefficients in all equations, while the LAFTA dummy is not significant in any equation and has relatively low coefficients.

Table 3.2. Percentage of Bilateral Trade Flows of Less than $10,000 Annually

Year	Total Exports	MAN	NRB
1971	27.1	39.5	50.0
1975	21.0	30.5	45.7
1979	18.6	27.6	46.2

The integration dummies' results reflect the various approaches to economic integration followed by each system. The CACM has been the most successful integration system in LAC.[15] It was formed by countries of similar size and while their income per capita levels vary, they do so less than among the LAFTA and AG countries. In 1960, when the CACM was created, modern manufacturing was not important in any of the five member countries. One of the main goals of the CACM was the development of manufacturing following an import substitution industrialization strategy which flourished as a common external tariff was put in place and intra-common market trade was freed swiftly. While the efficiency aspects of the development strategy followed could be questioned, it is undeniable that the CACM achieved a significant increased in intra-CACM trade, particularly in manufactures.

CARICOM has attempted to establish a very comprehensive system of economic integration, with varying degrees of success.[16] However, it did achieve a significant degree of trade liberalization that resulted in expanded trade flows, particularly from import-substitution projects.

The LAFTA dummy has proven to be statistically significant in a study similar to this one which includes all of South America and which uses the same data base.[17] The fact that this variable is not significant in this study shows that LAFTA's impact on intra-Latin American trade is due to its impact on trade among the other LAFTA members, while it has not contributed significantly to expanding trade relationships between Colombia, Mexico and Venezuela.

The relative weakness of the statistical results provided by the gravity equation is undoubtedly the result of the weak trade relationships among many of the Basin countries. As shown in Table 3.2, there are quite a few instances in which trade is virtually non-existent between the countries of the region. During the 1970s the very fast growth of trade strengthened the integration of the Basin; however, by 1979 still in almost 1 in 5 bilateral

Table 3.3. Cases of No-Bilateral Intra-Basin Trade (less than $10,000)

Number of Cases (Max. 14)	1971			1975			1979		
	TOT	MAN	NRB	TOT	MAN	NRB	TOT	MAN	NRB
Exports									
12		HA	HA					GY	
11	BB	BB-GY	BB		HA	ES-HA			HA
10	HA	DR	TT	BB	BB-GY	BB		HA	BB
9			ES-DR			GY	HA		ES-GY
8			GY-VZ	HA		DR-TT	BB-GY	BB	VZ
7	GU	JA-NI	JA-PA	GY		JA-PA			DR-TT
6		HO	CR	DR	NI-DR	CR			GU-JA
5	NI-DR	PA	HO-NI			VZ		JA-NI	CR-NI-PA
Imports									
11			GY						GY
10			HA-MK						
9			TT			BB-ES			BB
8	GY	CO	ES-GU HO-VZ			HO			NI-HO ES-HA-DR
7		BB-ES-GU GY-HO-MX			GY-BB	GU-MX-NI		ES	
6	BB	TT	CR-NI-DR	GY	ES-MX-NI	CO-CR	ES	CO-MX-NI	GU-MX
5	CR-ES	CR-HA-NI	BB-PA	ES	CR-HA	PA-DR	GY-NI	BB-GY-HO	CR-TT

BE = Barbados; CO = Colombia; CR= Costa Rica; DR =Dominican Republic; ES = El Salvador; GU = Guatemala; GY = Guyana; HA = Haiti; HO = Honduras; JA = Jamaica; MX = Mexico; NI = Nicaragua; PA = Panama; TT = Trinidad and Tobago, VZ = Venezuela.

trade possibilities, the trade volume was less the $10,000 — a proportion which increases to over 1 in 4 for MAN exports and to almost 1 in 2 for NRB exports!

The lack of economic relations among some of the countries is shown in Table 3.3 which presents the number of trade partners with which particular countries did not have any trade. Barbados, Guyana and Haiti do not export to most of the Basin countries. Even in 1979, after the substantial intra-Basin trade growth mentioned above, these 3 countries did not export to at least eight of the 14 other Basin countries. The lack of bilateral exports of these countries is as pronounced in MAN as in NRB exports, although for the Basin in general it is more noticeable in the case of NRB exports. Remarkably, in 1979, twelve of the fifteen Basin countries studied had at least five cases of bilateral exports of less than $10,000 in NRB products. Only Colombia, Mexico and Honduras were not in this group. Colombia and Mexico have the two most diversified economies of the Basin and, thus, a large number of possible export products; and Honduras is likely to be the most NRB intensive country of the Basin relative to its population.[18]

The ties in manufacturing trade have strengthened and, as a result, the number of countries that had five or more cases of no bilateral exports in MAN declined from eight in 1971 to five in 1975 and 1979.

Looking at the import side, it is clear that Guyana and Barbados and, to a lesser degree, Haiti import from very few of the other Basin countries. Thus, these three countries are particularly isolated from most of the Basin, although Barbados' and Guyana's trade within CARICOM is quite active.

Remarkably, the largest market among the LDCs of the Basin is one of the least exploited by the other countries, as Mexico imports less than $10,000 of MAN and NRB products from at least six of 14 countries in every year analyzed. Colombia, another good potential market, also does not import from many countries, although the tendency in this case is not as strong as that of Mexico.

It is thus clear that the bilateral exports of the Caribbean Basin show many empty cells. Trade is quite active within the two regional common markets, but the smaller countries of the region tend to have very weak ties with other countries, particularly outside their own common markets, while of the three larger countries, Mexico and Colombia appear to export to the Basin but to import very little. Venezuela, on the other hand, had imported from most of the Basin countries and, during the period covered by this study, had an extreme case of 'dutch disease' which made it into a very attractive market for the Basin's products.

4. CONCLUSIONS

The analysis of intra-Caribbean Basin trade using a gravity equation provides useful insights into the structure and characteristics of intra-Basin trade and into some of the problems faced by integration systems in the region.

One of the important characteristics of intra-Basin trade is that it has depended more on the total income of the exporting than of the importing countries. In general, bigger countries have succeeded in exporting more than smaller ones, generating a bilateral surpluses and deficits pattern which has been harmful to the promotion of economic integration. This pattern has been more pronounced in manufacturing exports. As long as this structural characteristic persists, integration systems in the area will be more likely to succeed if they are formed by countries of similar size.

Income per capita variables were not significant except for the exporter's income per capita which was significant in the case of total exports of 1975 and 1970, while the importer's was significant in 1979 for MAN and NRB products. These significant values are associated with the oil booms of some of the richest countries studied.

Physical distance is a very important determinant of bilateral trade flows in the Caribbean. Economic integration has increased faster among closer than among distant countries, many of which have non-existent trade flows. Therefore, it appears that decreasing the 'distance' between countries through improved communication and transportation systems could be one of the better ways to promote the integration of the region.

Two of the larger countries, Mexico and Colombia, have not provided good markets to the rest of the Basin, as they have had substantial trade surpluses. The opening of these markets is both a challenge and a contribution to the Basin's integration.

The integration systems of the region have had varying degrees of success in generating trade. Those that lowered trade barriers appear to be relatively more successful. The CACM and CARICOM appear to have had a substantial impact on intra-Basin exports, while LAFTA has failed to promote trade significantly in this subregion.

The gravity equation does not explicitly consider differences in country policies. However, the high value of the intercept indicates that they are an important element in determining intra-Basin trade.

APPENDIX

The Data Used

The export values for 1971, 1975 and 1979 were obtained from the United Nations International Trade Tapes, which had complete data sets for 15 countries: Mexico; the Central American countries except Belize; Colombia, Venezuela, Guyana, Jamaica, Haiti, the Dominican Republic, Barbados and Trinidad & Tobago. The data follow the Standard International Trade Classification (SITC). For the purposes of this study it was considered useful to use four different export concepts, total exports; total exports except fuels (Section 3 of the SITC); manufactured goods classified by material (Section 6), machinery and transport equipment (Section 7) and miscellaneous manufactured articles (Section 8); and natural resource based products except fuels which include food and live animals (Section 0), beverages and tobacco (Section 1), crude inedible materials (Section 2) and animal and vegetable oils and fats (Section 4). The trade data presented zero values for bilateral trade in several cases, particularly

between the poorer and smaller countries. Since the logarithmic specification of the equations estimated in this study gives more weight to very
small values, it was decided to use $10,000 as the bilateral trade for cases
where total trade and total trade less fuels was zero and $1,000 in similar
situations for the manufactured and other natural resource based exports.

The 1979 income and population data, except those for Barbados and
Guyana, were found in the World Bank, *World Development Report, 1981*;
these data for 1971 and 1975 came from ECLA, *Statistical Yearbook for
Latin America*. The income and population data for Barbados and Guyana
were obtained from Inter-American Development Bank estimates.

The physical distance between economic centers is a combination of
maritime distances found in US Defense Mapping Agency, *Distances Between Ports* (Fifth Ed.) 1985, and land distances obtained from several
country atlases. In some cases such as Colombia, there is no economic
center point, but rather, several economic center areas; thus; the distance
used was the closest one to either Barranquilla, Cali, or Bogota. Since
almost all of the intra-CACM trade is done by road, the land surface was
used for trade among these countries. However, as most other trade is done
by boat, maritime distances were used for the other countries.

The bilateral exchange rates were estimated using the following proce-
dure: the exchange rate data were obtained for each country for the 1960-
1984 period from the IMF, *International Financial Statistics*. A trend
equation of the form ln ER = a + bt was estimated for each country. Taking
the ratio of the actual to the estimated exchange rate for a particular year,
the degree of under or overvaluation that year with respect to the long term
trends is estimated. Finally, this ratio for the exporting countries is divided
into the one for the importing countries to obtain the bilateral exchange
rates.

The dummy variables for the integration systems used included Costa
Rica, El Salvador, Guatemala, Honduras and Nicaragua in the CACM,
except for the bilateral trade between El Salvador and Honduras which has
officially been zero since the 1969 'soccer' war.

The adjacency dummy was defined to reflect the existence of a common
land border in which there is active economic activity. Thus: Colombia
was paired with Venezuela; Costa Rica with Panama and Nicaragua; Honduras with Nicaragua and Guatemala, and Guatemala with El Salvador and
Mexico.

NOTES

1. Reprinted from *Social and Economic Studies*, Volume 38, No. 2, 1989, pp. 215-
233, by permission of the University of the West Indies, Kingston, Jamaica.

2. The opinions expressed in this essay are those of the author and do not necessarily reflect any position or policy of the Inter-American Development Bank. The author is grateful for comments to a previous draft from: R. Albert Berry, Jose Mendez and Simon Teitel; to Sergio Botero for his computing assistance; and to Magda Matamoros and Martha Rountree for their helpful typing.

3. See N.D. Aitken, "The Effect of the EEC and EFTA on European Trade: A Temporal Cross-Section Analysis, *American Economic Review*, Vol. 63, No. 5, 1973, pp. 881-892; V.J. Geraci and W. Prewo, "Bilateral Trade Flows and Transport Costs," *Review of Economics and Statistics*, Vol. LXI, No. 1, 1977, pp. 67-74; J. Pelzman, "Trade Creation and Trade Diversion in the Council of Mutual Economic Assistance: 1954-1970," *American Economic Review*, Vol. 67, No. 4, 1977, pp. 713-722; J. Tinbergen, *Shaping the World Economy: Suggestions for an International Economic Policy* (New York: The Twentieth Century Fund, 1962); J.C. Brada and J.A. Mendez, "Economic Integration Among Developed, Developing and Centrally Planned Economies: A Comparative Analysis," *Review of Economics and Statistics*, Vol. LXVII, No. 4, 1985, pp. 549-556; J.H. Bergstrand, "The Gravity Equation in International Trade: Some Microeconomic Foundations and Empirical Evidence," *Review of Economics and Statistics*, Vol. LXVII, No. 3, 1985, pp. 474-481, and "The Gravity Equation and the Factor-Proportions Theory in International Trade," The University of Notre Dame, mimeo, August 1986; and A. Sapir, "Trade Benefits Under the ECC Generalized System of Preferences," *European Economic Review*, Vol. 15, 1981, pp. 339-355, among others.

4. W. Prewo, "Determinants of the trade pattern among OECD countries from 1958 to 1974," *Jahrbucher Fur Nationalekonmie und Statistik*, 1978, 193.

5. J.H. Bergstrand, "The Gravity Equation and the Factor-Proportions Theory in International Trade," *op. cit.*

6. J.C. Brada and J.A. Mendez, "Economic Integration Among Developed, Developing and Centrally Planned Economies: A Comparative Analysis," *op. cit.*

7. J.E. Anderson, "A Theoretical Foundation for the Gravity Equation," *The American Economic Review*, Vol. 69, No. 1, 1979, pp. 106-116.

8. J.H. Bergstrand, "The Gravity Equation in International Trade: Some Microeconomic Foundation and Empirical Evidence," *op. cit.*, and "The Gravity Equation and the Factor-Proportions Theory in International Trade," *op. cit.*

9. LAFTA is not a Caribbean Basin Common market; however, since the three larger countries included in this study are LAFTA members, this variable was included.

10. The Appendix has a detailed discussion of each variable and their data source.

11. H. Linnemann, "Trade Flows and Geographical Distance or the Importance of Being Neighbors," in H.C. Boss (ed.) *Towards Balanced International Growth* (Holland: North Holland, 1969), pp. 111-128.

12. J.H. Bergstrand, "The Gravity Equation in International Trade: Some Microeconomic Foundations and Empirical Evidence," *op. cit.*

13. See the Appendix for a discussion of what is included in each category. The only other works that apply the gravity equation to desegregated data are Pelzman, *op. cit.*, Bergstrand, *op. cit.* and Sapir, *op. cit.*

14. Intra Latin America and Caribbean exports grew at 12.7 percent per year during the 1972-79 period, while extra regional exports were growing at 9.7 percent. See Inter-American Development Bank, *Economic and Social Progress in Latin America: Economic Integration, 1984 Report* (Washington, D.C., 1984).

15. The book edited by W.R. Cline and E. Delgado, *Economic Integration in Central America* (Washington, D.C.: The Brookings Institution, 1978), provides an excellent comprehensive analysis of the CACM's history and achievements. See also G. Rosenthal, "The Lessons of Economic Integration in Latin America: The Case of

Central America," in A. Gauhar (ed.), *Regional Integration: The Latin American Experience* (Boulder: Westview Press, 1985).

16. See G. Reid, "The Evolving Structure of the CARICOM Trade Regime," in *Ten Years of CARICOM* (Washington, D.C.: Inter-American Development Bank, 1984), pp. 102-117; A.T. Bryan, "The CARICOM and Latin American Integration Experiences: Observations of Theoretical Origins and Comparative Performance," in *Ten Years of CARICOM, op. cit.*; and W.G. Demas and J. Scotland, "Experiences in Regional Integration in Latin America," in A. Gauhar (ed.), *Regional Integration: The Latin American Experience, op. cit.*

17. See F. Thoumi, "Bilateral Trade Flows and Economic Integration in Latin America and the Caribbean, *World Development*, Vol. 17, No. 3, 1989, pp. 421–429.

18. The probable exception to this assertion is Guyana, which has many undeveloped natural resources.

PART 2

Industrialization and Trade in the Caribbean

CHAPTER 4

Industrialization and Trade in the Dominican Republic and Haiti

Irma T. de Alonso

1. INTRODUCTION

The purpose of this chapter is to determine the trade performance of goods manufactured by the two Caribbean Basin countries sharing the Island of Hispaniola, namely the Dominican Republic and Haiti. The Dominican Republic occupies 63 percent of Hispaniola's land mass (48,442 km^2 vs. 27,750 km^2). In 1988 the population of the island was 12.8 million, almost equally distributed between the two countries. However, the rate of population growth in the 1980s was proportionately higher in the Dominican Republic than that experienced in Haiti (2.4% as compared to 1.8%). Life expectancy at birth was also significantly higher in the former (64.1 years) as compared to the latter's (52.7 years).[1]

Marked differences can also be found in literacy rates. In the Dominican Republic, the literacy rate has been 69.4 percent, while in Haiti it has been a dismal 37.0 percent. This fact alone helps to explain why 65.4 percent of the labor force in Haiti is employed in agriculture as compared to the 23.6 percent in the Dominican Republic.[2]

In 1988, the GDP of Hispaniola was close to $12 billion (in 1988 prices), of this amount, the Dominican Republic generated 83 percent of it. Per capita GDP in this country was $1,509, while in Haiti it was a mere $319. Chronic unemployment is about 25 percent, and underemployment accounts for up to another 25 percent. These two factors combined largely characterize the labor force of the two countries. However, while Haiti has enjoyed relative price stability, with inflation rates below 5 percent, the Dominican Republic has, since 1981 grappled with inflation rates above 15

45

percent. In fact, inflation reached a high 44.4 percent at times, as was the case during 1988.[3]

Although the two countries have many marked differences, they share a similarity in their industrialization strategies. To supplement domestic investment, both countries have attracted foreign investment by relying on generous tax holidays and by offering high ceilings on profit repatriation, along with other incentives and subsidies. They have also banked on assembly operations to strengthen their manufacturing sectors. Although neither country belongs to any regional economic integration scheme,[4] both rely prominently on foreign trade. For example, in 1988 ratios of foreign trade (exports plus imports of goods and services) to GDP were as high as 43 percent in the Dominican Republic and 54 percent in the case of Haiti.[5]

The remaining part of this chapter is divided into the following parts: Section 2 provides a brief picture of the economic performance of the two countries under consideration; Section 3 analyzes the manufacturing sector, with special reference to its changing size and composition; and Section 4 presents trade patterns of manufactured goods for each country. The chapter concludes with a summary and assessment of perspectives for the future.

2. AN OVERVIEW OF ECONOMIC PERFORMANCE

2.1. Dominican Republic

Since the 1960s economic growth in the Dominican Republic has been erratic but substantial. Between 1961 and 1970 the average annual growth rate of GDP was 5.1 percent; this rate increased to 6.9 percent in the decade 1971-80, but then declined to 2.5 percent from 1981-88 [Table 4.1]. The economy has been affected by hurricanes, high energy prices, declining sugar prices, and lower international demand for its sugar, bauxite, and ferronickel. In addition, due to its large external debt, the government of the Dominican Republic has implemented a strict stabilization program, involving currency devaluations, tight monetary policies, tax increases, and tight fiscal policies.[6]

The proportion of value added in the agricultural sector has decreased from 26.7 percent in the 1960s to 16.5 percent in the 1980s, and the corresponding rate of growth has decreased as well. The share of manufacturing did increase from 14.9 percent to 17.5 for the same period, but the rate of growth in the 1980s has decreased considerably from the rates experienced in the previous two decades [Table 4.1]. Industrial tax free zone activities contributed to the creation of output expansion and employment, but this is not reflected in the official GDP statistics as these activities are considered part of exports of non-factor services.[7] Other sectors which have increased their share of value added include commerce, financial services, transportation and communications, government, and "other" sectors, among which tourism is included. The direction of the economy has moved away from a concentration in sugar production, towards a diversification in light industry, mining, and tourism, which together help lessen its dependence on sugar and the uncertainty of fluctuating world sugar prices.[8]

2.2. Haiti

Haiti is classified as one of the most underdeveloped countries in the world. It is the poorest nation in the Western Hemisphere and has the worst indices of social deprivation. In terms of rank, the World Bank classifies Haiti as the 29th poorest nation in the world.[9] The average rate of growth in the last three decades has been inconsistent. In the 1960s the average rate of growth of GDP was only 0.8 percent, in the 1970s it increased to 4.7 percent, and from 1980-88 it declined to –0.5 percent [Table 4.1].

Haiti is a country heavily dependent on international food relief programs and on foreign direct investment. In 1960, 84 percent of the GDP was comprised of public and private consumption; by 1988 the share had increased to 97 percent. During this time it has experienced a negative trade balance, and investment from domestic sources has been almost non-existent.[10]

In 1988 the Haitian GDP was estimated at $2.0 billion (in 1988 dollars), which was slightly less than the 1980 level. GDP per capita is even more reflective of Haiti's economic difficulties: the level achieved in 1988 was of $319, which was $12 less than the level achieved in 1960, and $67 less than the level achieved in 1980.[11] In addition, there is widespread income inequality, horrible deficiencies in overall nutritional levels, and also very little is spent on education.[12]

Haiti is predominantly an agricultural economy where two-thirds of the labor force is employed but where only one-third of the GDP is generated by that work force. The sector is characterized by low productivity and low agricultural yields per unit of acre as a result of the use of primitive technology: prevalent small farm plots, widespread use of basic and rudimentary tools, moderately low soil fertility, and lack of commercial fertilizers. The main cash crop is coffee followed distantly by sugar. In 1988 coffee and sugar provided 19 percent of export earnings, down from 33 percent in 1975, as a result of both decaying volume and smaller unit value of exports.[13] Crops for domestic consumption include maize, rice,

Table 4.1. Dominican Republic and Haiti: Growth of Production, 1960-1988

	GDP (Millions of 1988 dollars)				
	1960	1970	1980	1985	1988*
A. Dominican Republic					
GDP	2660	4364	8530	9209	10363
Value Added by:					
Agriculture	396	809	1557	1503	1744
Manufacturing	872	1014	1422	1561	1570
B. Haiti					
GDP	1215	1316	2092	1988	1998
Value Added by:					
Agriculture	162	171	382	318	304
Manufacturing	537	580	674	638	649

Average Annual Growth Rates (%)	Dominican Republic	Haiti
GDP		
1961-70	5.1	0.9
1971-80	6.9	4.7
1981-88	2.5	−0.5
Agriculture		
1961-70	1.5	0.8
1971-80	3.4	1.5
1981-88	1.2	−0.5
Manufacturing		
1961-70	7.4	0.5
1971-80	6.8	8.4
1981-88	1.4	−2.8

Source: InterAmerican Development Bank, Economic and Social Progress in Latin America, 1989 Report.
*Preliminary.

and beans, but agricultural production has not been sufficient to meet domestic consumption needs, thus, as mentioned, Haiti depends on imported food and food aid to feed its population.

Manufacturing has been a rapidly growing sector where 15 percent of GDP is generated and 6.5 percent of the labor force is employed.[14] Assembly of component parts operations is the main feature. These industries mainly produce apparel, electronic, toys, and sporting goods. The sector grew significantly from 1960 to 1980, but in the 1980s it contracted.[15] In the latter decade, the value added by both agriculture and manufacturing have had negative average annual rates of growth of –0.5 and –2.8 percent, respectively [Table 4.1].

3. THE MANUFACTURING SECTOR: SIZE AND COMPOSITION

3.1. Dominican Republic

Since the 1960s, every government in the Dominican Republic has consistently given its priority to industrialization and has sought to diminish the economy's dependence on sugar. The industrial policy framework which has dominated manufacturing in the Dominican Republic has been governed by the passage of the Industrial Incentives Law (Law # 299) in 1968, and by the approval of a parallel foreign exchange market in 1967. Both events encouraged inward development of the industrial sector. Priority was given to the production of consumer goods which replaced goods that were previously imported, and thus created a bias against the export of manufactured goods. For example, in 1970, manufactured goods constituted only five percent of merchandise exports, and these exports comprised an even lower proportion of manufacturing production. By 1987, the share of manufactured goods in total merchandise exports increased to 22 percent, after a peak value of 29 percent in 1986.

Law Number 299 imposed high tariffs on imported final goods and provided exemptions for imports of raw material and intermediate goods. Capital goods were imported at a lower exchange rate and this promoted the use of capital intensive technology and encouraged the use of imported inputs. At the same time, exports of manufactures were discouraged by the requirement that exporters were compelled to exchange their proceeds in part or in full at the official exchange rate, instead of the rate used for imports.

Because of high levels of effective protectionism, production was oriented towards the internal market rather than for exports.[16] This created a dualism between enterprises geared exclusively to exports in the free zones and those producing exclusively for the domestic market. The resulting effect was a bias against industries for exports, and instead towards those industries producing for the domestic market. Empirical studies clearly indicate that those domestically oriented industries are characterized by a high import content and a high level of excess capacity (an estimated 45 percent average excess capacity was found in 1983).[17] The combined effect of industrial incentives has provided and encouraged the production of final goods with imported inputs. Little stimulus has been given for the development of local intermediate goods.[18]

As a result of the provisions of these incentives, a series of new industries emerged: glass, textiles, assembly of electric and electronic equipment, small electric machinery, and pharmaceuticals, in addition to the traditional sugar refining.[19]

New government agencies were created to finance industrial development and to seek out new markets for Dominican products. The Corporation for Industrial Development (CFI) was established to act as a financial agency to assist those industries seeking to meet domestic consumption demands. The Investment Fund for Economic Development (FIDE) was formed to pool financial resources and to serve as a credit agency for new industries. The Dominican Institute for Industrial Technology (INDOTEC) has trained workers for the industrial sector. The Dominican Center for Promotion of Exports (CEDOPEX) was also created to aid local businesses seeking expanded markets for their products. In addition, public investment has been undertaken to provide the necessary infrastructure.[20]

The relative importance of the manufacturing sector as a percent of GDP has increased considerably. It represented an average 14.9 percent of GDP during the decade of 1960-69. From 1970-79 the sector had increased its average share to 18.6 percent, having stabilized at a level around 18 percent for most of the 1980s. By 1988, however, the share had decreased to 16.8 percent, reflecting a decline in domestic manufacturing activity while industrial activity in the tax free zones was flourishing.[21] The value added in manufacturing had a positive average annual rate of growth of 7.4 percent from 1961-70 and of 6.8 percent from 1971-80, but the rate decreased to 1.4 percent for the period 1981-88 [Table 4.1].

Much of the industry has been capital-intensive because of the system of incentives that has favored capital. As a result industrial activity has had a moderate effect on employment. In his study, Dauhajre found that the capital-labor ratio in manufacturing (excluding the sugar industry) decreased from 3.35 in 1973 to 2.32 in 1983. In the case of the sugar industry, the capital-labor ratio was also reduced from 3.33 to 2.27 for the same time period.[22]

Estimates of manufacturing activity in the Dominican Republic by the World Bank, reflect the status of manufacturing in the country.[23] Using an index of employment (1980=100) it was found that employment in the manufacturing sector increased from 71.4 in 1967 to 111.4 in 1985. The corresponding index for real output per employee also increased from 50.9 in 1967 to 90.7 in 1985, thus reflecting productivity weaknesses with respect to the levels achieved in 1980, but a substantial improvement over

Table 4.2. Dominican Republic and Haiti: Manufacturing Activity
(Index 1980=100)

	Employ-ment	Real Earnings per Employee	Real Output per Employee	Earnings as a % of value added
A. Dominican Republic				
1967	71.4	105.8	50.9	37.5
1970	75.8	124.9	63.0	35.3
1975	83.8	125.0	95.5	24.2
1980	100.0	100.0	100.0	26.9
1985	111.4	79.4	90.7	23.9
B. Haiti				
1967	53.7	117.5	na	na
1970	39.4	144.0	na	na
1975	74.0	91.3	na	na
1980	100.0	100.0	na	na
1985	115.5	101.7	na	na

Source: World Bank, World Tables 1988-89 Edition.

the level attained in 1967. The index of real earnings per employee decreased from 105.8 in 1967 to 79.4 in 1985, and earnings as percent of value added decreased from 37.5 percent in 1967 to 23.9 percent in 1985 [Table 4.2].

There has been a change in the composition of manufacturing output in the Dominican Republic over the period 1962 to 1985. Following the analysis of the rates of growth of the industrial production indices [Table 4.3] it can be concluded that from 1962-71 the sectors with the highest positive growth rates were electrical machinery, rubber products, paper products, plastic products, metal and non-metal products, whereas footwear and wood products had declines. For the period 1971-80 there were increases in the sectors of footwear, metal products, and those related to printing and publishing, while there were declines in textiles. For the more recent period from 1978 to 1985, it can be determined that the highest rates of growth were those experienced in the sectors of wearing apparel, paper products, plastic products, furniture, and printing. Negative rates or rates showing almost no growth were established for the same period in the sectors of iron and steel, food products, and rubber products.[24] The sectors

Table 4.3. Dominican Republic: Rate of Growth of Industrial Production, 1962-85

	ISIC Codes	Average Annual Growth Rates		
		1962-71 (1963=100)	1971-80 (1975=100)	1978-85 (1980=100)
311/12	Food Products	4.1	6.7	−2.1
313	Beverages	6.4	4.2	7.7
314	Tobacco	5.2	4.3	2.5
321	Textiles	5.3	−3.4	3.7
322	Wearing Apparel	2.8	1.2	12.1
323	Leather products	1.9	6.8	1.1
324	Footwear	−5.5	22.0	4.0
331	Wood products	−16.6	8.0	3.1
332	Furniture	4.1	5.6	7.7
341	Paper & Product	14.7	0.4	10.3
342	Printing, Publ.	5.4	12.0	7.1
351	Ind. Chemicals	7.2	4.6	3.7
352	Other Chem. prod.	7.7	7.1	7.4
355	Rubber prod.	15.6	3.1	−1.9
356	Plastic prod.	14.7	8.5	10.1
362	Glass prod.	7.2	−0.4	6.1
369	Non Metal Prod.	10.6	−1.5	5.5
371	Iron & Steel	na	−1.4	0.1
381	Metal prod.	11.9	21.2	3.5
383	Electrical Mach.	19.6	5.6	2.7
390	Other industries	na	−5.2	27.2
3	Manufacturing	4.8	5.9	4.4

Source: United Nations, Industrial Statistics Yearbook, various issues.

with consistently high rates of growth through the decades studied have been chemicals and plastic products (classifications 352 and 356 of the International Standard Industrial Classifications {ISIC}).

Statistics concerning the number of establishments, average number of employees, wages and salaries paid, and gross output by two-digit ISIC codes are given in Table 4.4. These statistics convey the importance of the high concentration of manufacturing activity in food producing sectors. In the 1960s, 80 percent of the output was generated in this activity. In the 1980s, the share has decreased to 54 percent, and there has been a surge with respect to chemical industry. Nonetheless, throughout the period,

Table 4.4. Dominican Republic: Manufacturing Statistics, 1963-1984

ISIC	Manufacturing	Number of Establishments			Number of Employees (thousands)			Wages and Salaries (million pesos)			Gross Output (million pesos)		
		1963	1970	1984	1963	1970	1984	1963	1970	1984	1963	1970	1984
31	Food, Beverage & Tobacco	936	509	1077	99.8	97.7	108.3	65.1	72.6	220.1	299	420	2298
32	Textiles & Apparel	484	228	222	5.2	4.2	9.5	4.8	5.7	27.3	22	26	217
33	Wood Products	378	116	117	1.8	0.6	2.1	1.3	0.7	6.2	5	4	47
34	Paper Products	96	42	69	1.4	1.7	4.3	2.0	3.4	16.8	11	18	184
35	Chemicals	125	74	163	2.1	2.8	9.0	3.4	5.3	43.7	24	44	996
36	Non-Metal Products	94	30	85	1.5	1.9	5.8	2.3	4.0	22.1	10	21	205
37	Basic Metals	7	7	9	0.8	0.8	1.1	1.2	1.8	6.1	–	7	126
38	Metal Manufactures	56	30	80	0.4	1.0	4.0	0.5	2.1	17.1	4	16	196
39	Other Manufactures	1	2	14	–	–	0.3	–	–	0.9	1	–	18
	Total	2177	1038	1036	113.1	110.6	144.4	80.6	95.6	360.3	376	556	4268

Source: United Nations, Industrial Statistics Yearbook, various issues.

more than 75 percent of the labor force has been employed in the food
industry.

Despite the incentives offered to foreign investment, nearly 89 percent
of manufacturing investment is nationally owned. It is concentrated in the
sectors of food, beverages, and tobacco, chemicals, petroleum derivatives,
rubber and plastic, basic metals, fabricated metals, and machinery. Many
of the industrial operations are in government hands as well. The extent of
public ownership was estimated to have averaged 29 percent in 1980, but
it was much higher in the following sectors: sugar (59.8%), petroleum
refineries (50%), and glass products (100%).[25]

The manufacturing sector has benefitted from foreign investment in the
industrial tax-free zones. These are zones where firms import raw materials
and component parts, mainly from the United States. Labor-intensive
methods are used to assemble the products in these zones, after which
finished assembled products are exported back to the United States. There
has also been foreign investment from East Asia as a way to escape the
import quota on clothing that has been imposed on them under the Multifiber Arrangement. The factories located within these zones enjoy tax exemptions, import incentives, export exemptions, and exemptions from
minimum wages.[26] Employment in these zones has also increased significantly. It is estimated that in 1988 employment in the sector approached
85,000 workers and that the value added from these operations corresponded to roughly 3 percent of the GDP.[27] By 1989 there were more
than 275 companies employing more than 115,000 workers.[28] The factories are largely geared to performing final assembly of wearing apparel
and electronic components. The incentives rendered via the United States
Tariff Schedule (USTS), Items 9802.00.60 and 9802.00.80 (formerly sections 806.30 and 807), and those of the Caribbean Basin Initiative have
encouraged the establishment of industrial complexes in these free zones,
whose products are destined exclusively for the United States market.

Nontraditional exports have been stimulated by an Export Promotion
Law (Law Number 69) implemented in 1979, and a Free Zone Law (Law
Number 145) approved in 1983. Law Number 145 offers producers in the
free zones important fiscal incentives, in terms of tax holidays and duty
free import of machinery and raw materials. On the other hand, Law Number 69 grants incentives to non-traditional exports by providing both
foreign exchange incentives and fiscal incentives.[29] The foreign exchange
incentive has proved to be more efficacious, while the fiscal incentives,
consisting of a tax certificate and a temporary import system has had little
impact, and subsequently have been abandoned. The foreign exchange
incentive consisted of a scheme permitting exporters of non-traditional
exports to keep a fixed portion of their foreign exchange earnings by

exempting them from the requirement that they had to surrender all foreign exchange earnings to the Central Bank. There are several factors taken into consideration in granting the exemption; the most important one being that of value added. To be eligible, the domestic value added must be at least 30 percent of the f.o.b. value.[30]

Despite the orientation of manufacturing to the local market, domestic demand for manufactured goods has been satisfied largely through imports [Table 4.6]. In 1967, according to World Bank estimates, imports of manufactures (cif) corresponded to 72 percent of total imports, while non-fuel primary products corresponded to 20 percent, and fuels the remaining eight percent. By 1980 the share of imported manufactured goods decreased to 54 percent while fuels increased to 25 percent. By 1987, however, manufactures rose again to 68 percent while fuels declined to 14 percent.[31]

3.2. Haiti

Industrialization efforts in Haiti began in the late 1940s, with an import-substitution strategy. Largely, most of the activities were devoted to the production of cement, shoes, textiles, paper products, essential oils, beverages, and food products. These industries received incentives through tariff protection and import bans, duty free import of equipment and supplies, and protection from local competition.[32] The Haitian based industries were highly capital-intensive, and were characterized by excess capacity and high operating costs, which translated into higher domestic prices in comparison to alternative imports of the same products.[33]

The low level of domestic demand attributable to the insignificant level of disposable income in Haiti meant a limited market for local import-substitution industries, and as a consequence output began to decline after a brief period of growth. An export promotion strategy was then launched in the 1960s, through the passage of the Law on New Industrial or Agricultural Enterprises. The incentives provided by this Law, which has been amended several times, provided exemptions of import duties on raw materials, machinery and supplies, exemptions of export duties on manufactured output, exemption of income and license taxes on all new industries for a period of five to ten years, and unlimited profit repatriation. But the political instability of the country during the 1960s was not conducive to investment. The situation changed somewhat during the 1970s and the country was able to attract foreign investment, and more than 200 enterprises were established.[34] There are no free-trade zones in Haiti to accommodate assembly operations. However, as a result of the provision of industrial estate facilities and of the existing infrastructure in the capital city, all industrial activity has concentrated in the Port-au-Prince region. Many U.S.-owned companies commenced assembly operations in Haiti in the 1970s, taking advantage of the proximity to the United States, Haiti's abundant and low-cost labor supply, and U.S. tariff provisions. It has been estimated that employment in the assembly industry, which had reached 60,000 in 1984, had declined to 40,000 by the end of 1987.[35] Wages paid to workers put them in the upper income groups in Haiti, as they earn slightly more than the minimum wage. The minimum wage of $3.10 per day was received by less than 20 percent of the full-time workers.[36]

In the case of Haiti, the manufacturing activities generated through assembly operations have been indisputable contributors to income, output, and employment. The exports of the manufacturing output has alleviated the difficult situation of the balance of payments. In addition, these operations have stimulated the banking, transportation, and communications sectors.

The most complete information about the status of assembly operations in Haiti comes from a survey undertaken of 51 firms and 500 workers during December 1979-January 1980.[37] The results of the survey denote that the main advantages derived from these experience are the development of Haitian entrepreneurship, the increase in the skill level of the work force, and the continuous flow of technical assistance. Backward linkages, although notably poor, have been established in some aspects, like the use of local raw material: leather for shoes and handbags, glue and core for baseballs and softballs, plastic shells for cassettes, as well as cartons, and other packaging material. However, the main linkage has been established by the consumption expenditures of the assembly workers. The assembly operations have exhibited some stability due to the diversification accomplished: many operations can be shifted, relatively easily, from one industrial sector to another, either by working simultaneously or by shifting the work force from one operation to another, as a response to external demands.

"Consumer non-durable goods" industries (classifications 31 and 32 of the ISIC, which consists of food, beverages, tobacco, textiles, apparel, leather, and footwear) have the been the leaders in Haiti's manufacturing sector. In the 1960s as well as in the 1980s, half of the value added in manufacturing corresponded to these two classifications. One-fourth of the value added corresponded to Classification 38 (metal products, machinery, and transportation equipment) which includes the assembly of electronic equipment. Table 4.5 portrays the status of manufacturing from 1968 to 1986. During this period, the number of establishments increased from 431 in 1968, to 992 in 1976, and then fell to 850 in 1986. The average number of employees, mainly women, increased from 13,502 in 1968 to 18,645 in

Table 4.5. Haiti: Manufacturing Statistics, 1960-1986

ISIC	Manufacturing	Number of Establishments			Number of Employees			Wages and Salaries (thous. gourdes)			Gross Output (million gourdes)		
		1968	1976	1986	1968	1976	1986	1968	1976	1986	1971	1976	1986
31	Food, Beverage & Tobacco	238	518	424	4728	5888	8500	14381	20751	96244	66.2	195.3	322.2
32	Textiles & Apparel	64	163	153	7030	6565	9763	8803	14606	74144	38.9	26.8	114.6
33	Wood Products	19	44	43	65	272	609	117	700	2663	2.5	na	na
34	Paper Products	7	12	30	36	126	461	72	526	4619	na	na	na
35	Chemicals	16	37	36	431	711	813	663	1661	6916	2.8	41.1	25.8
36	Non-Metal Products	14	30	35	438	780	1167	1986	4782	19355	8.5	33.6	39.7
37	Basic Metals												
38	Metal Manufactures	50	101	46	488	2026	3943	1457	9214	31535	46.4	58.3	177.5
39	Other Manufactures	25	92	76	286	2339	4898	993	6809	40829	9.3	200.7	108.9
	Total	431	997	843	13502	18707	30154	28472	62049	281237	174.6	663.6	788.7

Source: United Nations, Industrial Statistic Yearbook, various issues.

1976 and then to 30,165 in 1986. The index of employment in manufacturing in Table 4.2 shows the steady increase in employment.

The average payroll also increased from 28 million gourdes in 1968 to
62 million gourdes in 1976, and then to 281 million gourdes in 1986.
However, in real terms, the index of earning per employee does not show
improvement over the levels achieved in 1967 and 1970 [Table 4.2]. Value
added per worker, nonetheless, increased from 12,850 gourdes in 1968 to
35,590 gourdes in 1976, but then decreased to 26,149 gourdes in 1986.
Almost two-thirds of employment in the manufacturing sector is concentrated in food, beverages, tobacco, textiles, apparel, and leather industries. Ownership of these establishments is 40 percent Haitian, 30
percent foreign, and the remaining 30 percent are joint ventures. This
indicates that assembly activities rely to a great extent on Haitian
entrepreneurship.[38]

Domestic demand for manufactures has been satisfied mainly by imports: in 1987, 80 percent of imports were manufactured goods. At the
same time, 85 percent of the exports were manufactured goods [Table 4.6].

4. TOTAL TRADE AND TRADE OF MANUFACTURED GOODS

The objective of this section is to describe the pattern of total trade, granting special attention to the trade in manufactured goods. The percentage
compositions of imports and exports of the two countries, by the one-digit
Standard International Trade Classification (SITC) are presented in Tables
4.7 and 4.8.

4.1. Dominican Republic

The Dominican Republic is not a member of any economic integration
scheme but this country has signed a series of preferential trade and pay-
ment agreements with some Latin American countries, other Caribbean
islands, the United States, and also with the European Economic Community, through the provisions of the Lomé Convention.

The Dominican Republic has reported a consistently negative balance of
its current account since 1967, with the exception of 1975. The account
deficits have been financed by capital inflows: direct foreign investment
and borrowing. The external debt situation in the Dominican Republic has
reached crisis level, and rescheduling has been negotiated.

The value of exported merchandise (fob) in current US dollars has
increased from $150 million in 1967 to $961.9 million in 1980 [Table 4.6],
reflecting an average annual rate of growth of 19.9 percent. After 1981,

Table 4.6. Dominican Republic and Haiti: Exports and Imports by Classifications, 1967-1987 and Terms of Trade

	Total Exports (millions of current $)	Nonfuel Primary Products (percentages)	Manuf. (percentages)	Total Imports (millions of current $)	Nonfuel Primary Products (percentages)	Fuel (percentages)	Manuf. (percentages)	Terms of Trade (1980=100)
A. Dominican Republic								
1967	156.2	97.0	3.0	197.0	20.0	8.0	72.0	74.2
1970	214.0	95.0	5.0	304.0	20.0	7.0	73.0	94.8
1975	893.8	85.0	15.0	889.0	17.0	22.0	60.0	116.9
1980	961.9	83.0	17.0	1640.0	21.0	25.0	54.0	100.0
1985	735.2	73.0	27.0	1487.0	19.0	27.0	54.0	65.7
1986	717.6	71.0	29.0	1433.0	19.0	14.0	67.0	79.1
1987	711.3	78.0	22.0	1782.5	18.0	14.0	68.0	59.9
B. Haiti								
1967	32.9	77.0	23.0	37.6	31.0	6.0	62.0	117.3
1970	48.1	62.0	38.0	59.0	20.0	5.0	75.0	127.9
1975	142.9	34.0	65.0	193.3	24.0	7.0	69.0	94.0
1980	341.0	36.0	64.0	492.1	23.0	13.0	64.0	100.0
1985	332.6	31.0	69.0	449.2	21.0	4.0	74.0	97.3
1986	285.0	37.0	64.0	367.2	16.0	4.0	80.0	124.1
1987	260.7	15.0	85.0	378.2	17.0	3.0	80.0	108.6

Source: World Bank, World Tables, 1988-89.

Table 4.7. Dominican Republic: Exports and Imports by SITC Code, 1969-1985 (percentages)

	SITC Codes	Exports			Imports		
		1969	1974	1983	1969	1979	1985
0	Food & Live Animals	80.0	74.0	71.0	13.0	10.0	6.0
1	Beverages & Tobacco	7.0	6.0	4.0	2.0	1.0	0.0
2	Crude Materials, excluding fuel	9.0	18.0	1.0	1.0	4.0	4.0
3	Mineral Fuels	0.0	0.0	0.0	8.0	26.0	35.0
4	Animal & Vegetable Oil and Fats	0.0	0.0	0.0	2.0	5.0	1.0
5	Chemicals	3.0	0.0	4.0	11.0	13.0	12.0
6	Basic Mmanufactures	0.0	0.0	14.0	26.0	17.0	14.0
7	Macinery & Transportation Equipm.	0.0	0.0	4.0	31.0	19.0	23.0
8	Miscellaneous Manuf.	0.0	0.0	2.0	2.0	4.0	2.0
9	Special Transactions	1.0	2.0	0.0	2.0	0.0	0.0

Source: United Nations, International Trade Statistics Yearbook, various issues.

Table 4.8. Haiti: Exports and Imports by SITC Codes, 1968-1984 (percentages)

	SITC Codes	Exports			Imports		
		1968	1974	1984	1968	1974	1984
0	Food & Live Animals	57.0	45.0	36.0	16.0	14.0	18.0
1	Beverages & Tobacco	0.0	0.0	0.0	3.0	2.0	2.0
2	Crude Materials, excluding fuel	17.0	18.0	1.0	2.0	4.0	3.0
3	Minerals, Fuels, etc.	0.0	0.0	0.0	6.0	11.0	13.0
4	Animal & Vegetable Oil and Fats	0.0	0.0	0.0	6.0	7.0	7.0
5	Chemicals	8.0	9.0	3.0	11.0	9.0	9.0
6	Basic Manufactures	13.0	12.0	16.0	31.0	23.0	20.0
7	Machinery & Transportation Equipm.	0.0	2.0	0.0	12.0	17.0	20.0
8	Miscellaneous Manuf.	4.0	12.0	38.0	8.0	8.0	8.0
9	Special Transactions	0.0	0.0	0.0	0.0	4.0	0.0

Source: United Nations, International Trade Statistics Yearbook, various issues.

however, the value of exports decreased reaching an estimated $711 mil-
lion in 1987, due to declines in export prices, particularly the price of
sugar. The average annual rate of growth for the period 1981-87 declined
to –4.2 percent.[39] More than 75 percent of exports were comprised of
non-fuel primary products, and the remaining were manufactured goods.
This composition illustrates the heavy domestic bias of the manufacturing
sector.

Since 1973 the principal manufactured goods exported by the
Dominican Republic have been: sugar, gold and silver (dore), iron and
steel (ferronickel), cocoa and derivatives, meat and meat preparations,
processed fruits and vegetables, vegetable and animal oil and fat, various
food products, leather and leather products, fertilizers and pesticides, cement, lime, and plaster, and industrial machinery. Combined, these goods
represent slightly more than 95 percent of total exports of manufactured
goods, with sugar, ferronickel, and dore making up more than 80 percent
of that total.[40] Slight changes in the composition of exports by industrial
origin are revealed in Table 4.7.

The US was the principal export market for the Dominican Republic
with a percentage share of 76 percent in 1976. That share decreased to 56.7
in 1982, but then increased again to 76 percent in 1985 [Table 4.9]. Trade
with the US is particularly important because the Dominican Republic has
been a signatour to the following agreements: (1) the Generalized System
of Preferences (GSP), which gives duty free treatment to many items from
developing countries; (2) the US Tariff Schedule, former Sections 806.30
and 807, which allows duty free entry of that portion of a finished product
which is a US component; (3) the Caribbean Basin Initiative (CBI), which
also grants duty-free treatment to specified manufactured goods, provided
they meet the requirement of a 35 percent local value-added; (4) the extension of the Multifiber Arrangement, which is a bilateral agreement to
restrict textiles and clothing exports, but which has not affected the
Dominican Republic, as they have not filled their quotas; (5) "super 807",
which guarantees access to US markets for apparel assembled in the Caribbean without regard to quota levels, but with the specification that the
clothing be made entirely of US materials; and (6) the quotas on sugar,
which has affected the Dominican Republic more than any other country in
the Caribbean. The fluctuations in trade with the US has been related to
declines in both the sugar quota and the price of sugar.[41]

The second trade partner in importance is the EEC export market, but
their share has decreased from 16 percent in 1976 to 12 percent in 1985. It
is expected that, after 1990, through the stipulations of the Lomé Convention, the share of exports to Europe will increase again.

Table 4.9. Dominican Republic and Haiti: Percentage Composition of Imports and Exports by Sources and Destinations, 1968-1985

Country	USA	EEC	Latin America	Japan
A. Dominican Republic				
Sources of Imports				
1968	54.7	18.9	2.5	6.1
1976	57.1	15.8	5.1	9.1
1985	34.7	10.3	39.6	6.3
Destination of Exports				
1968	88.8	4.6	0.3	0.7
1976	76.0	16.2	0.5	0.7
1985	75.9	12.5	0.3	1.8
B. Haiti				
Sources of Imports				
1968	53.3	21.5	0.0	6.2
1975	74.2	20.8	0.0	6.8
1981	73.4	22.6	0.0	6.3
Destination of Exports				
1968	58.8	33.6	0.0	0.0
1975	74.2	20.8	0.0	0.0
1981	73.4	22.6	0.0	3.4

Source: United Nations, International Trade Statistics Yearbook, various issues.

US imports of Dominican manufactured goods more than doubled during the period 1980 to 1986, increasing from $303 million to $656 million, as a result of the industrial tax free zones and the other incentives provided by the US. Exports of manufactured goods to the EEC were second in importance, although their value has increased only slightly from $52 million to $57 million for the same period.[42]

The value of imported merchandise (cif), in current US dollars, increased from $197 million in 1967 to $1,640 million in 1980, which represents an average annual growth rate of 23.6 percent. During the 1980s and up until 1986, imports have been on the decline, reaching a low value of $1,433 million in 1986.[43] This decline corresponds to the economic recession that started in 1981, and also to the implementation of fiscal, monetary, and exchange rate policies aimed at reducing the volume of imports.[44] It is estimated that by 1987 imports rose again, to an estimated value of $1,782.5 million, and the average annual rate of growth declined to 1.2 percent for the period 1980-87.

The Dominican Republic's imports have changed in composition during the 1969-1985 period [Table 4.7]. Food, beverages and tobacco, as well as other consumer goods have decreased their shares, while fuels have increased their participation and the demand for machinery and transportation equipment has remained strong. The share of food dropped from 13 percent in 1969 to 6 percent in 1985, while fuels increased from 8 to 35 percent for the same period.

Few countries account for a large portion of the Dominican Republic's imports [Table 4.9]. The United States has been the leading supplier with 35 percent in 1985, which is a considerable decrease from the 57 percent attained in 1976. The countries of Latin America are also major suppliers, providing 40 percent of the imports in 1985 compared to only 5 percent in 1976. The main trading partners have been Venezuela (providing 27 percent in 1985, up from 0.8 percent in 1976) and Mexico (supplying 8 percent in 1985 up from 1.1 percent in 1976). The substantial increase in imports from both of them after 1982 is singularly due to the increase in oil imports negotiated as part of the San José Agreement, under which Venezuela and Mexico supply crude oil to specific Central American and Caribbean countries on concessionary terms. The countries of the European Economic Community supplied 16 percent of the Dominican imports in 1976, but by 1985 their share dropped to ten percent. (The Netherlands and Belgium are the main trading partners among the EEC.) At the same time, Japan decreased its share from 9.2 to 6.3 percent for the same period.

4.2. Haiti

Haiti's foreign trade has been in deficit since 1960, reflecting lower world coffee prices, declines in the volume of sugar and coffee exports, rising costs of fuels, and consistent import demand for food, industrial supplies and transportation equipment. Since the 1970s, manufactured exports have surpassed agricultural products as the main export revenue earner [Table 4.6].

Trade is strongly oriented towards the United States [Table 4.9]. More than 50 percent of imports come from the US and about three-fourths of the exports go to the US. The EEC is Haiti's second major trading partner.

The same special provisions granted by the US to the Dominican Republic explain the extensive trade between Haiti and the US: (1) the

Generalized System of Preferences (GSP); (2) the US Tariff System, former Sections 806.30 and 807; (3) the Caribbean Basin Initiative (CBI); (4) the extension of the Multifiber Arrangement (MFA); (5) the "Super 807", and (6) the sugar quotas.[45]

Up until 1970 exports were dominated by non-fuel primary products (mainly coffee), while manufactured goods prevailed in the import market. Table 4.8 shows that exports of manufactures have grown substantially as a result of assembly operations. However, the contribution of this activity to the local economy is minimal and represented chiefly by the salaries and wages paid to employees and the use of some local inputs.

5. SUMMARY AND PERSPECTIVES

The main findings of the study can be summarized as follows:

1. The Dominican Republic and Haiti have marked differences in their indices of social and economic progress, but they share the problem of high levels of unemployment.

2. Both countries have relied on attracting foreign investment to supplement their domestic industrial sector. The incentives offered include tax holidays and profit repatriation, among other incentives and subsidies.

3. In the Dominican Republic economic growth has been erratic, but substantial. Although there have been variations, the rate has been positive for the most recent decades. Conversely, in Haiti, economic growth has been unstable, varying from positive to negative, from decade to decade.

4. Agriculture has decreased as the main economic sector in the Dominican Republic, but has maintained a positive growth rate. In Haiti, agriculture remains an important sector but its rate of growth has been stagnant or negative, due to the primitive technology utilized.

5. The share of manufacturing to GDP has increased in the Dominican Republic, but the rate of growth achieved during the 1980s has been much lower (1.4%), than the high rates attained during the 1960s and 1970s: 7.4 and 6.8 percent, respectively. In the case of Haiti, the rate of growth in manufacturing value added has been negative during the 1980s (–2.8%), after a strong performance in the 1970s (8.4%).

6. In the Dominican Republic, the industrial policy framework has been determined largely by the passage, in 1968, of the Industrial Incentives Law. This Law has encouraged an inward development of the industrial sector, and under the incentives provided, the sector has become capital intensive and dominated by imported inputs. Many industries emerged producing consumer goods for the domestic market. Another industrial development was organized through tax free zones, designed to export assembled goods. The anti-export bias of the Industrial Incentives Law has started to be overcome, in part, by the passage of an Export Incentive Law and a Free Zone Law at the beginning of the 1980s.

7. In Haiti, the industrialization strategy followed was that of export promotion, after abandoning an inward orientation, due to the weak domestic market. By 1987, 85 percent of exports were manufactured output, mainly consumer non-durable goods. Foreign investment has been an important participant in that country's manufacturing activity.

8. Both the Dominican Republic and Haiti have had consistent negative balances of trade. Both exports and imports of the two of countries are heavily concentrated: the Dominican Republic exports mainly primary goods, and imports manufactured goods; Haiti exports primarily manufactured goods, and imports manufactured goods, as well.

9. The trade of the two countries is also heavily concentrated: the US is the main trading partner, as both nations take advantage of the incentives provided by the Generalized System of Preferences (GSP), the US Tariff System, mainly former Sections 806.30 and 807, and those of the Caribbean Basin Initiative.

The Dominican Republic has good prospects for expanding non-traditional exports. Among these, attention should be called to the potential that exists in the agro-industry and in light manufacturing. The country is endowed with an abundant labor supply which can be utilized to expand production in the processed food sector as well as in other sectors including: apparel, electronics, footwear, medical supplies, pharmaceuticals, leather products, and jewelry. The Dominican Republic offers many advantages to the possible investor in terms of (1) competitive wages, much lower than other possible alternative locations in the Caribbean Basin; (2) political stability; (3) governmental policies such as fiscal incentives supportive of investment in manufacturing can be more generous than possible inducements provided in other Caribbean countries; (4) easy access to US markets through arrangements like the Caribbean Basin Initiative, the Multifiber Arrangement (MFA), and the Generalized System of Preferences; (5) access to the EEC, through the provisions of the Lomé Convention, to which the Dominican Republic became a beneficiary in 1990; and (6) the possibility of getting investment funds through the "twin plant" concept being promoted in the Caribbean, by the Puerto Rico Government Development Bank, with funds from the US Tax Code Section 936, of which the Dominican Republic has been a major beneficiary.

However, in order to promote exports and manufacturing activity, the Dominican Republic will have to overcome serious deficiencies. In the first place, there is an acute need of financial capital, for both medium and long term projects. Due to tight monetary policies, the availability of funds has been diminished, and high interest rates prevail in the market. In the second place the assembly operations in the tax free zones should develop backward linkages with the rest of the economy. In this respect, ways should be explored to increase, among others, the use of local inputs, local supplies of packaging material, and local insurance services. Attempts should be made to provide needed infrastructure, in terms of sea and air transportation, which is at present costly and deficient, and in terms of electricity, which is expensive and unreliable. There is also the necessity to improve the level of marketing capabilities. There is a need for knowledgeable, trained, and experienced personnel, in dealing with the markets of the developed countries, if exports to those markets are going to continue escalating. But, above all, it is imperative that the anti-export bias be reduced. One way to accomplish this is by establishing a new tariff structure. The present one has been found deficient because it has promoted a capital intensive manufacturing sector and one which has relied strongly on imported raw material.

Haiti shares many of the problems that exist in the Dominican Republic, but at the same time offers many of the same advantages as the other. The main difficulty to venture manufacturing activities, not found in the Dominican Republic, is related to the political atmosphere and uncertainties present in Haiti. The tax incentives are not as generous in Haiti as in the Dominican Republic, but wages are lower in Haiti, so that this nation also offers some attractiveness to possible investors. Haiti also offers easy access to the US market, and the possibility of operating under the twin plant concept.

As indicated, the future of manufacturing and the capability of increasing exports of manufactured goods from the Dominican Republic, as well as in Haiti, depend on many factors, some of which are beyond the control

of their governments; such as the wave of protectionism sweeping many of
the developed countries.

NOTES

1. Interamerican Development Bank, *Economic and Social Progress in Latin America, 1989 Report* (Washington, D.C.: Interamerican Development Bank, 1989).
2. Interamerican Development Bank, *1989 Report.*
3. Interamerican Development Bank, *1989 Report.*
4. Both the Dominican Republic and Haiti have observer status in CARICOM.
5. Interamerican Development Bank, *1989 Report.*
6. J.A. Mathieson, "Dominican Republic," in *Struggle Against Dependence: Non-traditional Export Growth in Central America and the Caribbean*, edited by Eva Paus, pp. 41-63 (Boulder and London: Westview Press, 1988); World Bank, *Dominican Republic: Economic Prospects and Policies to Renew Growth* (Washington, D.C.: World Bank, 1985).
7. Interamerican Development Bank, *1989 Report.*
8. Interamerican Development Bank, *1989 Report.*
9. World Bank, *World Development Report, 1989.*
10. Interamerican Development Bank, *1989 Report.*
11. Interamerican Development Bank, *1989 Report.*
12. Some of the publications delineating the economic situation in Haiti are: A. Dupuy, *Haiti in the World Economy: Class, Race and Underdevelopment Since 1700* (Boulder: Westview Press, 1989); S.M. Fass, *Political Economy in Haiti: The Drama of Survival* (New Brunswick, N.J.: Transaction Books, 1988); M. Lundhal, *The Haitian Economy: Man, Lands and Markets* (New York: St. Martin's Press, 1983); D. Nicholls, *Haiti in Caribbean Context* (London: Macmillan 1985); R. Prince, *Haiti: Family Business* (London: Latin America Bureau, 1985); and R. J. Tata, *Haiti: Land of Poverty* (Lanham, Md.: University Press of America, 1982), among others.
13. International Monetary Fund, *International Financial Statistics Yearbook, 1989.*
14. Interamerican Development Bank, *1989 Report.*
15. Interamerican Development Bank, *1989 Report.*
16. World Bank, *Dominican Republic: Economic Prospects and Policies to Renew Growth, op. cit.*; Andrés Dauhajre, Jr., "República Dominicana: Comercio e Industrialización, 1973-1984," an IESCARIBE study presented to the Interamerican Development Bank (mimeo), 1987.
17. According to surveys undertaken by CERDOPEX (Centro Dominicano de Promoción de Exportaciones) and reported by A. Dauhajre, *op. cit.*
18. The Economist Intelligence Unit, *Country Profile: Dominican Republic, Haiti, Puerto Rico, 1989-90* (London: The Economist Publication Ltd., 1990).
19. In this aspect, see for example, A. Dauhajre, *op. cit.*, and J.K. Black, *The Dominican Republic: Politics, and Development in an Unsovereign State* (Boston: Allen & Unwin, 1986).
20. For more details, Dauhajre, *op. cit.*, and Black, *op. cit.*
21. Interamerican Development Bank, *1989 Report.*
22. Andres Dauhajre, *op. cit.*
23. World Bank, *World Tables, 1988-89* (Washington, D.C.: World Bank, 1990).
24. United Nations, *Industrial Statistics Yearbook*, various issues.

25. A. Dauhajre, *op. cit.*, based on data provided by Banco Central de la Republica Dominicana.

26. H. J. Wiarda and M. J. Kryzanek, *The Dominican Republic: A Caribbean Crucible* (Boulder: Westview Press, 1982).

27. Interamerican Development Bank, *1989 Report*.

28. The Economist Intelligence Unit, *Country Profile, op. cit.*

29. World Bank, *Dominican Republic, op. cit.*

30. World Bank, *Dominican Republic, op. cit.*, and A. Dauhajre, *op. cit.*

31. World Bank, *World Development Report, 1988-89* (Washington, D.C.: World Bank, 1990).

32. In this aspect, please refer, among others, to R. Prince, *Haiti: Family Business, op. cit.* and S.M. Fass, *Political Economy in Haiti: The Drama of Survival, op. cit.*

33. R. Prince, *op. cit.*, and S.M. Fass, *op. cit.*

34. Leslie Pean, "Trade in Manufactures: Haiti, 1970-79," an IESCARIBE study submitted to the Interamerican Development Bank (mimeo), 1987.

35. United Nations, *The Least Developed Countries, 1988 Report* (New York: United Nations, 1989).

36. Michael S. Hooper, "Haiti," in *Latin America and Caribbean Contemporary Record*, edited by Jack W. Hopkins (New York: Holmes & Meier, 1986), pp. 727-742.

37. L. Delatour and K. Voltaire, *International Subcontracting in Haiti* (Chicago: University of Chicago Press, 1980).

38. Grunwald, J. L., L. Delatour and K. Voltaire, "Foreign Assembly in Haiti" in *The Global Factory: Foreign Assembly in International Trade*, edited by Joseph Grunwald and Kenneth Flamm (Washington, D.C.: The Brookings Institution, 1985), pp. 180-205.

39. World Bank, *World Tables, 1988-89*.

40. Andres Dauhajre, *op. cit.*

41. World Bank, *The Caribbean: Export Preferences and Performance*.

42. World Bank, *The Caribbean, op. cit.*

43. World Bank, *World Tables, 1988-89*.

44. Andres Dauhajre, *op. cit.*

45. World Bank, *The Caribbean, op. cit.*

CHAPTER 5

Trade of Manufactured Goods in the English Speaking Caribbean

Irma T. de Alonso

1. INTRODUCTION

The English Speaking Caribbean has made various attempts at economic integration, the first being the Federation of the West Indies, created in 1958, but ultimately dissolved in 1962. Afterwards, the Caribbean Free Trade Area (CARIFTA) and the Eastern Caribbean Common Market (ECCM) came into existence in 1968. Subsequently, the Caribbean Community and Common Market (CARICOM), was initiated in 1973 by Barbados, Guyana, Jamaica, and Trinidad & Tobago. The Windward and Leeward Islands, and Belize, subsequently followed as members. The Bahamas is a member of the Community, but not of the common market.

The CARICOM, established by the Treaty of Chaguaramas in 1973 is still viable, but not simply as a trading arrangement, due that it embraces three major elements: (1) economic integration (through the Caribbean Common Market), (2) functional cooperation (including common services), in a number of areas, and (3) coordination of common foreign policies.[1] The effort at economic integration involved: (a) the expansion of intra-regional trade, (b) joint efforts to strengthen production selling to national, regional, and extra-regional markets, and (c) joint efforts at extra-regional trade and other external economic relations and transactions. CARICOM has achieved such objectives as the establishment of a common external tariff, a harmonized system of fiscal incentives for industry, double-taxation and tax-sparing agreements.[2] When these joint efforts were evaluated in 1981 it was determined that some slight progress was attained in the area of economic integration, but the consensus view was

71

widespread disappointment in the areas of functional cooperation and in the coordination of foreign policies.[3]

Together with the integration movement, a series of institutions were established. The Caribbean Development Bank (CDB) was set up in 1969 as the first ever regional lending institution, and to date it has been successful in mobilizing and disbursing development funds. The Caribbean Investment Corporation (CIC) was established in 1973 to promote industrial development within the less developed countries of the Community. A third organization, The Multilateral Clearing Facility (MCF), began operations in 1969, and was aimed at promoting greater liberalization of intra-regional trade. However the MCF was suspended in 1983 when credit line limits were reached, and following the incident it has remained inoperative. As a result, intra-regional payments continue to be settled on a bilateral basis.[4]

The CARICOM encompasses an archipelago in the Caribbean Sea plus two mainland countries on the continent of South America; Guyana and Belize. Since its inception, the CARICOM countries have been divided into two classifications: more developed countries (MDC) and the less developed countries (LDC). The Bahamas, Barbados, Guyana, Jamaica, and Trinidad & Tobago are classified as MDCs, while the Windward and Leeward Islands and Belize belonged to the LDCs.

The land mass covered by the CARICOM member countries is 271 thousand km^2. Guyana occupies 80 percent of the land mass, Belize, 8.5 percent, the Bahamas 5.1 percent, Jamaica 4.2 percent, and Trinidad & Tobago 1.9 percent. The remaining one percent is covered by the following islands: Antigua & Barbuda, Barbados, Dominica, Grenada, Montserrat, St. Kitts-Nevis, St. Lucia, and St. Vincent and the Grenadines. [Table 5.1].

The total population of this area is 5.5 million: 42 percent residing in Jamaica, 21.5 percent in Trinidad & Tobago, 14.4 percent in Guyana, 4.6 percent in Barbados, and 4.2 percent in the Bahamas. The remaining 13.3 percent is distributed among the other eight islands and accounts for one to three percent each.

In 1985 per capita GNP (in 1984 US dollars) was the highest in Trinidad & Tobago ($7,150), followed by $6,690 in the Bahamas, and $4,370 in Barbados. The remaining countries had much lower values, and the lowest value of $590 was found in Guyana [Table 5.1]. For the period 1980-85, seven of the thirteen countries had negative growth rates of GDP per capita. The most severe cases were those of Trinidad & Tobago, with average rates of –5.9 percent, followed by –2.9 percent in Guyana. Open unemployment rates in the range of 10 to 25 percent and inflation rates in the range of 6 to 20 percent have characterized these economies in the 1980s.

Table 5.1. English Speaking Caribbean: Basic Indicators, 1985

Country	Population (thou.)	Land Area (th.km2)	Per capita GNP (1984 US$)	Growth Real GDP Per capita	Percentage Composition of Real GDP			Unemployment Rates (%)		Inflation Rate 1980-85
					Agric.	Mining	Manuf.	1980	1985	
Antiqua & Barbuda	80.3	0.4	1860.0	5.9	4.9	0.6	6.1	na	21	na
Bahamas	232.0	13.9	6690.0	1.3	na	na	na	na	12	5.9
Barbados	252.7	0.4	4370.0	-0.5	9.7	1.0	11.8	11	18	7.8
Belize	166.4	23.0	1110.0	-0.8	25.0	0.3	9.0	na	na	na
Dominica	77.9	0.8	1010.0	2.7	29.0	0.8	8.0	19	na	na
Grenada	100.3	0.3	860.0	-0.6	22.0	1.0	5.0	18	20	na
Guyana	790.8	215.0	590.0	-2.9	26.0	9.0	11.0	na	na	19.7
Jamaica	2311.1	11.4	1150.0	-1.7	9.0	5.0	16.0	27	25	16.9
Montserrat	11.9	0.1	2644.0	1.1	5.0	1.0	9.0	11	na	na
St. Kitts-Nevis	45.8	0.3	1150.0	-1.3	14.0	0.3	14.0	12	na	na
St. Lucia	1368.0	0.6	1130.0	1.2	14.0	0.8	9.0	19	25	na
St. Vincent & the Grenadines	109.3	0.4	840.0	4.1	17.0	0.3	10.0	20	na	na
Trinidad & Tobago	1181.2	5.1	7150.0	-5.2	3.0	7.0	18.0	10	15	12.4
All countries	5496.5	271.8								

Source: Bourne, C., Caribbean Development to the Year 2000. Challenges, Prospects and Policies, Tables II.1, II.5, II.6, II.7, and II.8. InterAmerican Development Bank, Economic and Social Progress in Latin America, 1989 Report, Table II.7.

Agriculture is an important economic activity in the CARICOM countries, despite their small geographic area; in fact it is the major sector in six of the thirteen countries. Mining is another important sector for three of the countries, consisting of bauxite and alumina in Guyana and Jamaica, with petroleum, and to a lesser extent, natural gas, in Trinidad & Tobago. Manufacturing is the significant operation in Antigua & Barbuda, Barbados, Jamaica, and Trinidad & Tobago.

The purpose of this chapter is to determine the trade experience of manufactured goods within three of the most developed countries of the CARICOM, namely Barbados, Jamaica, and Trinidad & Tobago. These three countries were selected because they are the main CARICOM exporters of manufactured goods to both extra-regional markets and within the Caribbean Community. What remains of the Chapter is divided into the following sections: Part 2 will provide a brief overview of the performance of their economies since 1960; Part 3 will analyze the structure of manufacturing, while Part 4 will review the trade performance of manufactured goods of those three Caribbean islands. The Chapter concludes with a summary and perspectives for the future.

2. AN OVERVIEW OF ECONOMIC PERFORMANCE IN BARBADOS, JAMAICA, AND TRINIDAD & TOBAGO

The CARICOM member states are small trading nations; they rely on foreign trade, not to mention, foreign finance, and foreign technology, for their economic activities. In 1988 ratios of foreign trade (exports plus imports of goods and services) to Gross Domestic Product were as high as 61 percent in Trinidad & Tobago, 105 percent in Barbados, and 118 percent in Jamaica. Other CARICOM members had ratios near the 200 percent level.

All these nations, in some degree or another, are struggling to recover from the economic recession which impaired them significantly during the late 1970s and the beginning of the 1980s. The poor performance of the CARICOM countries during the last decade has been the result of both international and domestic factors. In the international setting they have experienced world-wide economic recession, high inflation rates, and waves of protectionism from the industrialized economies. In the domestic front they have suffered from inadequate domestic savings and investment as well as production weaknesses.[5]

The economic performance, from 1960 to the present, of the individual three nations under consideration can be shown from statistics prepared by the Interamerican Development Bank.[6]

Table 5.2. English Speaking Caribbean: Gross Domestic Product, and Value Added by Main Sectors, 1960, 1970, 1980 and 1988 (millions of 1988 dollars)

GDP and Main Sector	1960	1970	1980	1985	1988*
GDP					
Barbados	462.0	844.0	944.0	963.0	1075.0
Jamaica	2623.0	4419.0	4080.0	4094.0	4472.0
Trinidad & Tobago	3244.0	5060.0	8668.0	7417.0	6375.0
Value added by Agriculture					
Barbados	106.0	108.0	97.0	88.0	77.0
Jamaica	289.0	330.0	340.0	365.0	338.0
Trinidad & Tobago	229.0	262.0	217.0	230.0	274.0
Value added by Manufacturing					
Barbados	32.0	61.0	111.0	96.0	100.0
Jamaica	438.0	777.0	628.0	668.0	710.0
Trinidad & Tobago	538.0	714.0	849.0	701.0	663.0
Value added by Mining					
Barbados	na	1.0	5.0	9.0	8.0
Jamaica	197.0	312.0	363.0	213.0	231.0
Trinidad & Tobago	634.0	1268.0	2000.0	1637.0	1421.0
Value added by Construction					
Barbados	51.0	54.0	66.0	58.0	69.0
Jamaica	302.0	584.0	220.0	217.0	292.0
Trinidad & Tobago	223.0	349.0	1276.0	891.0	596.0
Value added by Commerce					
Barbados	90.0	143.0	183.0	180.0	211.0
Jamaica	700.0	944.0	611.0	599.0	714.0
Trinidad & Tobago	427.0	769.0	1200.0	867.0	488.0
Value added by Government					
Barbados	44.0	100.0	119.0	125.0	139.0
Jamaica	128.0	402.0	784.0	153.0	735.0
Trinidad & Tobago	388.0	626.0	1006.0	1125.0	1070.0

Source: InterAmerican Development Bank, Economic and Social Progress in Latin America, 1989 Report.

2.1. Barbados

In real 1988 dollars, the GDP in Barbados increased from $462 million in 1960 to $844 million in 1970, representing an average annual growth rate of 6.2 percent. Much of this growth can be attributed to the growth of its manufacturing sector which increased at an average annual rate of growth

Table 5.3. English Speaking Caribbean: Growth of Production in Real 1988 Dollars (percentages)

GDP and Sector	Average Annual Growth Rates		
	1961-70	1971-80	1981-88
Gross Domestic Product			
Barbados	6.2	1.6	1.0
Jamaica	5.4	−0.8	1.2
Trinidad & Tobago	4.5	5.5	−3.8
Value added by Agriculture			
Barbados	0.2	−1.1	−2.8
Jamaica	1.4	0.3	−0.1
Trinidad & Tobago	1.3	−1.9	3.0
Value added by Mining			
Barbados	na	na	na
Jamaica	4.7	1.4	−5.5
Trinidad & Tobago	7.3	4.5	−4.2
Value added by Manufacturing			
Barbados	6.5	6.2	−1.2
Jamaica	5.9	−2.1	1.5
Trinidad & Tobago	2.9	1.7	−3.0
Value added by Commerce			
Barbados	4.7	2.5	1.8
Jamaica	3.0	−4.2	2.0
Trinidad & Tobago	6.1	4.6	−10.6
Value added by Government			
Barbados	8.6	1.8	2.0
Jamaica	12.1	6.9	−0.8
Trinidad & Tobago	4.9	4.9	0.8

Source: InterAmerican Development Bank, Economic and Social Progress in Latin America, 1989 Report.

of 6.5 percent. The growth in the agricultural value added during the period was a dismal 0.2 percent [Tables 5.2 and 5.3]. During the 1960s, the proportion of manufacturing in GDP remained at seven percent, whereas the share of agriculture declined from 23 percent to 13 percent [Table 5.4]. In real terms the value added by manufacturing increased from $32 million in 1960 to $61 million in 1970, while the value added by agriculture remained nearly the same; increasing only from $106 million to $108 million.

Table 5.4. English Speaking Caribbean: Structure of Production, in Real 1988 Dollars (percentages)

Distribution of GDP	1960	1970	1980	1988*
Agriculture				
Barbados	23.0	13.0	10.0	7.0
Jamaica	11.0	7.0	8.0	8.0
Trinidad & Tobago	7.0	5.0	2.0	4.0
Mining				
Barbados	0.0	0.0	0.0	1.0
Jamaica	8.0	7.0	9.0	5.0
Trinidad & Tobago	20.0	25.0	23.0	22.0
Manufacturing				
Barbados	7.0	7.0	11.0	9.0
Jamaica	17.0	18.0	15.0	16.0
Trinidad & Tobago	17.0	14.0	10.0	10.0
Construction				
Barbados	11.0	6.0	6.0	6.0
Jamaica	12.0	13.0	5.0	6.0
Trinidad & Tobago	7.0	7.0	15.0	9.0
Government				
Barbados	10.0	12.0	12.0	13.0
Jamaica	5.0	9.0	19.0	16.0
Trinidad & Tobago	12.0	12.0	12.0	17.0
Commerce				
Barbados	19.0	17.0	18.0	20.0
Jamaica	27.0	21.0	15.0	16.0
Trinidad & Tobago	13.0	15.0	14.0	8.0

Source: InterAmerican Development Bank, Economic and Social Progress in Latin America, 1989 Report.

For the decade 1971-1980, the GDP grew at the estimated average 1.6 percent yearly, while the growth in manufacturing remained at a strong 6.2 percent average rate and agriculture subsided at a rate of −1.1 percent. The value added in manufacturing, in real terms, increased to $111 million in 1980, while the value added from agriculture decreased to $97 million. In proportion the manufacturing GDP increased to 11 percent, and that of agriculture decreased to 10 percent [Tables 5.2, 5.3 and 5.4].

The growth in the 1980s has been more sluggish than in the previous decades. GDP grew at an average annual rate of 1.0 percent, while both manufacturing and agriculture had negative rates: −1.2 percent and −2.8 percent, respectively. The proportion of both sectors in the GDP decreased from 1980 to 1988: agriculture decreased from 10 to seven percent and manufacturing declined from 11 to nine percent. The higher growth of the construction and tourism sectors during the 1980s accounted for the positive growth of GDP.

2.2. Jamaica

In real 1988 dollars, the GDP in Jamaica grew from $2.6 billion in 1960 to $4.4 billion in 1970. The value of GDP declined to $4.1 billion in 1980, and then it increased to $4.5 billion in 1988. The average yearly rate of growth of GDP has been uneven: 5.4 percent during the 1960s, −0.8 percent during the 1970s, and 1.2 percent during the 1980s [Tables 5.2 and 5.3].

The relative importance of agriculture has been declining with a rate of growth of 1.4 percent in the 1960s, later decreasing to 0.3 in the 1970s, and to −0.1 percent in the 1980s. However, the share of value added by agriculture in GDP, during 1980-88, has remained at eight percent, after sharply declining from 11 percent in 1960 to seven percent in 1970 [Table 5.4].

The importance of manufacturing in Jamaica increased significantly in the 1970s. From a value added of $438 million (in 1988 dollars) in 1960, it then increased to $777 million in 1970, but then decreased to $628 million in 1980. It was estimated that by 1988 the value added by manufacturing has increased again, to $710 million, after irregular performance during the 1980s. The share of value added by manufacturing in the GDP has declined from the proportion attained in 1970, although the rate of growth in the 1980s has been a positive 1.5 percent which followed a disappointing −2.1 percent decline in the 1970s, and a healthy rate of 5.9 percent in the 1960s [Tables 5.3 and 5.4].

A downward trend is evident in the mining sector with average yearly rates of 4.7, 1.4 and −5.5 percent for the 1960s, 1970s, and 1980s, respectively [Table 5.3]. This trend has been the result of shutting down mining operations of bauxite and alumina and declines in the global demand for aluminum.

2.3. Trinidad & Tobago

The combined economy of Trinidad and Tobago traditionally has been focused on the production of petroleum. Following the boom in the petroleum industry during the 1970s, the GDP in Trinidad and Tobago increased to an average yearly rate of 5.5 percent, after having attained a 4.5 percent rate in the previous decade.

As a result of the decline in the production of oil and the fall in oil prices, during the 1980s, the economy has contracted and the average yearly rate of growth of the GDP has been –3.8 percent [Table 5.3]. The substantial reduction in oil revenues had repercussions in other sectors of the economy, in particular those of distribution, construction, transportation, and manufacturing. The value of the GDP in 1988 (in real terms) was of $6.4 billion, representing 74 percent of the value reached in 1980 [Table 5.2].

By 1980, the shares of both agriculture and manufacturing had been declining from the values achieved in both 1960 and 1970. However, by 1988 the proportion had increased in agriculture while remaining constant in manufacturing [Table 5.4]. The agricultural value added recovered in the 1980s at a rate of 3.0 percent per year, after a gloomy –1.9 percent in the 1970s. In the case of manufacturing, during the 1980s, the sector had a –3.0 percent average annual rate, after achieving rates of 2.9 and 1.7 percent in the 1960s and the 1970s, respectively.

There has been a downward growth trend in the mining sector with average annual rates of growth of 7.3, 4.5, and –4.2 percent, in the 1960s, 1970s, and 1980s, respectively [Table 5.3]. The production of petroleum has decreased considerably when the price of oil fell and as oil reserves were depleted. Trinidad and Tobago is expanding its resource extraction operations to include the production of natural gas, and is considered the second exporter of ammonia in the world.

The government has initiated the revival of the economy by looking to export products other than petroleum alternatives. In this respect efforts have been addressed at strengthening the energy-based industrial sector. The government has also promoted agro-industry, as a result of the resurgence of the agricultural sector.

3. THE MANUFACTURING SECTOR: SIZE AND COMPOSITION

The manufacturing sector has been an important component in the economic development strategies of the CARICOM countries. The principal feature was the encouragement of foreign investment in the manufacturing sector to undertake production for both local and export markets.[7] However, since 1960, manufacturing has experienced a downward trend in Barbados and in Trinidad and Tobago, while Jamaica was successful in reversing the negative trend during the period 1980-88. The magnitudes of manufacturing value added attained in 1988 by both Jamaica and Trinidad & Tobago ($710 million and $663 million, respectively), were lower than

the values achieved in 1970 ($777 million and $714 million, respectively).
In the case of Barbados, the estimated value added by manufacturing in
1988 ($100 million) was less than the magnitude attained in 1980 ($111
million), as shown in Table 5.2.

The development strategy of these countries was chiefly one of import
substitution. Industrial production was mainly directed at domestic and
regional markets in response to the conditions for import substitution
created by each country and by integration arrangements.[8] The industrial
structure was sheltered by high tariff protective barriers. In addition, mas-
sive fiscal and other government incentives were offered. The firms were
allowed to import duty free raw materials, intermediate goods, and capital
goods. As a result, the industrial structure created has been determined
problematic and inadequate.

As expressed by Cox[9] in the 1960s the Government of Barbados recognized that industrialization based on import substitution was limited by the
small size of the domestic market and legislation was introduced providing
benefits to firms exporting all their output outside the CARICOM. Consequently, assembly-type operations were begun in Barbados as early as
1968. The Barbados Industrial Development Corporation was established
to foster industrial development and to diversify the economy. The Fiscal
Incentive Act of 1974 provided more generous tax holidays to firms exporting outside the region than those trading within the region, with both
types of firms importing duty-free raw materials destined for manufacturing.

Similar developments were taking place in Jamaica. Tax holidays and
liberal profit repatriation were offered by the Industrial Incentives Law, the
Export Industry Encouragement Law, and the Pioneer Industries (Encouragement) Law. In addition, the Jamaica Industrial Development Corporation has focused its activities on providing: (1) technical assistance,
(2) training and (3) construction/expansion of factory space.[10] Free zones
have been established around Kingston, the capital city, and around Montego Bay, for manufacturing and assembly operations.

Likewise, in Trinidad and Tobago, many new industrial plants have been
built under the "Pioneer" category. Incentives include tax concessions,
duty free import of raw materials and capital goods, accelerated depreciation, and subsidized rental space. The Industrial Development Corporation
promotes industrial investment and development, and operations have concentrated around Port of Spain, the capital city, and the San Fernando area.
Contrary to other CARICOM countries, state participation is a common
feature in Trinidad & Tobago, particularly in the areas of sugar and
petroleum production.

Despite the incentives offered, the manufacturing sector is relatively small in most areas. By 1988 the share of manufacturing value added in GDP was less than ten percent in both Barbados and Trinidad and Tobago, and only 16 percent in Jamaica. As mentioned in a previous section, these proportions represent decreases from the shares attained in past decades.

Manufacturing activities have been classified into two categories: those producing for the domestic market and those characterized as enclave-type in free zones, designed to assemble component parts of goods and re-export them back to the USA. Both Jamaica and Barbados have been successful as exporters of assembled goods, taking advantage of the benefits provided by the Tariff Schedule of the United States (TSUS), former Sections 806.30 and 807, in addition to the benefits granted by the Caribbean Basin Initiative (CBI). Both the European Economic Community (EEC) — through the provisions of the Lomé Convention, and Canada — through the provisions of CARIBCAN, offer the CARICOM countries the opportunity of exporting some manufactured goods under preferential treatment. Mention should also be made of the US and EEC Generalized System of Preferences (GSP), which provides duty-free treatment to most exports from the CARICOM, and the Multifiber Arrangement (MFA) which is an import restricting policy that does not affect the imports from CARICOM as they have not filled their quotas of textiles and garments.[11]

Table 5.5 portrays the structure of manufacturing by International Standard Industrial Classification (ISIC). Food and agricultural products (ISIC 31) has been the main industrial activity for these economies. The exception was in the 1970s, when Trinidad and Tobago, due to a surge in petroleum production, produced more petroleum derivatives than food. Most food processing has been related to some form of sugar output: raw sugar, refined sugar, molasses, and rum.

ISIC 38 (machinery and transportation equipment) has been second in importance, since the assembly of electronic components is included under this classification. Textiles and apparel (ISIC 32) has remained important as these enclave-type industries take advantage of the special provisions granted under TSUS, former section 807, for the re-export of assembled garments. Chemicals (ISIC 35) have also been significant and include the production of industrial chemicals, pharmaceutical products, refined petroleum products, rubber products, and plastic products.

Utilizing statistics compiled by the World Bank,[12] it is possible to analyze indices of manufacturing activity in the areas of employment, real earnings and real output per employee, as well as in earnings as a percentage of value added [Table 5.6]. The information as proxied by the indices exhibit ample fluctuations and from there it can be generalized that Barbados has been more successful in generating employment than Trinidad

IRMA T. DE ALONSO

Table 5.5. English Speaking Caribbean: Structure of Manufacturing 1970 and 1986

| | Distribution of Manufacturing Value Added (%, current prices) | | | | | | | | | |
| | Food & Agriculture | | Textiles & Clothing | | Machinery & Transport Equipment | | Chemicals | | Other Manufacturing | |
Country	1970	1986	1970	1986	1970	1986	1970	1986	1970	1986
Barbados	39	42	13	9	28	26	3	11	17	12
Jamaica	46	50	7	6	na	na	10	13	36	31
Trinidad & Tobago	18	41	3	5	7	15	2	7	70	32

Source: United Nations, Industrial Statistics Yearbook, various issues. World Bank, World Development Report, 1989.

Table 5.6. EnglishSpeakingCaribbean: IndicesofManufacturingActivity (1980=100)

	Employment	Real Earning per Employee	Real Output per Employee	Earnings as % of Value Added
Barbados				
1970	91.6	99.6	78.6	56.7
1975	107.2	75.9	77.5	53.1
1980	100.0	100.0	100.0	63.0
1984	142.9	115.9	77.8	61.3
Jamaica				
1970	104.3	111.4	na	42.6
1975	120.4	129.6	na	46.3
1980	100.0	100.0	na	46.6
Trinidad & Tobago				
1970	62.6	na	na	na
1975	83.1	100.2	73.2	36.8
1980	100.0	100.0	100.0	41.0
1984	66.4	120.3	105.4	41.0

Source: World Bank, World Tables 1988-89 Edition.

and Tobago, but that the latter has been more successful than Barbados in increasing both real earnings and real output per worker. These outcomes are the result of the composition of the two countries' industrial production. The indices of industrial production in Tables 5.7 and 5.8 indicate that Barbados has had more success in the sectors of food and wearing apparel, which are labor-intensive, while Trinidad and Tobago has been more productive in chemicals and non-metallic products, which are capital-intensive. Earnings as percent of value added are therefore higher in Barbados than in Trinidad and Tobago. However, earnings have tended to increase faster than productivity in both countries.

In the case of Jamaica, the indices of manufacturing value-added at constant prices, in Table 5.9, display a distinctive downward trend from the levels achieved in 1974. The only sectors showing some stagnation were the wood and wood products, and chemicals and chemical products. Additional information provided by the Planning Institute of Jamaica indicate

Table 5.7. Indices of Industrial Production: Barbados (1971 = 100)

Commodity	1977	1978	1979	1980	1981	1982	1983	1984
Food	152	160	168	174	165	153	143	145
Beverages & Tobacco	124	139	113	125	119	112	119	103
Wearing Apparel	169	160	166	168	169	173	175	150
Chemicals	110	119	118	149	150	131	129	114
Petroleum Products	115	119	128	133	137	136	133	136
Other non-metallic								
Mineral Products	77	81	98	105	116	100	95	92
Other Manufacturing	165	159	155	146	139	120	121	105
Total Manufacturing	145	148	144	147	139	132	130	120

Source: C. Bourne, Caribbean Development to the Year 2000. Table VII.4.

Table 5.8. Indices of Industrial Production: Trinidad and Tobago (1971 = 100)

Commodity/ Industries	1977	1978	1980	1981	1982	1983	1984	1985
Food Processing	106	116	122	126	128	133	131	120
Beverages & Tobacco	96	93	110	104	119	118	116	102
Wearing Apparel	99	96	105	83	71	64	60	47
Printing, Publishing, Paper	98	117	123	135	124	104	97	107
Wood and Related Products	89	119	122	90	95	88	76	43
Chemicals and Non-								
Metallic Products	126	129	139	116	152	180	193	244
Assembly-type and								
Related Products	112	115	124	126	120	131	268	224
Misc. Manufacturing	104	121	107	125	103	97	84	85

Source: C. Bourne, Caribbean Development to the Year 2000, Table VII.5.

that the trend in industrial production was reversed in 1983 and that the index of industrial production (1974=100) achieved its peak value in 1986, at a level of 119.0, which was accompanied by a corresponding increase in employment. The major subsectors responsible for the reverse of the trend were food processing, textiles and leather products, and chemical and chemical products.[13]

Research undertaken in regard to the industrial sector in the Caribbean Community indicates that the industry of member countries is not competitive by international standards. The cost of production has been increased

Table 5.9. Indices of Jamaican Manufacturing Value-Added at Constant
Price (1971 = 100)

Commodity	1977	1978	1979	1980	1981	1982	1983	1984	1985
Food (excl. sugar)	106	97	92	72	72	79	87	66	83
Beverages & Tobacco	97	97	100	100	98	104	97	91	93
Textiles Apparel	97	89	66	59	56	58	53	51	65
Wood and Wood Products	197	104	90	100	88	90	84	91	102
Furniture and Fixtures	68	53	40	33	34	42	41	49	46
Paper, Printing, Publ.	67	71	81	71	76	83	73	80	71
Chemicals and Chemical Products	94	100	90	75	86	87	101	101	91
Non-metallic Products	79	73	68	40	40	61	68	66	65
Metal and Metal Products	82	79	61	56	69	66	75	63	61
All Manufacturing	90	86	82	72	73	78	80	75	77

Source: C. Bourne, Caribbean Development to the Year 2000, Table VII.6.

by both the importation of raw material and capital goods, and the high
wages demanded by labor unions (which are particularly strong in both
Jamaica and Trinidad and Tobago). Since the member states of the
CARICOM did not coordinate their industrialization efforts, the activities
have become uneconomically duplicative. The high transportation costs
among the member states has not allowed much coordination of their
industrialization efforts. Excess capacity has been another feature of the
industrial activity. Last but not least, the sector has been vulnerable to
fluctuations in world supply and world prices. As an example, the production of electronics in Barbados has been subject to wide fluctuations as
result of the closure of a US firm in the presence of high costs of production.[14]

4. TRADE PERFORMANCE OF MANUFACTURED GOODS

In current dollars, the value of total merchandise trade grew at high rates
during the 1970s [Table 5.10]. For the period 1970-80, exports grew at an
average annual rate of 17.5, 11.2 and 23.8 percent for Barbados, Jamaica,
and Trinidad and Tobago, respectively. The corresponding rates for imports
were 16.1, 8.4, and 19.3 percent. Nevertheless, much of this growth is
attributable to inflation. As reported by Bourne,[15] the unit value prices of
both imports and exports were nearly constant for the period between 1963
and 1974, but after 1974, the unit value price started rising until 1980.

Table 5.10. English Speaking Caribbean: Growth of Merchandise Trade, 1970-1987

Country	Merchandise Trade						Average Annual Growth Rates (%)				Terms of Trade (1980=100)		
	Exports			Imports			Exports		Imports				
	1970	1980	1987	1970	1980	1987	1970-80	1980-87	1970-80	1980-87	1970	1985	1987
A. Millions of Current US$:													
Barbados	39.0	196.0	155.9	117.3	522.0	520.0	17.5	-3.2	16.1	-0.1	62.7	74.5	71.4
Jamaica	334.9	964.6	649.0	525.4	1177.7	1207.2	11.2	-5.5	8.4	0.6	117.1	95.2	99.9
Trinidad & Tobago	481.5	4080.0	1462.4	543.4	3180.0	1218.7	23.8	19.3	-12.8	73.1	96.0	96.0	61.1
B. Millions Constant 1980 US$:													
Barbados	244.9	196.0	221.7	461.1	522.0	528.1	-2.2	1.8	1.2	0.2			
Jamaica	1194.7	964.6	690.2	2193.6	1177.7	1283.1	-2.1	-4.7	-6.0	1.2			
Trinidad & Tobago	9058.5	4080.0	2262.7	7470.4	3180.0	1152.8	-7.7	-8.1	-8.1	-13.5			

Source: World Bank, World Tables 1988-89 Edition.

After 1980, prices declined in Barbados and Jamaica, but in the case of Trinidad and Tobago, import prices continued the upward trend, while export prices declined.

In constant 1980 prices, the rate of growth of exports was negative for the three countries for the 1970-80 period: −2.2, −2.1 and −7.7 percent, for Barbados, Jamaica, and Trinidad and Tobago, respectively. Imports grew at a positive pace in Barbados, but at a negative pace in the other two countries.

For the period 1980-87, in current prices, exports maintained negative growth for the three countries (−3.2, −5.5, and −13.6 percent, respectively), while imports remained stagnant in both Barbados (−0.1%), and Jamaica (0.6%), and they fell significantly in Trinidad and Tobago (−12.8%), as shown in Table 5.10. At constant prices, export growth was negative for Jamaica (−4.7%) and Trinidad and Tobago (−8.1%), while it was 1.8 percent for Barbados. The growth of imports remained negligible in Barbados (0.2%), dismal in Jamaica (1.2%), and deteriorated significantly in the case of Trinidad and Tobago (−13.5%).

Throughout the period, both Barbados and Jamaica have had chronic trade deficits, while Trinidad and Tobago has frequently experienced surpluses. The absolute value of the trade deficit measures the foreign exchange gap, which affects the economy's capacity to import. The terms of trade [Table 5.10] show deteriorating conditions with respect to 1980, especially in the case of Trinidad and Tobago, as a result of the decrease in the price of oil; and in Barbados, as a result of decreases in the price of sugar.

Tables 5.11 and 5.12 show the changing composition of merchandise exports and imports. In terms of exports, with the exception of Barbados, there is a heavy concentration on primary commodities (food, fuels, minerals, metals, and others). Measures of the Hirschman commodity export concentration indices for the CARICOM from 1970 to 1983 indicate this high level of concentration.[16] In Barbados, electrical components, sugar, and apparel comprised 80 percent of total merchandise exports; in Jamaica, alumina, bauxite, and sugar encompassed 60 percent; in Trinidad & Tobago, 88 percent of merchandise exports were crude petroleum, petroleum products, and ammonia. This extreme concentration makes these countries extremely vulnerable to supply and price fluctuations.

The three countries mentioned have been able to increase their exports of manufactured goods (SITC 5-8). In the case of Barbados, manufacturing exports increased from 26 percent in 1969 to 67 percent in 1986, with a significant rising trend. Regarding Jamaica and Trinidad and Tobago, the share of manufactured goods exported has not remained constant throughout the period, but there has been an upward trend, increasing from

Table 5.11. English Speaking Caribbean: Structure of Merchandise Exports, 1969 and 1986

Country	Fuels, Minerals & Metals		Other Primary Commodities		Machinery & Transport. Equipment		Manufactures Basic & Miscellaneous		Chemicals	
	1969	1986	1969	1986	1969	1986	1969	1986	1969	1986
Barbados	12.9	16.7	60.4	15.5	12.1	47.7	11.3	14.7	3.5	5.4
Jamaica	60.7	68.4	30.7	19.0	0.2	2.1	6.0	7.9	2.3	2.5
Trinidad & Tobago	77.7	71.8	8.6	4.5	0.7	1.4	3.1	8.0	9.5	14.1

Percentage Share of Merchandise Exports

Source: United Nations, International Trade Statistics Yearbook, various isses. World Bank, World Tables 1988-89 edition.

Table 5.12. English Speaking Caribbean: Structure of Merchandise Imports, 1974 and 1986

| | Percentage Share of Merchandise Exports | | | | | | | | |
| | Food | | Fuels | | Industrial Supplies | | Machinery & Transp. Equip. | | Other Consumer Goods | |
Country	1974	1986	1974	1986	1969	1986	1974	1986	1974	1986
Barbados	23.1	13.9	15.8	10.2	28.7	23.3	13.3	34.1	19.1	18.6
Jamaica*	19.3	16.4	20.9	28.9	34.8	28.0	17.8	18.5	7.3	8.1
Trinidad & Tobago**	6.3	18.1	71.8	4.2	12.3	36.2	6.3	31.0	3.3	10.5

Source: United Nations, International Trade Statistics Yearbook, various issues. World Bank, World Tables 1988-89.
*1974 and 1982. **1974 and 1987.

8.6 to 12.5 percent from 1969 to 1984, in the case of Jamaica, and from 13.3 to 23.4 percent, in the case of Trinidad and Tobago. Barbados has concentrated in the export of electronic components, Jamaica in miscellaneous manufactures, and Trinidad and Tobago in the export of chemicals.[17]

It can be highlighted that there is a domestic orientation of manufacturing as a result of the import substitution strategy which was implemented in the 1960s, and of the protective nature of incentives. Even in the case of Barbados, which has been the most successful in promoting exports of manufactured goods, an export bias and high effective protection have been found evident.[18] In the cases of Jamaica,[19] and of other CARICOM countries, the same conclusion has been reached.[20]

The percentage structure of merchandise imports show heavy reliance on industrial supplies and capital goods, which reflects a low local capacity to produce these type of goods and it is indicative of the constraint faced by these nations in their attempt at reducing dependence on imported inputs and investment goods.[21] The composition of imports also shows that these countries are heavily dependent of the importation of food and other consumer goods. In the case of Jamaica, their share of imported fuel in 1986 exceeded those of Barbados and Trinidad and Tobago. The imports of fuels by Trinidad and Tobago, for refining, decreased significantly after 1974, and as a consequence there has been a significant re-structuring of their imports.

Analyzing trade patterns by principal countries, Table 5.13 provides the percentage composition of imports and exports by sources and destinations. There is a substantial concentration of foreign trade for these CARICOM countries. The US has kept its place as the main trading partner, followed distantly by the EEC and Canada. Other CARICOM countries are important both as a destination of exports and as suppliers of imports, but most of this trade takes place among the MDCs.

5. SUMMARY AND PERSPECTIVES FOR THE FUTURE

The main conclusions of the research can be summarized as follows:

1. The English Speaking Caribbean has attempted economic integration many times, including the Federation of the West Indies, the Caribbean Free Trade Area, the Eastern Caribbean Common Market, and the Caribbean Community and Common Market (CARICOM). Of all these efforts, the CARICOM has been the most ambitious, and as such it has not accomplished all the objectives sought.

Table 5.13. English Speaking Caribbean: Percentage Composition of Imports and Exports by Sources and Destinations

Country	USA	EEC	Canada	Caribbean
Barbados:				
Sources of Imports				
1969	22.0	37.8	10.7	10.1
1978	29.0	27.1	7.4	17.1
1987	32.2	11.6	7.8	13.4
Destinations of Exports				
1969	22.6	38.3	4.0	4.0
1978	34.6	25.1	6.2	27.3
1987	21.5	17.8	4.2	22.9
Jamaica:				
Sources of Imports				
1968	38.6	30.1	9.5	2.7
1980	31.5	11.3	6.0	19.7
1984	45.4	10.3	5.5	17.0
Destinations of Exports				
1968	39.2	25.3	14.4	0.9
1980	36.7	20.6	3.5	6.8
1984	48.2	14.3	14.3	8.2
Trinidad & Tobago:				
Sources of Imports				
1968	15.1	19.2	4.2	–
1980	26.8	14.2	3.9	2.7
1987	41.9	21.7	6.7	4.9
Destinations of Exports				
1968	45.1	15.3	4.3	7.0
1980	59.9	11.5	–	9.3
1984	58.3	12.4	1.9	13.6

Source: United Nations, International Trade Statistics Yearbook, various issues.

2. The CARICOM groups together a number of countries which are divergent in terms of size, population, and level of income. They share the common problems of unemployment and inflation.

3. Barbados, Jamaica, and Trinidad and Tobago are among the more developed countries within the CARICOM which have managed to increase the importance of the manufacturing sector in the GDP, while the importance of agriculture and mining has been diminished.

4. Although the share of manufacturing has increased from the previous two decades, it has exhibited a negative trend in both Barbados and Trinidad and Tobago during the 1980s, while Jamaica has been able to reverse this trend.

5. Incentives offered by the governments of these countries to foster industrialization include, among others: tax concessions, duty-free imports of raw materials and capital goods, profit repatriation, accelerated depreciation, and subsidized rental space. Considerable investment in the sector has been foreign.

6. The manufacturing sector is relatively small in the CARICOM: it represents 10 percent of GDP in both Barbados and Trinidad and Tobago, while it is 16 percent in Jamaica.

7. The structure of manufacturing is heavily concentrated on food and agricultural products. Other subdivisions of importance include those relating to machinery and transportation equipment, among which assembly of electronic components is included; textiles and apparel, given the incentives provided by the TSUS, former Section 807; and chemicals, mainly related to petroleum products.

8. Indices of real earnings and gross output per worker are higher in Trinidad and Tobago than in Barbados, while the reverse is true for the index of employment. This reflects the nature of industrial production in the two countries: capital-intensive in Trinidad and Tobago and labor-intensive in Barbados. Similar information is not available for Jamaica, but the Planning Institute of Jamaica reports that the negative trend in industrial production was reversed in 1983, with the corresponding increase in employment.

9. Research undertaken concerning the industrial sector in CARICOM countries reveals that industry is not competitive by international standards, due to the high costs of production, high wages, excess capacity, and high transportation costs.

10. In current prices, the level of merchandise trade grew at high rates during the 1970s, but not so in constant prices. During the 1980s, both exports and imports had negative or stagnant growth, in both current and constant prices. Trinidad and Tobago had the most drastic reductions in both imports and exports, as a result of declining petroleum production.

11. Measures of the Hirschman commodity export concentration indices signify a high level of concentration in primary commodities.

12. Barbados, Jamaica, and Trinidad and Tobago have been able to increase their exports of manufactured goods, with an upward trend: the first one has concentrated in the export of electronic components, the second in miscellaneous manufactures, and the third in chemicals.

13. Manufacturing has been classified into two activities: those activities producing for the domestic market and those involved in assembly operations which are designed to export all their output. An export bias has been found in manufacturing production, given the incentives provided.

14. Merchandise imports are heavily dominated by industrial supplies, capital goods, food, and other consumer products.

15. The US is the main trading partner of these nations, followed by the European Economic Community and Canada. Other CARICOM nations are also important trading partners, but most of the trade takes place among the MDCs.

Given this picture, the Group of Caribbean Experts which evaluated the CARICOM in the 1980s, recommended, among others, that the industrial strategy of import substitution should be complemented by export promotion:

the regional development strategy must seek to stimulate simultaneously industrial activities designed to satisfy regional demands and activities to exploit extra-regional markets.[22]

However, the Group of Experts recommends that in devising the program for export industries, attention should be given to local subcontracting activities and to local or joint venture export operations, in addition to the traditional assembly-type operations. The Group cautions that this industrial development will be achieved if there is risk capital available, if there is training in export marketing technology, and if there are arrangements for the provision of export finance. In order to market the output, it will be equally necessary to maintain both the level of supply and the level of quality control.

The report prepared for the Caribbean Community Secretariat,[23] also provided valuable recommendations in order to achieve growth through foreign trade. Among the main proposals put forth, the following require careful consideration: (1) increase cost-competitiveness, which would require some combination of unit factor cost reductions and technological improvement; (2) reduction of the anti-export bias, by phasing out and selective dismantling of the existing protective mechanisms; (3) targeting the market of other less developed economies, which requires the identification of possible markets, and the exercise of market skills; and (4) restraining import growth by fiscal and credit policies.

The possibilities of the CARICOM to augment its economic growth through the expansion of exports will have to originate within CARICOM. In this respect, member states will have to become more competitive in world markets. The major impediments of the CARICOM that need to be overcome include: (1) a weak external marketing capacity, in terms of lack of trained, knowledgeable, and experienced personnel; (2) a lack of price competitiveness, due to higher wages than in other alternative locations in the Caribbean, although automation has made labor intensive methods less attractive; and (3) a weaknesses in decreasing imports, due to their productive structure which requires imported raw material and capital goods.

Nevertheless, there are good prospects for the CARICOM member states to increase their exports. As expressed by Alister McIntyre:

> Basically, the large majority of Caribbean countries have to transform their patterns of development from one centered around the utilization of natural resources, to one relying upon the utilization and upgrading of their human resources.[24]

These countries will have to consider, in addition: (1) diversifying their production, by concentrating in agro-industry, (2) expanding non-traditional exports, (3) taking advantage of the provisions granted by the main trading partners in the US, the EEC, and Canada, and (4) expanding the size of the regional market by adding other members in the Caribbean, such as the Dominican Republic and Haiti, which after many years still remain observers rather than members.

NOTES

1. Group of Caribbean Experts, *Caribbean Community in the 1980s* (Barbados: Coles Printery Ltd., 1981).

2. K.R. Hope, *Economic Development in the Caribbean* (New York: Praeger, 1986).

3. Group of Caribbean Experts, *Caribbean Community in the 1980s, op. cit.*

4. Caribbean Development Bank, *Annual Report, 1989* (Barbados: Caribbean Development Bank, 1990).

5. C. Bourne, et al., *The Caribbean Development to the Year 2000: Challenges, Prospects and Policies* (London: Commonwealth Caribbean and Georgetown, Guyana: Caribbean Community Secretariat, 1988); George Beckford and Norman Girvan (eds.), *Development in Suspense* (Kingston, Jamaica: Friedrich Ebert Stiftung, in collaboration with the Association of Caribbean Economists, 1989); W. Demas, "Perspectives on the Future of the Caribbean in the World Economy," *Caribbean Affairs*, Vol I, No. 4, October-December 1988; R. Palmer, *Problems of Development in Beautiful Countries* (Lanham, Md.: North-South Publishing Co., 1984).

6. Interamerican Development Bank, *Economic and Social Progress in Latin America, 1989 Report* (Washington, D.C.: Interamerican Development Bank, 1989).

7. Karl Bennett, *Trade and Payments in the Caribbean Common Market* (Kingston, Jamaica: Institute of Economic and Social Research, University of West Indies, 1982).

8. Group of Caribbean Experts, *Caribbean Community in the 1980s, op. cit.*, page 50.

9. W. Cox, "The Manufacturing Sector in the Economy of Barbados," in *The Economy of Barbados, 1946-1980*, edited by DeLisle Worrell (Bridgetown, Barbados: The Central Bank of Barbados, 1982).

10. Planning Institute of Jamaica, *Economic and Social Survey, Jamaica, 1985* (Kingston, Jamaica: Planning Institute of Jamaica, 1986).

11. P. Whitney, "The CBI: important incentives for trade and investment," *Department of State Bulletin*, Vol. 88, June 1988; World Bank, *The Caribbean: Export Preferences and Performance* (Washington, D.C.: World Bank, 1988).

12. World Bank, *World Tables, 1987, The Fourth Edition* (Washington, D.C.: World Bank, 1988).

13. Planning Institute of Jamaica, *Economic and Social Survey, 1986, op. cit.*, Chapter 10.

14. C. Bourne, E.B.A. St. Cyr, and M. Howard, "Industrialization and Foreign Trade in the Caribbean Basin: The Case of CARICOM Countries," an IESCARIBE study presented to the Interamerican Development Bank (mimeo), 1987; C. Bourne, et al., *The Caribbean Development to the Year 2000, op. cit.*; D. Worrell, *Small Island Economies: Structure and Performance in the English Speaking Caribbean* (New York: Praeger, 1987).

15. C. Bourne, et al., *Caribbean Development to the Year 2000, op. cit.*

16. C. Bourne, et al., *Caribbean Development to the Year 2000, op. cit.*; C. Brathwaite and H. Codrington, "The External Sector of Barbados, 1946-1980" in *The Economy of Barbados, 1946-1980*, edited by DeLisle Worrell, *op. cit.*

17. United Nations, *International Trade Statistics Yearbook*, various issues.

18. P. Whitehall, "Protectionism in the Manufacturing Sector of Barbados," *Quarterly Economic Review*, Central Bank of Barbados, Vol. 11, No. 2, 1984, pp. 9-27.

19. M. A. Ayub, *Made in Jamaica: The Development of the Manufacturing Sector, World Bank Staff Occasional Papers*, No. 31 (Baltimore, Maryland: The John Hopkins University Press, 1981).

20. G. Ranis, et al., "Production and Export Incentives in the CARICOM Region" (mimeo). Report of a Group of Experts to the Caribbean Community Secretariat, May 1982.

21. C. Bourne, et al., *Caribbean Development to the Year 2000, op. cit.*

22. Group of Caribbean Experts, *The Caribbean Community in the 1980s*, *op. cit.*, page 51.

23. C. Bourne, et al., *Caribbean Development to the Year 2000*, *op. cit.*

24. Alister McIntyre, "The International Economic Situation: Elements for a Policy Agenda" in *Development in Suspense*, edited by George Beckford and Norman Girvan (Kingston, Jamaica: Friedrich Ebert Stiftung, in collaboration with the Association of Caribbean Economists, 1989).

CHAPTER 6

Economic Impact in Puerto Rico of its Exports to the Caribbean: An Input-Output Analysis

Juan A. Castañer and *Angel L. Ruiz*[1]

1. INTRODUCTION

Neoclassical literature on economic development emphasizes the importance of exports to a country as well as its trade linkages with the rest of the world. Another important consideration is the impact of *intra-regional trade* on the development of the home country and the region as a whole. The latter issue is addressed here from an empirical perspective; focusing specifically on Puerto Rico's trade relations with the rest of the Caribbean, and how the structure of its exports are changing to promote intra-regional trade. This analysis is significant in that it provides an empirical basis for examining 'regional integration' as a strategy for economic development.

Regional integration is one of the motivations behind the US sponsored Caribbean Basin Initiative (CBI) of 1984. CBI was instrumental in shaping and defining several subsequent initiatives taken by the Puerto Rican government to increase commercial activity at the local and regional level. The impact of these initiatives are examined here within an input-output framework,[2] with two goals in mind: First, to understand not only the structure of economic linkages within the region but also to identify export-oriented industries which offer the greatest potential for national income, employment and production. And second, to understand the economic impact of intra-regional trade on the region as a whole. The insight gained here is useful in explaining current trade phenomenon and in formulating sound policy recommendations.

This chapter is organized into several parts: Part 2 examines the initiatives and objectives which motivate the strengthening of trade linkages between Puerto Rico and the rest of the Caribbean. This can be viewed specifically as a process of restructuring the Caribbean economy and the readjustment of economic dependency in Puerto Rico. Part 3 examines the structure and trends in Puerto Rico's intra-regional trade links since 1986, specifically with respect of its exports. This section also serves as a backdrop for Part 4 which presents the results of an input-output analysis, showing the economic impact and multiplier effects of Puerto Rico's exports on employment and production in the region. Part 5 summarizes the study with conclusions and observations.

For the purpose of this study, the CBI definition of the Caribbean is used which includes Panama and the Commonwealth Caribbean. Major emphasis is placed on the Dominican Republic, Haiti and Jamaica, which together along with The Netherlands Antilles constitute Puerto Rico's main trading partners in the region.

2. INITIATIVES AND OBJECTIVES

This section examines two recent policies (since 1985) adopted by the Puerto Rican government: *Twin-Plant* and *936 Financing*. These policies were designed to improve and modify trade links with the rest of the region, and since neither policy operates in an economic vacuum, their impact is considered together with the changing structure of world capital; that is, the internationalization of capital and production.[3]

The underlying objectives of the policies above are: (1) the reformulation of the *role of the State*, and (2) the enhancement of Puerto Rico's influence in the Caribbean.[4] The government of Puerto Rico has been an active participant in internal economic affairs since its initial stages of industrialization (from 1940 to 1946). In the decades that followed it assumed a somewhat more passive role, but nevertheless remained significant. Political forces at work today are aiming to reduce the government's role still further through policies such as the two mentioned above. One reason for the changing role of the State stems from the economic crisis of the mid-1970s which brought to light the limitations of the government's economic model. The new model now calls for the stimulation of private investment (rather than public investment) through fiscal reform, special legislation and the diversification of the external sector. *Twin-Plant and 936 Financing* are two of a growing number of policies which direct domestic and foreign investment into the external sector where intra-regional as well as international trade is encouraged.

A critical issue for Puerto Rico now is how responsive is the rest of the region, economically and/or politically, to its external strategy; and is this the right formula for economic development at home as well as for the

Caribbean as a whole. Whatever the outcome, given its size and resource base, and the transformations already in progress throughout the region, Puerto Rico is destined to play an increasing economic role.[5]

3. TRADE LINKS WITH THE CARIBBEAN

The economic structure of Puerto Rico has changed substantially over the last three decades. These changes are evident not only in the sectoral composition of employment and output but also in the structure of exports and the dependence on external commercial and financial transactions. These have acquired strategic importance over the years, as is the case for many other developing economies, where it has been realized that the external sector is not only an important source of economic stimuli but also a vehicle for the *internationalization of world capital.*

Structural change in Puerto Rico is largely the result of the ever-increasing importance of manufactured products in the external sector. Commodity and geographic concentration in the external sector have been lessened since the 1950s as a result of Puerto Rico's efforts to diversify. Some studies have shown a decisive reduction in the concentration of manufactured goods for export but only a slight reduction in terms of its geographic destination and in the composition of imports.[6] Nevertheless, there are encouraging signs on the horizon, as will be discussed in subsequent sections.

For the purpose of this study, three important facts are highlighted which more-or-less characterize the evolution of Puerto Rico's external trade. The first is that the external sector is highly specialized in the production and export of goods destined to a single market; the US market. This was the situation when the external sector was originally developed and has not changed much over the years, as is evident in Graph 6.1. The concentration of exports bound for the US continues to be very high but has been declining gradually in recent years. The reason for this decline is due in part to the industrial strategy adopted by US transnational corporations to develop more dynamic sectors of the economy. Given their enormous technological and financial resources, US corporations have imprinted certain characteristics onto the domestic industrialization process. Domestic producers, large and small, are adopting many of the production techniques in the external sector and utilizing the same flows of goods and services. Therefore, a similar transformation can be noted in the structures of both domestic and external market production.

The second characteristic is that intra-regional exports are very small in proportion to total exports. This characteristic is often described as the 'legacy of colonization.' However, what little intra-regional trade exists is

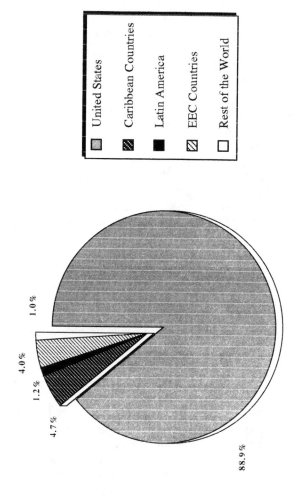

Graph 6.1. Distribution of total exports by country and region, 1987. *Source: Puerto Rican Planning Board, Bureau of Economic Analysis.*

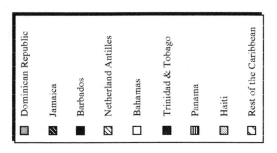

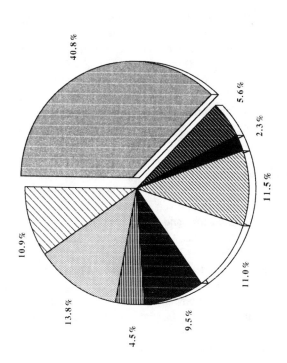

Graph 6.2. Distribution of exports to the Caribbean by country, 1987. *Source: Puerto Rican Planning Board, Bureau of Economic Analysis.*

also characterized by a concentration of exports to a single market; in this case the Dominican Republic (Graph 6.2). As will be shown later, this trade link is very important to Puerto Rico's economy.

And third, total exports are now dominated by manufactured products from capital-intensive and technology-intensive industries rather than from labor-intensive industries, as once was the case. This has led to rising unemployment throughout the economy. In contrast intra-regional exports are dominated by products from labor-intensive industries. The impact of this will be examined in greater detail below.

Tables 6.1 and 6.2 and Graphs 6.1 and 6.2 present data describing the degree of geographic concentration, the composition and the distribution of Puerto Rico's exports. Note from Graph 6.1 the concentration of exports to the US market. In 1987, 88.9 percent of total exports were destined for the US while only 4.7 percent of total exports were destined for the Caribbean; a proportion that has remained more-or-less the same during the past three years.

Several intra-regional trends have emerged during the 1980s that are worth mentioning. One is the marked decline in the volume of trade (in current prices) between Puerto Rico and the rest of the Caribbean, which persisted from as early as 1980 up until 1986. This reduction is explained by a decline in oil imports from the Netherlands Antilles and Trinidad and Tobago, as a result of rising oil prices. The trend however has been reversed in 1986 and intra-regional exports are now on the rise (see Table 6.2 for 1986/7 export figures). A second trend refers to Puerto Rico's trade balance with the Caribbean. Table 6.1 indicates that the balance has improved significantly between 1986 and 1988: In 1986 there was a trade balance deficit of $103.5 million which by 1988 was turned into a surplus of $61.0 million. This dramatic improvement is due in large part to an increase in exports to the Dominican Republic (which is a direct result of Twin-Plant and 936 Financing) and to the continued reduction of imports from the region. A third and last trend to be noted refers to the increasing concentration of trade between Puerto Rico and the Dominican Republic. Graph 6.2 indicates that in 1987, 40.8 percent of Puerto Rico's exports to the Caribbean were destined for the Dominican Republic. Of all such exports, 44.6 percent were goods and services generated from labor-intensive industries. This contrasts sharply with the composition of Puerto Rico's total exports, wherein the majority (64.9 percent) of goods and services originate in technology-intensive industries, and less than a third (28.2 percent) originate in labor-intensive industries (*see* Graphs 6.3 and 6.4). Thus, intra-regional exports have important implications with respect · to employment generation in Puerto Rico and its major trading partner, the

Table 6.1. Trade of Puerto Rico with Caribbean Countries, 1986-1988 (Millions of Dollars)

Country	1986			1987			1988		
	Exports	Imports	Balance	Exports	Imports	Balance	Exports	Imports	Balance
Bahamas	17.6	114.7	-97.1	6.3	120.2	-113.9	6.9	37.3	-30.4
Barbados	14.3	108.0	-93.7	12.8	28.3	-15.5	9.8	9.7	0.0
Belize	0.2	0.0	0.2	0.3	0.1	0.2	0.3	–	0.3
Costa Rica	9.9	35.9	-26.0	1.3	44.2	-42.9	2.0	54.9	-52.9
Dominican Republic	189.9	95.7	94.2	230.5	146.8	83.6	312.0	184.7	127.4
El Salvador	4.2	1.8	2.4	3.5	1.7	1.9	2.7	2.5	0.2
Guatemala	6.9	10.6	-3.6	6.1	6.7	-0.6	6.5	12.0	-5.5
Haiti	69.9	43.8	26.2	78.1	35.0	43.1	62.6	37.4	25.2
Honduras	6.1	5.7	0.4	9.8	9.9	-0.1	3.0	13.2	-10.2
Jamaica	19.0	4.0	15.0	31.4	3.9	27.5	31.7	2.1	29.7
Leeward and Windward Islands[a]	46.2	12.0	34.2	47.9	11.0	37.0	39.4	12.1	27.3
Netherlands Antilles	44.6	141.5	-96.9	64.8	118.7	-17.4	51.0	125.2	-74.2
Panama	22.2	23.5	-1.2	25.5	23.6	1.9	19.6	23.1	-3.4
Trinidad and Tobago	61.0	18.6	42.5	47.3	18.5	28.8	53.8	26.1	27.7
Total*	512.1	615.6	-103.5	565.7	568.6	-2.9	601.3	540.3	61.0

Source: Puerto Rico Planning Board, Bureau of Economic Analysis.

Note: The years for Puerto Rico are fiscal years.

[a]Includes Antigua and Barbuda, The British Virgin Islands, Dominica, Grenada, St. Christopher-Nevis, St. Lucia, St. Vincent, and The Grenadines.

*Includes merchandise not classified.

Table 6.2. Exports of Merchandise, 1986-1988 (in millions of dollars)

SIC		1986	1987	1988
01-09	Agriculture	60.9	72.2	84.7
10-14	Mining	4.1	3.5	6.9
20	Food	1815.2	1966.7	2142.8
2091-2092	Fish and shellfish	620.7	540.5	595.1
21	Tobacco (manufactured)	42.2	68.4	91.4
22-23	Textiles and apparel	771.3	656.9	711.1
24-25	Wood and wood products	27.1	38.0	61.0
26-27	Paper, printing and publishing	63.3	55.0	60.9
28	Chemical products	3964.3	4481.0	5042.8
283	Drugs and pharmaceutical preparations	2753.2	3375.8	3735.3
29	Petroleum refining and related products	381.5	269.7	316.6
30	Rubber and plastic products	142.4	126.5	186.3
31	Leather and leather products	192.1	208.5	224.6
32	Stone, glass, clay and concrete products	81.3	73.3	93.0
33	Primary metal products	64.4	55.7	82.0
34	Fabricated metal products	58.5	58.1	88.6
35	Machinery, except electrical	1410.5	1348.4	1433.8
3573	Electronic computers	1116.4	1021.7	1090.4
36	Electrical machinery	922.5	1049.9	1110.6
37	Transportation equipment	371.7	244.2	217.4
38	Professional and scientific instruments	873.9	899.6	923.5
39	Miscellaneous manufacture	219.1	233.8	181.9
	Total	11,466.3	11,909.4	13,059.9

Source: Puerto Rico Planning Board, Informe Económico al Gobernador 1988 (San Juan: Bureau of Economic Analysis, 1989).

Note: Excludes returned merchandise and unclassified merchandise.

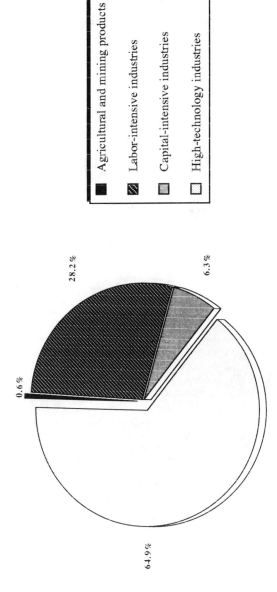

Graph 6.3. Distribution of exports by type of industry, 1987. *Source: Puerto Rican Planning Board, Bureau of Economic Analysis.*

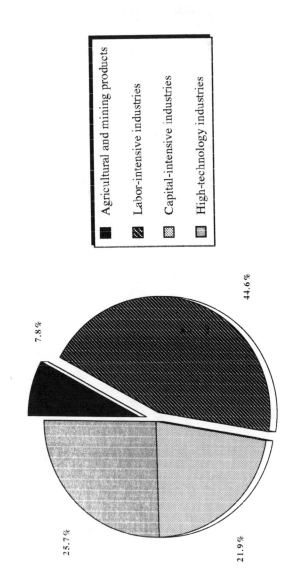

Graph 6.4. Distribution of exports to the Caribbean by type of industry, 1987. *Source: Puerto Rican Planning Board, Bureau of Economic Analysis.*

Dominican Republic. (*See* Graph 6.6 for employment distribution by industry.)

The advantages that Caribbean countries derive from preferential trade agreements with the United States vary considerably from country to country, and over time. These trade agreements, in turn, influence the structure of Puerto Rico's intra-regional imports. Of those commodities entering the US duty-free from the region, the value and proportion of goods exported under US tariff item 806.3/807 [there is a new classification under the Harmonized Tariff System] has increased since 1983 along with those under the CBERA.[7] In 1987, according to the Planning Board of Puerto Rico, 41.0 percent of intra-regional imports entered under the CBERA, which represents a significant increase over previous years. Half of these imports were products from the pharmaceutical industry (SIC 283); in other words, intra-firm transactions. This is not typical in terms of the changes in product composition taking place elsewhere. Since not all imports entered under the CBERA, only those from Barbados, the Dominican Republic and Haiti will be highlighted.

Of the total imports from Barbados, 92.5 percent entered through the preferential tariff systems mentioned above. In 1986 about 98.0 percent of the imports from these countries were classified as electronic products and circuits (SIC 35), of which a significant proportion can be attributed to one twin-plant belonging to INTEL, which later closed. This explains the reduction in Barbados' exports to Puerto Rico after 1986 (see Table 6.1). In the case of the Dominican Republic, its exports to Puerto Rico are concentrated in products from the textile and apparel industries (SIC 22-23), and electronics (SIC 35). Textiles and apparels represented 40.0 percent of total imports to Puerto Rico. Excluding US imports, over 45.0 percent of Puerto Rico's imports of textiles and apparel originated in the Dominican Republic. These items are not eligible under the CBI but do fall within the TSUS. One possible explanation for this concentration is the increase in the number of complementary plants established in the Dominican Republic. In the case of Haiti, products from these industries (SIC 22-23) represent almost two thirds of total exports to Puerto Rico. In sum, the pattern emerging for non-traditional intra-regional trade is that of product concentration in labor-intensive industries and geographic concentration (see Graphs 6.4 and 6.5).

3.1. Structure and Industry Composition of Exports

For analytical purposes the evolution of Puerto Rico's manufacturing sector is divided into three basic stages: (a) the development of labor-intensive industries; (b) the development of capital-intensive industries, and (c) the

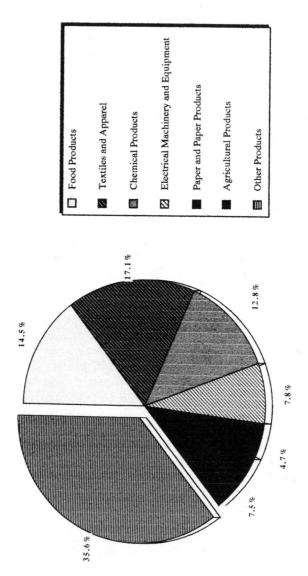

Graph 6.5. Distribution of exports to the Caribbean by industrial sector, 1986. *Source: Puerto Rican Planning Board, Bureau of Economic Analysis.*

development of technology-intensive industries. The composition of exports has followed this pattern of industry development over the last three decades, with the latter type products and industry now prevalent (Graph 6.6). Table 6.3 presents the industry grouping that will be used to examine the structure of exports and compare them with the industry composition of employment.

The structure of merchandise for export has passed through several stages since the 1960s. During these years the importance of labor intensive industries, which were centered around textiles and apparel, started to decline while that of capital-intensive industries such as petrochemicals and electronic products began to rise. By the mid-1970s much of the emphasis on the technology-intensive industries centered on the expansion of the pharmaceutical and electronic industries which were geared for the export markets of the US and Europe. A current picture of the relative importance of each industrial sector is presented in Graph 6.6, which compares the composition of exports with that of employment in manufacturing and agriculture. In 1987, the exports of technology-intensive industries represented 64.9 percent of total exports (as mentioned previously), while those of the capital-intensive industries represented only 10 percent and those of the labor-intensive industries only 28.2 percent. Employment levels in these industry groups do not correspond with the magnitude of their respective exports by reason of the fact that capital-intensive and technology intensive industries tend to use less labor. Nevertheless, changes which affect the competitive position of labor-intensive industries in Puerto Rico cannot be understated since employment in the latter industries represent approximately 45.0 percent of total employment in manufacturing and agriculture (Graph 6.6). It is precisely these industries, and specifically apparel and textiles, which have seen their competitive position in the US market decline over the years.

The encouraging note here is that the fastest growing intra-regional export products are generated within the textile and apparel, and electronics industries (Table 6.4); the former of course being the more labor-intensive. Graph 6.7 summarizes Puerto Rico's intra-regional export growth rates for the period 1980 to 1987 by selected industry and for the region as a whole. While total exports to the Caribbean grew at an annual average rate of 3.6 percent, textile and apparel exports grew at 7.8 percent, with agricultural and mining products growing at only 2.8 percent. It is obvious that the exports of the textile and apparel industries, which grew at over twice the rate as the overall average, are responsible for much of the growth during this period.

Table 6.3. Industry Groupings (SIC codes in parentheses)

Technology-intensive industries undertaking relatively large amounts of R&D and using relatively more skilled labor:

Chemicals and related products	(28)
Drugs and pharmaceutical preparations	(283)
Machinery, except electrical	(35)
Electronic computers and related equipment	(3573)
Electrical machinery and supplies	(361-362; 364; 366-367; 369)
Professional and scientific instruments	(38)

Capital-intensive industries producing products with large amounts of capital, generally undertaking less R&D and more capital than the first group:

Paper and related products and printing & publishing	(26-27)
Oil refining and related products	(29)
Rubber and plastic products	(30)
Fabricated metal products	(34)
Electrical machinery and supplies	(363; 365)
Transportation equipment*	(37)
Professional and scientific instruments	(386-387)

Labor-intensive industries using larger amounts of less skilled labor, generally undertaking less R&D and using fewer skilled workers and less capital than the other two groups:

Food and related products	(20)
Tobacco products	(21)
Textiles	(22)
Apparel and related products	(23)
Wood and products made of wood, and furniture	(24-25)
Leather and leather products	(31)
Stone, clay, glass and cement products	(32)
Primary metal products	(33)
Miscellaneous manufacture	(39)

---

*In the case of Puerto Rico, this sector does not include manufacturing of motor vehicles or other types of vehicles.

4. IMPACT ANALYSIS

This part of the analysis presents the results of an input-output study showing the impact or multiplier effect of commodity exports to the Caribbean on Puerto Rico's economy. The analysis was performed using the interindustry econometric model of the Planning Board of Puerto Rico

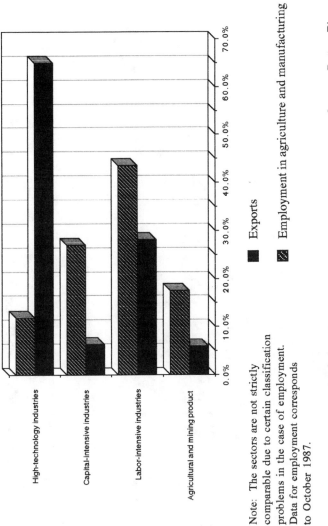

Note: The sectors are not strictly
comparable due to certain classification
problems in the case of employment.
Data for employment corresponds
to October 1987.

Graph 6.6. Distribution of exports and employment by type of industry, 1987. *Source: Puerto Rican Planning Board, Bureau of Economic Analysis.* Informe Economico al Gobernador, 1987.

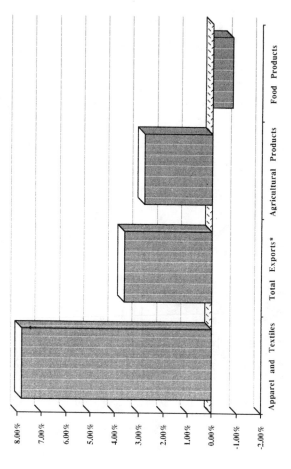

* Information corresponds to period 1981-1988.

Graph 6.7. Rate of growth of exports to the Caribbean, 1981 to 1987. *Source: Puerto Rican Planning Board, Bureau of Economic Analysis.*

Table 6.4. Exports to the Caribbean and Selected Countries at Constant Prices, 1986 (Millions of Dollars: 1977=100)

Industrial Sector	Costa Rica	Jamaica	Haiti	Dominican Republic	Barbados	Trinidad Tobago	Sub-total	Rest of Caribbean	Total
Agricultural Products	23,865	483,901	2,027,364	25,244,325	66,096	1,413,597	29,259,147	1,525,155	30,784,302
Mining	48,943	1,628	6,264	218,034	15,033	40,456	330,359	108,004	438,363
Food Products	362,216	4,324,954	4,736,738	10,437,632	2,095,835	13,349,483	35,306,859	37,915,567	73,222,426
Tabacco Products	—	23,285	127,353	113,357	4,362	48,659	317,016	445,574	762,590
Textiles and Apparel	278,596	1,735,914	11,790,673	39,256,020	3,259,538	991,107	57,311,848	6,563,238	63,875,086
Furniture and Wood Products	14,234	153,831	159,127	1,460,321	215,194	157,084	2,159,792	2,564,958	4,724,750
Paper and Allied Products	273,921	991,887	1,002,520	6,692,304	278,041	3,712,349	12,951,021	1,641,730	14,592,751
Printing and Publishing	99,037	83,845	40,120	923,714	26,692	725,316	1,898,726	158,403	2,057,129
Chemical Products	2,128,000	2,049,900	2,220,726	7,119,877	1,444,200	5,447,889	20,410,593	21,650,423	42,061,016
Refineries and Petroleum Products	952,279	665,699	396,667	1,881,409	107,162	865,172	4,868,387	12,826,170	17,694,557
Rubber and Plastic Products	113,595	212,844	1,083,793	6,267,262	182,803	1,671,699	9,531,996	1,094,322	10,626,318
Leather and Leather Products	—	—	1,757,843	5,889,197	42,367	92,583	7,781,990	341,893	8,123,883
Stone, Clay and Glass Products	182,796	58,253	248,001	1,136,319	63,680	556,595	2,245,644	597,331	2,842,975
Primary Metal Products	246,318	52,736	487,422	1,519,835	151,380	1,281,321	3,739,013	1,026,534	4,765,547
Fabricated Metal Products	411,223	146,486	630,662	1,522,284	428,576	2,239,009	5,378,240	4,616,161	9,994,401
Machinery Except Electrical	840,461	1,190,517	1,947,052	8,913,144	530,106	6,835,457	20,256,737	5,065,148	25,321,885
Electrical Machinery	282,772	1,296,964	11,613,846	5,458,470	676,946	3,442,351	22,771,349	4,339,406	27,110,755
Transportation and Equipment	138,009	48,204	274,589	5,542,833	40,106	206,759	6,250,500	2,331,330	8,581,830
Professional and Scientific Instruments	285,880	370,136	1,001,829	1,995,164	393,494	1,225,326	5,271,829	3,494,940	8,766,769
Miscellaneous Manufacturing Industries	40,938	43,096	5,758,036	740,564	41,200	562,940	7,186,773	575,551	7,762,324
Non-Classified Merchandise	46,020	408,153	1,058,014	3,520,714	340,126	797,860	6,170,887	3,023,645	9,194,532
Total	6,769,103	14,342,233	48,368,639	135,852,779	10,402,937	45,663,012	261,398,706	111,905,483	373,304,189

Source: Estimated using the price indexes from the Planning Board and the U.S. Department of Labor; Time Series Data for Imput–Output Industries, June 1986.

(ECOINTER) and the multipliers derived therefrom. This model combines aggregate econometric equations with the input-output matrix. The endogenous matrix consists of 100 equations. Of these, 50 are interindustry equations (input-output balance equations), 16 form a rectangular matrix of value added components, two row vectors of imports of goods and services, and the rest are definitional and stochastic equations for macroeconomic variables such as Gross National Product, national income, consumption and others. The exogenous matrix consists of variables such as investment (machinery and equipment, and construction), exports of goods and services by industrial sectors, government expenditures, transfer payments from the US and others.

Two sets of multipliers for Puerto Rico's exports were derived from 1986 sample data; one set represents the impact of each industrial sector as a whole while the other desegregates this sectoral impact across selected countries of the Caribbean. Exports and production together with employment were classified by industry according to the Standard Industrial Classification system, (see Table 6.2). The selected Caribbean countries where chosen based on their degree of trade participation with Puerto Rico. Table 6.1 identifies all the Caribbean countries considered in this analysis.

4.1. Methodology

The first step was to construct price indices with which to deflate exports by industrial sectors and convert them into 1977 prices; which is the base year for the model. The data used for this purpose was unpublished estimates of price indices provided by the Planning Board of Puerto Rico. Whenever price indices were not available for a specific industrial sector, proxies were used based on the producer price indices reported by the U.S. Department of Labor.[8] Aggregate macroeconomic variables were deflated using implicit price deflators. Once converted into constant prices, exports vectors were then multiplied by the inverse of the endogenous matrix to obtain solution vectors of domestic output necessary to deliver the constant dollar amount of exports, plus value added and other aggregate macroeconomic variables. To measure the impact of Puerto Rico's exports on local employment, a vector of labor coefficients (employment per million dollar of output) was estimated and then multiplied by the corresponding output vector obtained from the solution of the model.

Mathematically the model can be expressed as follows:

$$(I - A)^{-1}Ec = Xe \qquad (1)$$

where $(I - A)^{-1}$ is the matrix of direct plus indirect requirements per unit of final demand (inverse matrix); Ec is exports to the Caribbean; and Xe is the vector of output and values for macroeconomic variables generated locally;[9]

$$E/X = N \tag{2}$$

where E is the employment by industrial sector; X is output defined in input-output methodology (in millions of dollars); and N is the vector of employment coefficients (employees per million dollars of output);

$$Ee = N \cdot Xe \tag{3}$$

where Ee is the employment generated locally by the exports of merchandise to the Caribbean. The other vectors are defined as above.

4.2. Analysis of the Results

Tables 6.5, 6.6 and 6.7 present the results of this analysis, measuring the production and employment generated in the Puerto Rican economy by intra-regional exports. These results are listed by selected countries and the region as a whole; and by industrial sector. Although the information is for 1986, it gives a concrete picture of how important this trade is, not only to the home economy but also to the region as a whole, and in particular to Puerto Rico's main trading partners. Table 6.6 lists the contribution of each dollar of export from each industrial sector to Gross National Product, imports and compensation to employees. Both tables can be used to identify those industrial sectors which benefit the most from or receive the greatest impact from this trade. In terms of developing economic policy, these tables identify sectors that should be targeted for special attention.

Table 6.5 presents output and employment by industrial sector generated by Puerto Rico's exports to the Caribbean and to selected countries. The estimates obtained show that $261.4 million (at constant prices) in exports to Jamaica, Haiti, the Dominican Republic and Barbados generated $401.3 million in output, and created 11,212 jobs or 70 percent of the total jobs generated by the exports to the Caribbean. For the region as a whole the corresponding impact on output and employment were $575.3 million and 16,016 jobs, respectively. In other words, each million dollars of exports generated $536,000 of additional (indirect) output, implying a domestic output multiplier of 1.536; and an employment multiplier of 43 jobs per million dollars of exports. When looking at the table sector-wise in terms of jobs created, the textile and apparel industry is one of the most important industries based on its contribution to employment and output, followed by agriculture and wholesale and retail trade. These findings corroborate the structure of specialization discussed in Part 3.

Table 6.5. Production and Employment Generated in the Economy: Multiplier Impact

Industrial Sector	Jamaica		Haiti		Dominican Republic		Barbados		Rest of Caribbean Basin Countries*		Rest of Caribbean		Total			
	Out.	Employ-ment	Out.	Employ-ment	Out.	Employ-ment	Out.	Employ-ment	Out.	Employ-ment	Out.	Employ-ment	Out.	Employ-ment	Out.	Employ-ment
Agriculture	1.4	107	4.7	361	13.1	1015	1.0	78	5.1	392	10.8	836	36.0807	2789	0.0635	77.29
Mining and construction	0.2	7	0.7	24	2.0	68	0.2	5	0.8	26	1.7	56	5.5115	187	0.0097	34.01
Manufacturing, total:																
Food Products	2.6	31	8.8	104	24.7	291	1.9	22	9.5	112	20.3	240	67.7294	799	0.1192	11.80
Tobacco Products	0.1	2	0.3	5	0.9	15	0.1	1	0.3	6	0.7	13	2.3864	42	0.0042	17.67
Textiles and Apparel	2.4	124	8.1	419	22.8	1177	1.7	90	8.8	454	18.8	970	62.7293	3235	0.1104	51.57
Furniture and Wood Products	0.2	6	0.5	19	1.5	55	0.1	4	0.6	21	1.2	45	4.1479	150	0.0073	36.27
Paper and Related Products	0.3	4	1.1	12	3.0	35	0.2	3	1.2	14	2.5	29	8.3525	96	0.0147	11.51
Printing and Publishing	0.2	4	0.5	15	1.5	41	0.1	3	0.6	16	1.2	34	4.0910	113	0.0072	27.54
Chemicals Products	1.7	8	5.7	27	15.9	77	1.2	6	6.2	30	13.1	63	43.8082	211	0.0771	4.81
Refineries and other Petroleum Products	2.7	3	9.1	10	25.6	29	2.0	2	9.9	11	21.1	24	70.4568	80	0.1240	1.13
Rubber and Plastic Products	0.4	10	1.2	33	3.5	92	0.3	7	1.3	35	2.9	75	9.5458	251	0.0168	26.34
Leather and Leather Products	0.4	18	1.2	61	3.4	171	0.3	13	1.3	66	2.8	141	9.3753	470	0.0165	50.11
Stone, Glass, and Clay Products	0.3	6	0.9	19	2.4	53	0.2	4	0.9	20	2.0	43	6.5911	144	0.0116	21.89
Primary Metals Products	0.2	3	0.6	10	1.7	29	0.1	2	0.7	11	1.4	24	4.6592	81	0.0082	17.36
Fabricated Metals Products	0.5	10	1.7	35	4.7	98	0.4	7	1.8	38	3.9	81	12.9550	269	0.0228	20.75
Machinery, except Electrical	0.8	10	2.6	34	7.3	95	0.6	7	2.8	36	6.0	78	20.1711	260	0.0355	12.88
Electrical Machinery	1.3	23	4.3	78	12.2	220	0.9	17	4.7	85	10.0	181	33.4670	605	0.0589	18.08
Transportation Equipment	0.1	4	0.4	14	1.2	39	0.1	3	0.5	15	1.0	32	3.2387	107	0.0057	33.12
Professional and Scientific Instruments	0.3	11	1.2	37	3.3	103	0.3	8	1.3	40	2.7	85	9.0344	284	0.0159	31.45
Miscellaneous Manufacturing	0.6	13	2.1	45	5.9	127	0.4	10	2.3	49	4.8	105	16.1369	349	0.0284	21.64
Transportation	0.4	12	1.2	41	3.5	115	0.3	9	1.3	44	2.9	95	9.6026	316	0.0169	32.87
Communications	0.6	16	2.0	55	5.6	153	0.4	12	2.2	59	4.7	126	15.5119	422	0.0273	27.18
Public Utilities	0.5	7	1.6	25	4.5	69	0.3	5	1.8	27	3.7	57	12.5004	189	0.0220	15.15

(Continued)

Industrial Sector	Jamaica		Haiti		Dominican Republic		Barbados		Rest of Caribbean Basin Countries*		Rest of Caribbean		Total			
	Out.	Employ-ment	Out.	Employ-ment	Out.	Employ-ment	Out.	Employ-ment	Out.	Employ-ment	Out.	Employ-ment	Out.	Employ-ment	Out.	Employ-ment
Trade	1.1	67	3.8	226	10.7	634	0.8	48	4.1	245	8.8	522	29.4328	1742	0.0518	59.17
Finance, Insurance and Real Estate	1.0	10	3.3	32	9.2	91	0.7	7	3.6	35	7.6	75	25.3417	250	0.0446	9.85
Hotels and Lodging Places	0.0	2	0.1	8	0.4	21	0.0	2	0.1	8	0.3	18	1.0228	59	0.0018	57.28
Personal Services	0.1	6	0.3	19	0.7	54	0.1	4	0.3	21	0.6	44	2.0455	148	0.0036	72.50
Repair Services	0.2	4	0.5	15	1.5	41	0.1	3	0.6	16	1.2	34	4.0910	112	0.0072	27.47
Business Services	0.8	25	2.8	85	7.8	238	0.6	18	3.0	92	6.4	196	21.3075	653	0.0375	30.64
Medical and Health Services	0.2	18	0.6	61	1.6	171	0.1	13	0.6	66	1.3	141	4.4888	470	0.0079	104.78
Other Services	0.4	28	1.4	94	4.0	263	0.3	20	1.5	101	3.3	216	10.9663	722	0.0193	65.83
Government	0.2	16	0.8	53	2.4	150	0.2	11	0.9	58	1.9	123	6.4775	411	0.0114	63.52
Total Domestic Output and Employment	22.0	614	74.3	2075	208.6	5829	15.9	445	80.5	2249	171.9	4803	573.2570	16016	1.0089	1093.5
Imports	0.0	0.0	29.3		82.3		6.3		31.8		67.8		217.4308		0.3979	
Value Added	8.1		27.3		76.8		5.9		29.6		63.3		210.9158		0.3712	
Compensation to employees	3.0		10.1		28.4		2.2		10.9		23.4		77.9570		0.1372	
Propietors income	3.6		12.0		33.8		2.6		13.0		27.9		92.9007		0.1635	
Other value added	1.5		5.2		14.6		1.1		5.6		12.0		40.0581		0.0705	

*Includes Trinidad and Tobago, and Costa Rica. Source: Own estimates.

It is interesting to note that the leading industry — refineries and other petroleum products — generated only 80 jobs. One reason for this is the relatively low requirement of workers per output and workers per capital. The above situation can be observed in other sectors such as food products, chemical products, electrical machinery and finance. For example if the petroleum refining and chemical products industries are combined, $59.8 million of exports to the Caribbean generated $114.3 million in output ($1.91 million for each million dollar of exports), but only created 291 jobs or five jobs for each million dollars of exports. The last column of Table 6.5 shows the output and employment multipliers for each industrial sector. These two columns identify the industries with the highest employment multipliers: agriculture, textiles and apparel, and leather products in the case of manufacturing, and hotel, medical and health services and others in the service sector. The last rows of the table show the dollar impact of exports on imports and value added.[10] Import requirements amounted to $217.4 million, which represents 38 percent of the output generated by exports. Also, value added in the form of compensation to employees represented only $78.0 million while proprietor's income (profits) amounted to $92.9 million. Most of the profits are classified as returns on external investment originating in Puerto Rico.

4.3. Macroeconomic Impacts

Table 6.6 describes the impact of exports on other selected macroeconomic indicators, Table 6.7 lists the multipliers for these variables, and Table 6.8 presents the multipliers for four variables originating in each industrial sector. An examination of these tables reveals that if the criteria for the allocation of resources is to maximize the value added in the form of compensation to employees then the exports of industries or sectors such as textiles and apparel, scientific instruments, and agriculture, should be specifically promoted. These industries also have high personal income multipliers. However, a very important criteria to bear in mind is the import requirements of these industries per dollar of exports. Examining the import multipliers by industrial sector reveals there are few sectors with multipliers lower than 0.58 (the average for the economy generated by exports is 0.582).

Finally, an analysis by country of destination shows the Dominican Republic as contributing the most to job creation, value added and output in Puerto Rico. For instance, in fiscal year 1986 exports to this country amounted to $135.8 million (at 1977 prices). They generated $208.6 million in output, 5,829 jobs and $76.8 million in value added. Most of the jobs created were in manufacturing industries, such as textiles and apparel,

Table 6.6. Contribution of Exports to Macroeconomic Variables to the Caribbean Countries (in millions of dollars: 1977=100)

Macroeconomic Variables	Jamaica	Haiti	Dominican Republic	Barbados	Rest of Caribbean Basin Countries*	Total Caribbean Basin Countries	Other Caribbean Countries	Total
Personal Consumption Expenditures	4.4	14.8	41.5	3.2	16.0	79.9	34.2	114.1
Durable Goods	0.6	2.0	5.6	0.4	2.2	10.8	4.6	15.4
Non-Durable Goods	2.1	7.1	20.1	1.5	7.7	38.5	16.5	55.0
Services	1.7	5.7	15.8	1.3	6.1	30.6	12.9	43.5
Domestic Savings	1.9	6.4	18.1	1.4	7.0	34.8	14.9	49.7
Government Revenues	1.8	6.0	16.7	1.3	6.5	32.3	13.8	46.1
Gross National Product	6.2	21.0	59.0	4.5	22.7	113.4	48.6	162.0
Net National Income	5.7	19.2	53.8	4.1	20.7	103.5	44.3	147.8
Personal Income	4.9	16.6	46.6	3.6	18.0	89.7	38.4	128.1

Source: Multipliers of the Puerto Rico Planning Board ECOINTER Model.
*Includes Costa Rica and Trinidad and Tobago.

Table 6.7. Contribution by Dollar of Exports to Selected Macroeconomic Variables By Industrial Sector (1977=100)

Industrial Sector	Gross Product	Employee Compensation	Imports
Agricultural Products	0.9009	0.2915	0.6170
Mining	0.0583	0.0195	0.9725
Meat Products	0.5312	0.1868	0.7552
Dairy Products	0.2076	0.0790	0.9079
Grain Meal Products	0.2117	0.1002	0.8458
Bakery Products	0.7287	0.3602	0.6858
Beer and Malt Products	0.5348	0.2073	0.7306
Alcoholic Beverages	0.7445	0.2475	0.4363
Non-Alcoholic Beverages	0.5910	0.2974	0.4174
Miscellaneous Food	0.3466	0.1735	0.7493
Tobacco Products	0.7581	0.2263	0.2967
Textiles and Apparel	0.6662	0.3689	0.6468
Furniture and Wood Products	0.4545	0.2007	0.7985
Paper and Allied Products	0.3920	0.1585	0.7842
Printing and Publishing	0.9649	0.4749	0.5379
Petrochemical Products	0.4716	0.1832	0.6343
Other Petrochemical Products	0.4716	0.1832	0.6343
Refined Petroleum Products	0.1257	0.0493	0.9142
Other Petroleum Products	0.2130	0.0868	0.8163
Rubber and Plastic Products	0.4801	0.2552	0.5879
Leather and Leather Products	0.3789	0.2263	0.8000
Stone, Clay and Glass Except Cement	0.6100	0.2526	0.7526
Primary Metal Products	0.2564	0.1244	0.8872
Fabricated Metal Products	0.3202	0.1397	0.7447
Machinery Except Electrical	0.4156	0.2355	0.4167
Electrical and Electronic Equipment	0.3261	0.2271	0.3112
Transportation and Equipment	0.2545	0.1299	0.8660
Professional and Scientific Instruments	0.4195	0.2934	0.3810
Miscellaneous Manufactured Products	0.3077	0.1632	0.7796

Source: Puerto Rico's Planning Board, multipliers of the industrial econometric model.

and electrical machinery, and in agriculture. Although one cannot establish a hypothesis, it would be very interesting to observe whether there is a similarity in structure with the complementary plants established elsewhere in the region.

As a general conclusion, after examining the data obtained it can be said that the local impact of Puerto Rico's trade with Caribbean countries can be considered relatively small. In some sectors, however, this relatively small volume of trade has important consequences for the economy. It should also be noted that, given the data, there is great potential for intra-

Table 6.8. Multiplier Impact of Selected Macroeconomic
Variables Per Dollar of Exports (1977 = 100)

Variables	Multiplier
Domestic Production	1.536
Imports	0.582
Value Added	0.565
Compensation to employees	0.209
Proprietor income	0.249
Other value added	0.107
Personal Consumption Expenditures	0.306
Durable goods	0.041
Non-durable goods	0.147
Services	0.117
Total Domestic Savings	0.153
Government Income	0.123
Gross National Product	0.434
Net National Income	0.396
Personal Income	0.343

Source: Puerto Rico Planning Board, ECOINTER Model.

regional trade with the resulting benefit of an increase in job creation and
the generation of value added for all countries involved. Much of the
output, value added and job creation can be induced by exports to a few
countries and by a few industrial sectors, most falling within the category
of labor-intensive industries. It is of great importance that these exports be
more diversified, targeting industries such as electrical machinery and
electronic equipment.

5. SUMMARY AND OBSERVATIONS

The analysis presented here shows several important facts with respect to
Puerto Rico's trade with the Caribbean. The first is that the volume of
intra-regional trade is low, and its economic impact on the economy relatively small. Yet, by desegregating this impact across industrial sectors and
macroeconomic variables, the importance of this trade is greater in those
industries which have been losing their competitiveness in the US market.
Secondly, the degree of concentration by type of industry, namely labor-intensive; and by country, namely the Dominican Republic, is very high,

representing almost the opposite structure of that found in total exports. Third, economic relations between Puerto Rico and the Dominican Republic are deepening. The structure of this trade is centered around labor-intensive industries, and seems to be configured by the development of the complementary plants of an assembly-type nature established in the latter by Puerto Rico. The multiplier analysis performed here also corroborates at a detailed level the structure of this trade, and identifies certain economic changes taking place which should be the subject of future studies; namely the impact of intra-regional trade on the remaining Caribbean countries.

NOTES

1. The authors are grateful to Javier Renta and Debby McPartlan for their assistance, to the Economic Advisory Council for the use of their facilities, and to the Planning Board of Puerto Rico for statistical information provided.
2. Juan A. Castañer and Angel L. Ruiz, "Vinculación comercial de Puerto Rico con el resto del Caribe," *Caribbean Studies*, 21, July-December 1988.
3. See Hilbourne Watson, "The Changing Structure of World Capital and Development Options in the Caribbean," 1989, pp. 1-9.
4. Commonwealth of Puerto Rico, Economic Development Administration, *Puerto Rico's Caribbean Development Program* (San Juan: Caribbean Development Office, September 1988).
5. William G. Demas, "The Caribbean Economy," *Caribbean Affairs*, 1, October-December 1988.
6. See Fuat and Suphan Andic, "Concentration in the External Trade of Puerto Rico," *Caribbean Studies*, Vol. 4, October 1964.
7. U.S. International Trade Commission, *Annual Report on the Impact of the Caribbean Basin Economic Recovery Act on US Industries and Consumers, Third Report, 1987* (Washington, D.C.: USITC, September 1988).
8. U.S. Department of Labor, Bureau of Labor Statistics, "Time Series Data for Input-Output Industries" (unpublished), June 1986.
9. This inverse matrix is not exactly the Leontief Inverse since the Planning Board model includes macroeconomic variables as endogenous. Therefore, the solution vector obtained is not merely the interindustry output but also includes the impact of macroeconomic variables.
10. Imports required to produce output generated by exports.

PART 3

Export Assembly Manufacturing in the Caribbean

CHAPTER 7

Export-Oriented Assembly Operations in the Caribbean

Gregory K. Schoepfle and *Jorge F. Pérez-López*[1]

1. INTRODUCTION

Often lacking the necessary infrastructure for industrialization, but abundant with labor resources, some developing economies have recently adopted new strategies to attract investment in export-oriented assembly operations that promote domestic employment opportunities, foreign exchange earnings, and industrial development.

One institutional arrangement that has become increasingly popular is the "export processing zone." Developing countries have established export processing zones (EPZs) as special enclaves to attract foreign investment through various incentives such as waiver of import tariffs, tax holidays, and subsidized rental of industrial shelters and other infrastructure. In many cases, these assembly operations have become a dynamic source of employment generation in these countries.

The expansion of EPZs in developing countries, however, may not necessarily be the *sine qua non* for industrialization. Firms operating in these zones often are not integrated into the domestic economy and, in most cases, are precluded or limited from selling their output in the host country's domestic market. This separation of domestic and export markets raises questions as to whether the full benefits of these investments are being realized and how long they will continue. In some cases, the costs of establishing EPZs (e.g., development of zones and infrastructure, foregone revenues from incentives offered to foreign investors, etc.) may be much greater than the benefits derived.[2] While assembly operations may provide immediate employment for large pools of unemployed workers, they often replace jobs in primary-commodity export production (e.g., sugar) that previously yielded more value-added and earned more net foreign ex-

125

change per unit of output. In many cases, new entrants (especially young women) have been attracted into a labor force where substantial numbers are already under- or unemployed.

On the other hand, the expansion of EPZs in developing countries is seen by many as a positive vehicle to foster industrialization, develop a work ethic, and promote potential backward linkages that encourage economic growth.

This chapter focuses on export-oriented assembly operations in the Caribbean, a preferred location for assembly facilities by many U.S. manufacturers.[3] First, export-oriented assembly facilities in the Caribbean are described briefly. Next, trends in U.S. imports of assembled products from the Caribbean are examined with special emphasis on those assembled from U.S.-origin components. Then, the implications of export-oriented assembly operations on the economies of the Caribbean are discussed. The chapter closes with some general observations about the growth in offshore assembly operations and their potential contribution to the economic development of the Caribbean.

2. EXPORT-ORIENTED ASSEMBLY OPERATIONS IN THE CARIBBEAN

2.1. Incentives Offered for Export-Oriented Assembly Operations

Most export-oriented assembly operations in the Caribbean are located in export processing zones (EPZs) and industrial estates or are located outside designated zones but accorded special status. EPZs are enclaves within a country where foreign components and materials can be brought in duty-free for further processing or assembly, in some cases by posting a bond which is refunded when the items leave the country. Imported components and materials are processed within EPZs — typically they are assembled into a finished product — and then exported. In addition, machinery, equipment, and other capital goods necessary for processing and assembly can be brought in duty-free. Customs duties or other taxes are not assessed on imported materials unless they leave the EPZ and enter into the national customs territory of the host country.[4]

Host governments generally grant fiscal and other incentives to companies that locate in these enclaves or agree to export their products.[5] Tax holidays are frequently offered to investors (i.e., preferential treatment with regard to taxes for a specified period of time). For example, members of the Caribbean Common Market (CARICOM) grant an exemption from income taxes anywhere from 10 to 15 years to assembly firms that export their products outside of CARICOM.[6]

Host countries in the Caribbean offer a myriad other incentives to attract investors. One of the most common incentives is subsidized rental of factory shells (particularly in those countries with EPZs), government-supported worker training, reduced (subsidized) public utility rates, credit assistance, guarantees that profits may be repatriated, permission to sell a share of the output in the domestic market, special treatment with regard to currency convertibility restrictions and repatriation of earnings, and subsidized feasibility studies.

Firms that locate in EPZs are generally not subject to the restrictions and red tape that apply to other firms located outside the zones (e.g., domestic ownership, local content, performance requirements); however, most export-oriented assembly firms must register with various host-government agencies (e.g., investment boards, taxing authorities, etc.) and be approved to receive special benefits.

In some countries, the basic elements underlying EPZs (viz., duty-free importation of equipment and materials to transform or finish goods that are exported and incentives to attract investors) are also present in other forms of export-oriented facilities that are not necessarily formally called EPZs or located in an enclave industrial park, special economic zone, or customs in-bond territory. In some cases, individual export-oriented firms may be granted special tax or customs status without regard to their location; often, this may be the case for very small island nations where the entire country is considered, *de facto*, a free-zone.

In addition to fiscal and infrastructure incentives, labor costs are another important consideration in outsourcing decisions by foreign manufacturers. A U.S. International Trade Commission survey of U.S. firms involved in offshore assembly of U.S.-sourced components found that savings on labor costs for labor-intensive operations abroad are a more significant factor than the many others offered in influencing the location of assembly facilities. Survey respondents overwhelming indicated (91 percent) that labor cost differentials exerted a positive influence on decisions on where to locate, while 47 percent indicated that such differentials were the single most-important in the decision to locate facilities abroad.[7]

Labor costs in the Caribbean are reportedly competitive with those at alternative offshore assembly locations in the Americas such as Mexico and Colombia. For example, the following table, based on data developed by a private-sector consultant, presents a comparison of illustrative assembly labor costs (hourly wages in U.S. dollars) in the Caribbean for the years 1983 and 1988:

Country	1983	1988
Mexico	$1.01	$0.90
St. Kitts	0.83	na
Colombia	0.62	0.89
Costa Rica	0.28	0.67
Dominican Republic	0.66	0.60
Honduras	0.45	0.60
Guatemala	na	0.58
Haiti	0.33	0.53
Jamaica	0.45	0.41

Source: International Business and Economic Research Corporation (IBERC), "Analisis Comparativo de Costos en Zona Franca, 1983" (Washington D.C.: IBERC, 1983) and cited in Abreu et al, Las Zonas Francas Industriales *(Santo Domingo, R.D.: Centro de Orientación Económica, 1989), pp. 128-130.*

Another source has provided the following estimates of average labor costs per hour (including fringe benefits) in the Caribbean in early 1988: $1.00 in Costa Rica, $0.61-0.88 in Guatemala, $0.44-0.48 in the Dominican Republic, and $0.36 in Jamaica.[8]

The labor-cost savings associated with foreign assembly operations — and the cost advantage of the Caribbean — can be illustrated by examining data for 1987, which were developed by the U.S. International Trade Commission, on labor costs to produce 4 typical garments (women's blouses, men's sports coats, brassieres, and men's casual slacks). According to these estimates, the cost of assembling any of these 4 garments in the Caribbean ranged from about a half to a third of the cost of similar work performed in the United States. At the same time, the costs of assembly in the Caribbean were about three-fourths of the cost of assembly in Hong Kong. For example, costs for labor and overhead associated with the assembly of women's blouses were: $4.75 per unit in the United States, $2.20 in Hong Kong, and $1.66 in the Caribbean. For men's sports coats, the assembly and overhead costs were $15.66 per unit in the United States, $7.24 in Hong Kong, and $5.24 in the Caribbean.[9]

2.2. Major Locations of Assembly Facilities

In most Caribbean countries, EPZs and other export-oriented facilities housing assembly operations were initially established in urban areas, near an international port and/or airport. Such location ensured that a transportation infrastructure was already in place to permit the importation of materials for assembly and the export of the finished goods. Certain Caribbean countries have begun recently to encourage the establishment of assembly operations in less-developed and rural regions, but this policy has had limited success to date. For example, Haiti grants a 15-year tax exemption (and also a lower minimum wage) to assembly firms that locate outside of the Port-au-Prince area, compared to only a 5-year exemption for those that locate within that area.[10]

In 1986, the following Caribbean nations reportedly had either EPZs or some other form of legal regime that supported export-oriented facilities: Antigua and Barbuda, the Bahamas, Barbados, Belize, Dominica, the Dominican Republic, Grenada, Haiti, Jamaica, Montserrat, the Netherlands Antilles-Aruba, Puerto Rico, St. Kitts-Nevis, St. Lucia, St. Vincent, and Trinidad and Tobago. With the exception of those facilities located in the Bahamas, the Netherlands Antilles-Aruba,[11] and Trinidad and Tobago,[12] which provided mainly warehousing or banking facilities or engaged in oil refining, export-oriented facilities in the Caribbean consisted primarily of assembly plants.

Some of the leading assembly locations in the Caribbean are located in the larger island nations and include:

- **Dominican Republic:** Export-oriented assembly operations in the Dominican Republic are located in industrial free zones (*zonas francas industriales*). The first zone was located at La Romana and began operations in 1969. Since then, similar zones have been established elsewhere in the country: San Pedro de Macorís in 1973, Santiago in 1974, and Puerto Plata in 1983. Five other zones, several of them located in the interior of the country, began operations in 1986 or 1987 at Bani, La Romana II, San Cristóbal, La Vega, and San Isidro. During 1988, six new EPZs were opened and more than a dozen additional locations were under active development.[13] In August 1989, the Dominican Republic inaugurated the 18th free zone at San Francisco de Macorís.[14]

  Activity in the Dominican free zones started out slowly but accelerated in the second half of the 1980s. Over the period 1969-71, only 6 plants were in operation in the single free zone at La Romana. Over the period 1973-83, the number of plants in the free zones rose from 22 to 103. In subsequent years, the number of new plants established in the free zones was as follows: 15 in 1984, 5 in 1985, 16 in 1986, 41 in 1987, and 44 in 1988. In 1988, 224 plants were in operation in Dominican free zones.[15] In 1990, it was estimated that there were 330 firms operating in the free zones.[16]

About two-thirds of the firms in Dominican free zones are engaged in apparel assembly for the U.S. market. Other significant assembly operations include footwear and leather products, electronics products, cigars, processed foods, jewelry, and furniture. Some newly-opened firms are engaged in precision tooling, data entry, computer graphics, and other service operations.[17]

- **Haiti:** Export-oriented assembly operations were established in 1960 in Haiti, but they did not become economically significant until over a decade later. Two industrial parks were created in Port-au-Prince in the late 1970s as the result of the growth of assembly plants. However, many export-oriented assembly firms are still located outside the industrial parks, and most are located near the airport in Port-au-Prince.[18]

  In 1966, there were 13 assembly firms operating in Haiti; by 1981, the number of assembly firms had grown to 154.[19] Haitian assembly firms primarily produce apparel, electronics products, sporting goods (especially baseballs and softballs), and toys.[20]

- **Jamaica:** In 1971, Jamaica led the Caribbean countries in assembled product exports, with about 25 assembly plants in operation.[21] The Kingston Export Free Zone, first established in 1976 as a warehousing and transshipment facility, was converted into an EPZ in 1982. By 1988, 12 of the 15 enterprises operating in the Kingston zone were assembly-type operations (10 of these firms assembled garments), up from 8 of the 17 firms in operation in 1984.[22] A second EPZ located at Montego Bay was opened in 1984 and housed 7 firms (3 apparel and 4 data entry) at the end of 1988. A third EPZ (the Garmex Free Zone) began operations in 1987 with 8 firms (7 apparel and one footwear) in operation at the end of 1988. A fourth free zone is under construction at Spanish Port.

- **Barbados:** Since 1969, Barbados has granted fiscal incentives to Bajan firms exporting outside the CARICOM area. In 1973, Barbados increased these incentives and began to promote industrial estates as a way to attract enclave enterprises; grants for new factories were also offered. Assembly facilities are situated primarily in industrial parks, administered by the Industrial

Development Corporation, and are located throughout the nation.[23]

In 1985, there were 23 enclave enterprises operating in industrial estates: 13 assembled electronic, electrical, and precision instruments; 5 assembled apparel and leather goods; and 5 were engaged in data processing activities. The Barbadian Government has targeted electronics, medical supplies, high quality apparel, and data processing as the main focus of future enclave activities.[24]

Smaller-scale export assembly operations are located in other Caribbean nations. For example,

- **Belize:** While there are no export processing zones in Belize, there is an offshore assembly sector. In 1989, it was reported that there were 5 companies that assembled garments for export.[25]

- **Dominica:** In 1989, there were three industrial estates with a total of 11 firms, plus 6 firms located outside of the industrial estates, that engaged in export assembly activities in Dominica. Unlike most other Caribbean assembly locations, no firms in Dominica were engaged in the assembly of electronic products. Two firms were engaged in the assembly of garments for the U.S. market, while the balance produced a variety of products (e.g., lumber, paint, bottled water, and soap) destined for other Caribbean countries.[26]

- **St. Lucia:** In 1989, it was reported that there were 5 industrial estates (similar to EPZs) and one facility located outside of the estates that engaged in production for export. In 1988, there were close to 20 firms operating in the estates, mostly producing apparel (12 firms) and electronic components (5 firms) for the U.S. market. The facility located outside of the estates was engaged in data processing services.[27]

- **St. Vincent and the Grenadines:** In 1989, it was reported that there was one government-administered industrial estate with 7 firms, with another in the planning stages. In addition, there were 4 export-oriented firms located outside of the estates. Together, these offshore assembly operations produced a variety of products: 7 firms assembled garments, 2 produced electronic components, and 1 produced state-of-the-art tennis rackets; two others (a brewery and a flour/rice mill) also produced for the local market.[28]

3.   U.S. IMPORTS OF ASSEMBLED PRODUCTS FROM THE CARIBBEAN

3.1. Special U.S. Tariff Provisions

The United States has several tariff provisions that contribute to the economic feasibility of U.S.-based manufacturers engaging in offshore assembly operations. These special provisions assess import duties only on the foreign value-added in products further processed or assembled abroad which are made of materials or components produced in the United States. The provisions were known formerly as items 806.30 and 807.00 in the Tariff Schedules of the United States (TSUS) and now as items 9802.00.60 and 9802.00.80 in the new Harmonized System nomenclature introduced on January 1, 1989. In what follows, these provisions will be referred to by their former designations.

Item 807.00 of the TSUS, in effect since 1963, is by far the more important of the two provisions. It provides for duty-free treatment of U.S.-made components used in the assembly of products for the U.S. market. The other provision, item 806.30, applies only to the treatment of nonprecious metals that are sent abroad for processing and then imported for further processing in the United States. In recent years, item 807.00 imports have accounted for over 99 percent of U.S. imports under these two provisions.[29] In what follows, U.S. imports under item 807.00 will be used as a measure of offshore assembly activities.

While U.S. imports under TSUS 807.00 do provide a rough measure of the rapid growth of offshore assembly for the U.S. market, they tend to understate the dynamism of this phenomenon as they fail to capture all exports from processing zones or other assembly facilities (e.g., items exported to countries other than the United States or items produced in the zones or other facilities which are exported to the United States under other available tariff provisions).[30]

In addition to the special tariff provision for items assembled abroad from U.S. components, the United States has several tariff preference programs for U.S. imports from developing countries. These programs offer even greater trade preferences (duty-free entry) for certain assembled products if a sufficient amount of host-country labor and materials (i.e., domestic valued added) have been incorporated to meet rules-of-origin requirements. Two of these programs, the U.S. Generalized System of Preferences (GSP)[31] and the Caribbean Basin Initiative (CBI),[32] are available to nearly all of the nations in the Caribbean. In addition, the United States has granted special access to the U.S. market for textile and apparel imports from certain Caribbean countries that use fabrics made and cut in the United States.[33]

3.2. U.S. Imports of Assembled Products from the Caribbean

Table 7.1 presents the total value of assembled product U.S. imports under item 807.00 from 27 Caribbean Basin countries over the period 1983 to 1989. Over this period, the value and the proportion of total U.S. imports from the Caribbean Basin entered under item 807.00 have expanded rapidly. U.S. imports of assembled products (807.00 items) from the Caribbean Basin have grown steadily from $751 million in 1983 to $1,570 million in 1989. Over the period 1983-89, U.S. imports of assembled products under item 807.00 from the Caribbean Basin have outperformed overall U.S. imports from the same region, increasing at an average annual rate of 13.1 percent, compared to a 4.0 percent average annual *decline* in overall imports.

In 1989, about 22 percent of all U.S. imports from the Caribbean Basin (31 percent of those subject to duty) entered the United States under item 807.00, compared to 8 percent (11 percent of those subject to duty) in 1983.

The U.S.-content value of offshore assembly imports (under item 807.00) from the Caribbean is substantially greater than that from most other countries (nearly 70 percent for those from the Caribbean compared to an average of about 20 percent from all sources). This is not surprising since many export items produced in the Caribbean primarily involve labor-intensive assembly of materials imported from the United States. Hence, the value-added to the export product consists mainly of the labor costs of assembly. Over the 1983-89 period, the share of foreign value-added in U.S. imports of assembled products from the Caribbean Basin has remained at about 31 percent.

Leading Sources of Assembled Products in the Caribbean Basin

Since 1983, the top-8 assembler nations in the Caribbean Basin (the Dominican Republic, Haiti, Jamaica, and Barbados in the Caribbean and Costa Rica, Guatemala, Honduras, and El Salvador in Central America) have accounted for nearly all (94 percent in 1983 and 97 percent in 1989) of all item 807.00 imports from that region (see Table 7.1). Over this

Table 7.1. U.S. Imports of Assembled Products under Item 807.00 from the Caribbean Basin: 1983–1989 (Customs Value in Thousands of Dollars; Share in Percent)

Country	Value of U.S. imports under item 807.00				Share of total U.S. imports from country				Share of value-added in item 807.00 imports			
	1983	1985	1987	1989	1983	1985	1987	1989	1983	1985	1987	1989
Caribbean Basin, total	750,513	783,085	1,093,117	1,569,648	8.3	11.4	17.7	22.4	30.7	30.4	30.8	31.9
Dominican Republic	160,958	246,796	428,068	662,679	20.0	25.6	37.4	40.5	30.7	28.4	31.3	31.3
Costa Rica	78,800	98,439	145,641	275,341	20.4	20.1	21.7	28.4	23.0	28.1	33.1	32.0
Haiti	197,406	221,138	231,268	219,582	58.5	57.2	58.7	59.0	29.4	28.1	29.4	30.0
Jamaica	15,495	41,482	115,820	163,959	5.9	15.5	29.4	31.1	44.9	29.7	26.3	28.9
Guatemala	1,357	9,367	31,291	80,051	0.4	2.3	6.4	13.2	38.1	39.2	34.9	47.4
Honduras	25,589	29,415	43,014	67,840	7.1	7.9	8.9	14.9	31.1	29.3	31.1	26.9
El Salvador	78,901	22,571	29,959	43,662	22.0	5.7	11.0	17.9	43.0	22.2	21.8	32.2
Barbados	154,885	69,218	17,252	13,331	76.7	34.2	29.2	34.4	28.0	36.7	50.5	46.9
Belize	6,398	14,383	14,262	12,446	23.4	30.6	33.2	28.9	27.3	27.8	28.3	28.5
St. Lucia	3,555	7,884	10,032	11,587	75.6	57.1	56.2	48.3	30.1	30.0	30.6	31.4
St. Kitts-Nevis-Anguilla	8,571	6,219	10,164	4,792	45.7	38.2	42.4	22.0	28.2	25.2	36.0	29.4
Grenada	5	204	1,059	3,525	2.4	15.6	29.2	44.8	55.9	28.7	30.3	42.8
Panama	1,851	3,776	2,484	2,643	0.6	1.0	0.7	1.0	29.9	27.5	31.3	37.6
St. Vincent & Grenadines	3,496	3,563	3,199	2,445	81.8	36.9	37.7	26.4	50.7	49.9	44.2	45.1
Bahamas	240	415	34	2,162	0.0	0.1	0.0	0.5	31.1	11.6	55.5	99.0

(Continued)

Country	Value of U.S. imports under item 807.00				Share of total U.S. imports from country				Share of value-added in item 807.00 imports			
	1983	1985	1987	1989	1983	1985	1987	1989	1983	1985	1987	1989
Trinidad & Tobago	41	–	477	1,161	0.0	.	0.1	0.2	62.1	.	66.3	37.2
Guyana	3,663	426	2,366	941	5.4	0.9	4.0	1.7	42.8	29.8	41.9	25.1
Montserrat	787	1,387	1,237	669	85.1	38.3	51.3	29.3	32.0	22.3	33.4	28.5
Dominica	171	114	222	528	70.9	0.8	2.2	6.9	33.7	19.1	1.2	32.6
Netherlands Ant.-Aruba	2,319	502	12	303	0.1	0.1	0.0	0.1	48.0	36.1	23.8	28.1
Antigua	5,794	5,763	5,180	–	65.8	23.3	60.1	.	20.9	25.7	30.4	.
British Virgin Islands	3	4	–	–	0.3	0.0	.	.	44.8	15.2	.	.
Cayman Islands	–	8	–	–	.	0.1	.	.	.	24.8	.	.
Turks & Caicos	–	–	76	–	.	.	1.6	.	.	.	28.9	.
Nicaragua	–	11	–	–	.	0.0	.	.	.	13.6	.	.
Suriname	–	–	–	–	.	.	.	.	.	.	.	.

Note: – or . equals zero; 0 means less than $500 or 0.05 percent. *Source: Compiled from official statistics of the U.S. Department of Commerce.*

period, the share of total 807.00 imports from the Caribbean Basin accounted for by the leading supplier nations in the region has changed dramatically: both the Dominican Republic and Costa Rica doubled their shares, and Jamaica and Guatemala have each increased their's 5-fold. In contrast, Honduras has maintained its share over the period, while Haiti's share of the region's total has fallen by a half and the share for both El Salvador and Barbados has fallen precipitously. By 1989, the major exporters of assembled products in the Caribbean (the Dominican Republic, Haiti, and Jamaica) accounted for $938 million or two-thirds of all item 807.00 U.S. imports from the Caribbean Basin — up from $240 million or about half of the total from the region in 1983.

Importance of Assembled Product Exports

For certain Caribbean nations, products assembled from U.S.-sourced components for export to the U.S. market represent a major portion of all products exported to the United States. Further, the U.S. market is the primary destination for most of these countries' exports. Based on the importance of assembled products in total exports to the United States over the 1983-89 period, these countries can be grouped in three export assembly reliance classes: high, medium, and low.

Caribbean countries that have a *high reliance* on assembly exports (over half of their exports to the United States) include Antigua, Montserrat, St. Lucia, and Haiti; however, the significance of assembly exports to the United States has been declining sharply for Antigua, Montserrat, and St. Lucia.

Countries that have a *medium reliance* on assembly exports (between one-quarter and one-half of their exports to the United States) include Belize, the Dominican Republic, Jamaica, Grenada, St. Kitts-Nevis, Barbados, and St. Vincent and the Grenadines. Belize, the Dominican Republic, Jamaica, and Grenada have shown an increasing reliance on assembly exports to the United States, while the significance of assembly exports to the United States has declined sharply for Barbados and St. Vincent and the Grenadines. Finally, there are a number of Caribbean countries that appear to have a *low reliance* on export assembly. At present, the export to the U.S. market of assembled products of U.S. components does not appear to be important for the following Caribbean countries: Dominica, Turks and Caicos Islands, Bahamas, Netherlands Antilles-Aruba, Trinidad and Tobago, Cayman Islands, and the British Virgin Islands.

Leading Assembled Product Exports from the Caribbean Basin

U.S. imports from the Caribbean Basin under item 807.00 have been concentrated in a few product categories (see Table 7.2). In 1989, 86 percent (up from 48 percent in 1983) of the value of all item 807.00 entries from the Caribbean Basin were apparel products and represented 79 percent (down from 92 percent in 1983) of all apparel imports from the Caribbean Basin. The other major categories of item 807.00 entries from the Caribbean Basin countries in 1989 were electrical machinery, miscellaneous manufactures, scientific instruments, leather and leather products, and textile mill products.

Over the period 1983-89, three import product groups from the Caribbean Basin (rubber and miscellaneous plastics, electrical machinery, and miscellaneous manufactures) have shown a significant decline in the share of products entered under item 807.00, as larger amounts qualified for duty-free entry under either GSP or CBI. In the case of miscellaneous manufactures, most sporting goods and toys qualified for duty-free entry under CBI or GSP, leaving primarily jewelry of precious metals (3-4 percent value-added) and softballs (23 percent value-added) as the major items entered under item 807.00. Similarly, a restructuring of the composition of precision instrument item 807.00 imports from the Caribbean Basin is evident over this period, as more labor-intensive assembly of gauges, medical instruments, and clock mechanisms has gained importance within assembly exports while other instrument exports were able to utilize benefits under the CBI and GSP.

Apparel and electrical machinery assembled products dominate U.S. imports from the Caribbean Basin, accounting for nearly 90 percent of total 807.00 entries from the region. However, the relative importance of these two categories of assembled products has changed dramatically since 1983.

As total U.S. imports of electrical machinery from the Caribbean Basin have fallen from $345.1 million in 1983 to $239.4 million in 1989, so too have those from the Caribbean Basin under item 807.00 (from $295.1 million to $91.3 million). In part, this reflected some changes in world demand patterns as well as a restructuring of global production and sourcing by multinational enterprises.

Over the 1983-89 period, five countries (the Dominican Republic, Haiti, El Salvador, Costa Rica, and Barbados) have provided nearly all electrical machinery 807.00 items from the Caribbean Basin. Imported products from the Caribbean Basin in this product category consist primarily of

Table 7.2. Commodity Distribution of U.S. Imports of Assembled Products under Item 807.00 from the Caribbean Basin: 1983-1989 (Percent)

| | Share of total item 807.00 U.S. imports from country | | | | | | | | | | | |
| Country | Apparel products (SIC 23) | | | | Electrical products (SIC 36) | | | | Misc. manufactures (SIC 39) | | | |
	1983	1985	1987	1989	1983	1985	1987	1989	1983	1985	1987	1989
Caribbean Basin, total	48	70	80	86	39	16	8	6	7	8	7	2
Dominican Republic	85	83	82	84	7	6	9	7	4	8	8	–
Costa Rica	76	86	94	92	19	11	5	3	–	–	1	2
Haiti	39	52	60	75	32	22	11	7	19	17	16	11
Jamaica	83	95	89	92	–	–	–	–	2	2	1	–
Guatemala	100	93	97	99	–	–	–	–	–	–	–	–
Honduras	78	80	91	100	–	–	–	–	22	19	9	–
El Salvador	7	39	57	75	92	61	43	23	–	–	–	–
Barbados	14	36	55	40	80	47	19	35	–	–	–	1
Belize	100	100	100	100	–	–	–	–	–	–	–	–
St. Lucia	75	95	94	84	21	4	5	13	–	–	–	–
St. Kitts-Nevis-Anguilla	57	92	91	96	43	6	7	4	–	–	–	–
Grenada	20	100	100	64	–	–	–	–	–	–	–	–
Panama	100	99	99	100	–	–	1	–	–	1	–	–
St. Vincent & Grenadines	43	92	84	54	57	8	16	46	–	1	–	–
Bahamas	–	–	100	–	100	82	–	–	–	–	–	–

(Continued)

Share of total item 807.00 U.S. imports from country

Country	Apparel products (SIC 23)				Electrical products (SIC 36)				Misc. manufactures (SIC 39)			
	1983	1985	1987	1989	1983	1985	1987	1989	1983	1985	1987	1989
Trinidad & Tobago	–	–	97	100	100	–	3	–	–	–	–	–
Guyana	100	100	100	100	–	–	–	–	–	–	–	–
Montserrat	3	18	–	–	97	64	55	46	–	–	1	–
Dominica	100	58	–	96	–	–	–	–	–	42	100	–
Netherlands Ant.-Aruba	1	28	–	–	42	21	17	25	–	–	–	–
Antigua	100	95	99	–	–	5	1	–	–	–	–	–
British Virgin Islands	100	100	–	–	–	–	–	–	–	–	–	–
Cayman Islands	–	100	–	–	–	–	–	–	–	–	–	–
Turks & Caicos	–	–	–	–	–	–	–	–	–	–	–	–
Nicaragua	–	–	–	–	–	–	–	–	–	–	–	–
Suriname	–	–	–	–	–	–	–	–	–	–	–	–

Note: – means zero or less than 0.05 percent. *Source: Compiled from official statistics of the U.S. Department of Commerce.*

electronic components and accessories (e.g., semiconductors and capacitors) and electrical lighting, wiring, and switching equipment.

The substantial decline in electrical machinery 807.00 imports from the Caribbean Basin has been the result of several factors. First, there have been large declines in imports of these items from Barbados (from 80 percent of all U.S. 807.00 imports from that country in 1983 to 35 percent in 1989)[34] and El Salvador (from 92 percent of all U.S. 807.00 imports from that country in 1983 to 23 percent in 1989). In part, the decline in electrical machinery 807.00 imports from the Caribbean Basin reflects the fact that a smaller share of all U.S. electrical machinery imports is now entered under the 807.00 provisions because these items can qualify for duty-free entry under the CBI. In the case of the Dominican Republic, there was a rise in 807.00 U.S. electrical machinery imports over the 1983-87 period, mostly in items with too little value-added to qualify for duty-free entry under CBI. By 1987, electrical machinery assembly was secondary to apparel assembly in all the major Caribbean Basin assembler countries.

Caribbean Basin apparel exports to the United States (nearly all of which are excluded from GSP and CBI benefits) exploded over the period 1983-89, rising from $393.9 million in 1983 to $1.7 billion in 1989; by 1989, the Caribbean Basin provided 7.6 percent of all U.S. apparel imports. Most of the surge in Caribbean apparel exports to the United States was attributable to apparel assembled, in part, from U.S. materials. Item 807.00 apparel imports from the Caribbean Basin have grown from $362.4 million in 1983 to $1.3 billion in 1989 (with over two-thirds U.S.-content value). By 1987, slightly over three-quarters of all 807.00 apparel imports from the world were provided by the top-5 supplier countries: Mexico, the Dominican Republic, Costa Rica, Haiti, and Jamaica; however, total 807.00 apparel imports accounted for only 6.5 percent of all U.S. apparel imports.

In the Caribbean Basin, the top-4 supplier countries of 807.00 apparel products in 1989 (the Dominican Republic, Costa Rica, Haiti, and Jamaica) have accounted for approximately 80 percent of all 807.00 apparel imports from the region over the 1983-89 period. Barbados, the fourth-largest Caribbean supplier in 1983, has experienced a dramatic decline since 1985 in the provision of assembled apparel products to the U.S. market, while some other countries (e.g., Jamaica, Guatemala, El Salvador, St. Lucia, and Grenada) have experienced a rapid rise. Over the 1983-89 period, Barbados, Guatemala, and St. Vincent have led other Basin suppliers in the share of value-added in assembled apparel (between 40 and 50 percent). Overall, the U.S.-content share in 807.00 apparel imports from the Caribbean Basin has declined slightly since 1983, perhaps due to the use of non-U.S. sourced materials by an increasing number of Asian (primarily Korean and Chinese) investors in the region.

Miscellaneous manufactured products (primarily jewelry, toys, and sporting goods) have been the third largest category of assembled products exported to the United States from the Caribbean Basin over the 1983-89 period. While the value of 807.00 entries of these items has increased moderately over this period, value-added has fallen dramatically. Nearly all miscellaneous manufactures 807.00 imports from the Caribbean Basin were supplied by the top-5 supplier countries (Haiti, the Dominican Republic, Honduras, Jamaica, and Costa Rica); Haiti and the Dominican Republic have accounted for nearly 90 percent of these items since 1983.

Other groups of U.S. imports of assembled products from the Caribbean (that have accounted for a substantial portion of several countries' assembled product exports to the United States) include: scientific instruments (the Dominican Republic, Barbados, Montserrat), leather and leather products (Haiti, Jamaica), textile mill products (Jamaica), primary metal products (Haiti, the Dominican Republic), and rubber and miscellaneous plastics products (Barbados).

4. IMPACT OF ASSEMBLY OPERATIONS ON CARIBBEAN COUNTRIES

4.1. Employment

One of the primary reasons why developing countries promote the establishment of assembly facilities — and offer incentives to enterprises that locate in their countries — is to create and expand employment in the manufacturing sector and to provide jobs (both direct and indirect) for the large number of new entrants into the labor force. Although data on employment created by assembly operations are sparse, fragmentary information suggests that they have been relatively successful on this score.

Assembly operations in developing countries tend to employ primarily unskilled or semi-skilled production workers. Employment opportunities in managerial activities — such as production planning, marketing, etc. — are very limited, as many of these functions are carried out abroad by parent companies. Although local talent is hired for mid-level management and engineering positions, key managerial posts are often filled with foreign nationals from the parent company.[35] In the Caribbean, some countries (e.g., Barbados and Haiti) offer tax incentives, cash grants or other subsidies to assembly operations that provide professional education and worker training programs.[36]

Workers in assembly operations in the Caribbean are primarily women, especially young women (in the 16-25 age group). Reasons for the high proportion of young women in the labor force of assembly plants range from their alleged better manual dexterity, which makes them more efficient in assembly tasks, to charges of their greater vulnerability to exploitation.[37] The very high participation of women in assembly operations holds for other nations as well; of an estimated 1.3 million workers in EPZs in developing nations in the mid-1980s, about 1 million (77 percent) were females.[38]

Table 7.3 presents estimates of employment in EPZs and other offshore manufacturing facilities in selected Caribbean nations in 1975, 1986, and 1988/89.[39] Also included in Table 7.3 are official statistics on paid employment in the manufacturing sector in those countries over a comparable period. According to the estimates in Table 7.3, EPZs and offshore manufacturing facilities in the Caribbean employed at a minimum 44,100 workers in 1975; by 1988/89, the total had risen to nearly 201,500 workers. While these employment levels appear small when compared with the aggregate economically active population in the region — about 4 percent of the estimated labor force in these countries of 6 million persons — they are significant for some countries. For example,

- **Haiti:** In the early 1970s, the 20,000 direct jobs associated with assembly industries accounted for about 25 percent of the total labor force in manufacturing and construction.[40] According to data in Table 7.3, assembly employment accounted for about 20 percent of manufacturing employment in 1975. By 1986, there were 43,000 jobs associated with assembly operations, compared with employment in the manufacturing sector of 122,000 in 1983. In 1988, assembly operations in Haiti provided about 55,000 jobs compared to a total paid employment in manufacturing of 115,490.

  Around 1979, women comprised 75 percent of the labor force of assembly plants.[41] More recent estimates indicate that assembly plant workers are primarily female (60-70 percent) and that the average age of workers is between 25 and 35 years old.[42]

- **Dominican Republic:** Assembly operations in the industrial free zones provided about 5 percent of manufacturing employment in 1975; by 1986, this had risen to about 25 percent. According to other sources, assembly operations employed 6.3 percent of total urban wage earners in 1985,[43] and provided about 22 percent of the country's manufacturing employment.[44] Free zone direct and

Table 7.3. Employment in EPZs and Other Offshore Manufacturing Facilities in Selected Caribbean Nations: 1975, 1986, 1988/89

Country	Labor force 1988	Employment in EPZ & other offshore manufacturing			Employment in all manufacturing			EPZ & offshore share of			
								All mfg.			Labor force
		1975	1986	1989	1975	1986	1988	1975	1986	1989	1988/89
Barbados	113,200	3,000	6,865	8,718d	13,800a	11,000	12,200	22	62	71	8
Montserrat	5,100	na	220	na	250	533b	522e	–	41	–	4
Haiti	2,400,000	25,000	43,000	55,000d	122,300	121,690b	115,490	20	35	48	2
Dominican Republic	1,750,000	6,500	48,600	112,112	122,131	140,840c	na	5	25	–	6
Jamaica	1,100,000	6,100	8,000	18,000	73,900	115,300	131,400e	8	7	14	2
Belize	49,000	na	200	1,060	na	na	na	–	–	–	2
Dominica	35,000	na	200	850	na	na	na	–	–	–	2
St. Lucia	54,000	3,500	na	2,780d	na	na	na	–	–	–	5
St. Vincent	45,000	na	844	2,740	na	na	na	–	–	–	6

a = 1976; b = 1983; c = 1985; d = 1988; e = 1987; na = not available.

Sources: Labor Force: Alfredo Berges, "Reto del Caribe, Aumentar el Turismo y Exportaciones," 4 July 1988, cited in Miguel Ceara Hatton, Las Economías Caribeñas en la Década del Ochenta (Santo Domingo, D.R.: Centro de Investigación Económica, Inc., 1988), p. 57. Employment in EPZs and other manufacturing facilities: International Labour Organisation and United Nations Centre on Transnational Corporations, Economic and Social Effects of Multinational Enterprises in Export Processing Zones (Geneva, 1988), p.163; Starnberg Institute, Working Conditions in Export Processing Zones in Selected Developing Countries, report prepared for U.S. Department of Labor, Bureau of International Labor Affairs, October 1989; and various reporting telegrams from American Embassies. Total paid employment in manufacturing: International Labour Office, Year Book of Labour Statistics 1989-90 and earlier issues.

indirect jobs now account for over 8 percent of national employment and over 50 percent of all manufacturing jobs.[45]

According to statistics from the Industrial Development Corporation in the Dominican Republic, employment in Dominican free zones in the 1980s has been as follows: 19,456 in 1981; 19,235 in 1982; 21,387 in 1983; 25,099 in 1984; 22,720 in 1985; 48,603 in 1986; 72,735 in 1987; and 85,000 in 1988.[46] Over the period 1985-87, employment in the free zones more than tripled, from 22,720 to 72,735 workers.

With the opening of 6 new free zones since March 1988, total direct employment in the zones soared to approximately 90,000 workers in March 1989 and an estimated 112,112 workers in late 1989. Females comprised around 70 percent of workers in the free zones.[47]

- **Jamaica**: In 1975, assembly operations in Jamaican free zones provided about 8 percent of manufacturing employment; this share of manufacturing employment remained relatively unchanged over the next decade (in 1986 it was 7 percent). However, employment in the zones has grown rapidly since 1986 as new apparel assembly firms have begun operations (in part, due to the U.S. special access program for apparel). Zone employment has grown from 8,000 workers in 1986 to 18,000 workers in 1989 which accounted for 14 percent of total manufacturing employment in Jamaica. Over 90 percent of the export free zone employment is in apparel assembly. Most free zone workers are between the ages of 18 and 24; over 90 percent of the zone workers are women.

- **Barbados**: In 1975, assembly operations in Barbados accounted for about 3,000 jobs and provided over 20 percent of manufacturing employment; by 1986, the number had more than doubled, growing to 6,865 jobs which accounted for over 60 percent of employment in manufacturing. More recent data for 1988 indicate that assembly operations account for 8,718 jobs and over 70 percent of manufacturing employment. Around 1984, women constituted 94 percent of the work force of assembly operations.[48]

- **Smaller Caribbean Countries**: In 1989, it was reported that apparel export assembly operations in **Belize** employed 1,060 workers out of a total country work force of 58,000; 90-95 percent of these assembly workers were female.[49] Export assembly activities in **Dominica** were reported to have employed 850 workers out of a total labor force of approximately 35,000 to 40,000 in 1989.[50] By the end of 1988, it was reported that there were 2,780 workers employed in offshore assembly operations out of a total labor force of about 54,000 in **St. Lucia** and that the government had forecasted 1,900 new jobs in manufacturing and data processing as new operations were expected to open in 1989.[51] In 1989, it was reported that 2,740 workers were engaged in offshore export assembly operations out of a total labor force of approximately 40,000 to 45,000 in **St. Vincent and the Grenadines**; the vast majority of these workers were women and a substantial number (1,500) of all assembly workers were employed by one apparel firm in cottage industries (i.e., production at home).[52]

Another way to assess the impact of assembly operations on employment is by focusing on the share of new jobs they have created. This is particularly critical for the Caribbean region, as the labor force in these nations has grown more rapidly than the sluggish industrial sectors have been able to absorb.[53] For the Dominican Republic, it has been estimated that since their establishment, EPZs have been responsible for over 30 percent of new manufacturing employment in that nation.[54]

Assembly operations also generate indirect employment from the purchase of local inputs (backward linkages) and from local expenditures by assembly workers (multiplier effects). While the indirect employment impacts of assembly operations are more limited than those of other forms of investment — the assembly operations receive most of their inputs from abroad and generally export most of their output — they are nevertheless significant. For example, in the Dominican Republic, it has been estimated that the 30,737 workers employed in assembly operations in 1984 supported an additional 5,777 workers (19 percent) supplying components, raw materials, parts, and machinery.[55]

A conservative estimate is that the number of jobs created in the local economy as the result of expenditures by assembly workers is at least of the same order of magnitude as the direct employment attributed to assembly operations.[56] Dominican economists estimate that each direct job in assembly operations generates 1.5 indirect jobs in the economy at large. Thus, in 1988 free zones in the Dominican Republic generated 85,000 direct jobs and 127,500 indirect jobs, for a total of 212,500 jobs.[57]

4.2. Export Earnings

Another positive contribution of assembly operations to the economies of host countries relates to the balance of payments. Exports of assembled products are a significant source of export earnings of developing countries. The significance of assembled products as a source of foreign exchange earnings has become more acute in recent years as international prices of basic commodities, the traditional exports of developing countries, have remained weak.

For the most part, statistics on the foreign exchange earnings associated with assembly operations in the Caribbean are not available. One exception is the Dominican Republic, for which statistics are available on the amount of foreign exchange (dollars) sold by industrial free zones to the Central Bank. Free zones in the Dominican Republic generated, on average, $4.8 million per annum in the first half of the 1970s, $26.7 million in the second half of the 1970s, $55.4 million in the first half of the 1980s, and $44.4 million in 1985, $88.3 million in 1986, $97.1 million in 1987, and $129.0 million in 1988.[58] Also, reports from the two major free zones in Jamaica (Kingston and Garmex) indicate that free zones in Jamaica provided about $31 million in foreign exchange earnings in 1988, compared to $2.4 million in 1984 and $10.8 million in 1986.[59]

One way to estimate the contribution of assembly operations to foreign exchange earnings is to use as a proxy for such earnings the dutiable (i.e., foreign value-added) portion of U.S. item 807 imports. While this proxy probably underestimates overall earnings from assembly operations because: (1) it deals only with exports to the United States; and (2) it fails to take into account assembly products that might enter the United States duty-free under GSP or CBI, nonetheless it probably provides a reasonable indication of foreign exchange earnings.

Table 7.4 presents the share of merchandise exports accounted for by assembled products during 1983-89 for selected Caribbean countries, calculated as the foreign value-added content of U.S. item 807 imports for each nation as a percent of that nation's merchandise exports to the world. Assembled products have contributed significantly to export earnings of Haiti and the Dominican Republic. In the case of Haiti, assembled products contributed over one-third of total merchandise export earnings over the 1983-88 period. In the case of the Dominican Republic, assembled products' share of merchandise exports increased steadily, doubling between 1983 and 1986, and accounting for over one-fifth of total merchandise exports in 1988 and 1989.

For Barbados, the situation was quite different: While assembled products constituted 13.5 percent of total merchandise exports of Barbados in 1983, this share fell throughout the 1980s, so that assembled products constituted only 3.3 percent of the value of exports in 1989.

Table 7.4. Assembled Product Exports as a Share of Total Country Exports from Selected Caribbean Nations, 1983-89 (Percent)

Country	1983	1984	1985	1986	1987	1988	1989
Haiti	35.0	34.7	41.3	34.8	30.9	37.8	na
Dominican Republic	6.3	7.1	9.5	13.0	18.8	20.4	22.4
Belize	2.2	4.4	4.4	4.1	4.0	4.0	na
Barbados	13.5	11.3	7.2	3.7	5.6	4.6	3.3
Jamaica	1.0	1.3	2.2	3.3	4.3	5.0	4.9

na = not available.
Source: Calculated using the dutiable portion of U.S. item 807.00 imports as a proxy for exports of assembled products over total exports from International Monetary Fund, International Financial Statistics Yearbook 1990; total exports were converted from domestic currency to U.S. dollars using official annual average exchange rates.

4.3. Exports of Manufactured Products

Data on manufactured goods exports were not available for a sufficiently large number of countries in the Caribbean to permit the estimation of the contribution of assembled products' exports to total exports of manufactured goods. Table 7.5 presents, for selected Caribbean countries, the value of leading primary commodity exports and of assembled products exports over the period 1983-89. In part, because primary-commodity prices have been depressed (and the volume of exports of these items has fluctuated greatly) over this period, assembled products (which, in most cases, have expanded steadily) have gained in importance in the export basket of several nations, in some cases displacing primary commodity exports.

Over the period 1983-88, assembled products were more important than coffee as an export earner for Haiti; in 1987 and 1988, the value of assembled product exports was twice as large as that of coffee. In the Dominican Republic, assembled products have been the most steady contributor to export revenues, with revenues from assembled products exceeding those from coffee, cocoa bean, and gold ore exports in recent years.

4.4. Impact on the Economic Structure of Exports

The United States is the most important customer for the merchandise exports of the nations of the Caribbean, with over half of their exports destined for the U.S. market. Given the importance of the U.S. market to

Table 7.5. Leading Primary Product Exports and the Value of Assembled Product Exports from Selected Caribbean Nations, 1983-89 (Millions of U.S. Dollars)

Country/ leading products	1983	1984	1985	1986	1987	1988	1989
Barbados							
Sugar	18.7	26.3	25.0	26.1	28.3	28.0	23.4
Assembled products	43.3	44.0	25.4	10.2	8.7	7.9	6.2
Belize							
Sugar	34.2	32.5	22.9	31.5	27.0	35.0	na
Citrus products	6.8	9.8	12.1	11.1	15.5	17.7	na
Assembled products	1.7	4.1	4.0	3.8	4.0	4.8	3.6
Dominican Republic							
Sugar	276.4	300.0	190.1	146.2	145.2	142.1	217.8
Coffee	76.4	94.9	57.6	115.9	61.4	66.2	87.6
Gold ore	164.5	131.8	113.6	111.8	120.0	98.1	88.8
Ferronickel	83.5	108.5	120.7	77.8	115.2	308.8	372.0
Cocoa beans and products	60.9	75.9	64.8	67.8	72.4	69.7	49.9
Assembled products	49.4	61.6	70.2	93.2	134.0	181.3	207.4
Grenada							
Nutmeg	2.9	2.1	4.2	9.7	14.6	na	na
Cocoa beans	6.0	4.2	5.0	4.2	4.0	na	na
Bananas	3.0	2.9	3.2	3.7	4.1	na	na
Mace	0.8	0.9	0.9	2.0	2.7	na	na
Assembled products	0.0	0.0	0.1	0.0	0.3	1.3	1.5
Haiti							
Coffee	55.5	47.4	45.3	55.9	24.9	36.6	na
Sugar	1.5	0.4	0.0	1.0	0.1	1.0	na
Assembled products	58.0	62.3	71.9	64.7	68.0	69.0	65.8
Jamaica							
Alumina	337.1	333.0	208.1	210.8	199.8	243.1	436.9
Bauxite	113.7	149.9	84.8	97.5	114.3	105.4	125.7
Sugar	58.2	43.6	45.4	43.7	61.6	78.4	63.3
Assembled products	7.0	9.5	12.3	19.3	30.4	41.7	47.4
St. Kitts-Nevis							
Sugar	10.0	11.6	8.8	11.8	na	na	na
Assembled products	2.4	2.6	1.6	3.1	3.7	2.3	1.4
St. Lucia							
Bananas	18.6	23.8	30.2	55.5	na	na	na
Coconut oil, unrefined	0.7	0.8	0.4	1.8	na	na	na
Coconut oil, refined	2.1	2.4	1.2	0.1	na	na	na
Assembled products	1.1	1.2	2.4	2.4	3.1	4.0	3.6
St. Vincent & Grenadines							
Bananas	11.0	11.9	16.9	19.4	na	na	na
Assembled products	1.8	0.9	1.8	0.9	1.4	0.9	1.1

na = not available.

Source: The dutiable portion of U.S. item 807.00 imports is used as a proxy for exports of assembled products. Country exports by product are from International Monetary Fund, International Financial Statistics Yearbook 1990; *country exports were converted from domestic currency to U.S. dollars using official annual average exchange rates.*

Table 7.6. Industrial Composition of U.S. Imports from Selected Caribbean Nations, 1983-89 (Percent of Total)

SIC-based division	Dominican Republic				Haiti				Jamaica			
	1983	1985	1987	1989	1983	1985	1987	1989	1983	1985	1987	1989
Agriculture, forestry, and fishery products	19	18	13	7	8	5	3	3	2	5	3	2
Mining and mineral products	0	0	0	0	0	0	0	0	38	19	27	20
Manufactured products	75	79	84	90	89	92	94	94	57	72	68	74
Other commodities	6	3	3	3	3	3	3	3	3	3	2	4

Source: Compiled from official statistics of the U.S. Department of Commerce.

these nations, it is instructive to look at how the structure of their exports to the United States has changed over the 1983-89 period.

Table 7.6 presents the broad industrial composition of U.S. imports from the three major Caribbean supplier countries: the Dominican Republic, Jamaica, and Haiti. In 1989, these three Caribbean nations provided: 36 percent (up from 16 percent in 1983) of all U.S. imports from the Caribbean Basin, 70 percent (up from 50 percent in 1983) of all item 807.00 entries from the Caribbean, and 49 percent (up from 33 percent in 1983) of all GSP or CBI duty-free entries from the Caribbean.

Over the 1983-89 period, manufactured goods have accounted for an increasing share of these Caribbean nations' exports to the United States. This increase in share of manufactured exports has occurred as other major export sectors in these countries — agricultural, forestry, and fishery products (in the Dominican Republic and Haiti) and mining and minerals products (in Jamaica) — either have grown less rapidly or have contracted. Manufactured products constitute the majority of merchandise exports to the United States from these countries.

Table 7.7 presents the leading product groups of U.S. imports of manufactured products from the same three Caribbean countries considered above; the share of each leading product group entered under item 807.00 is also presented. The industrial concentration of manufactured goods exports to the United States from these countries is evident; the top-4 product groups over the 1983-89 period accounted for over four-fifths of each country's manufactured product exports to the United States.

Table 7.7. Leading Product Groups of U.S. Imports of Manufactured Products from Selected Caribbean Nations, 1983-89 (Percent of Total)

Country and leading products groups	Share of total manufactured imports				Share of product group entered under item 807.00			
	1983	1985	1987	1989	1983	1985	1987	1989
Dominican Republic								
SIC 23 – Apparel	24	30	42	45	94	89	88	84
SIC 33 – Primary Metals	23	21	16	11	0	0	2	1
SIC 20 – Food & Kindred Prod	36	27	14	14	0	0	0	0
SIC 39 – Misc. Manuf. Prod	2	6	9	7	46	40	36	2
Haiti								
SIC 23 – Apparel	28	37	43	54	92	87	87	88
SIC 39 – Misc. Manuf. Prod	17	18	20	15	75	57	53	45
SIC 36 – Electrical Machinery	23	23	17	14	91	59	39	33
SIC 31 – Leather Products	15	9	6	6	24	21	47	15
Jamaica								
SIC 23 – Apparel	9	28	64	52	99	73	60	74
SIC 28 – Chemicals	61	43	14	29	0	0	0	0
SIC 20 – Food & Kindred Prod	18	16	8	7	0	0	0	0
SIC 22 – Textiles	0	0	4	6	0	98	99	52

Source: Compiled from official statistics of the U.S. Department of Commerce.

The three countries exhibit some interesting similarities. As certain non-assembly export-oriented manufacturing activities such as food and kindred products (sugar) in the Dominican Republic and Jamaica, primary metals (ferronickel and gold) in the Dominican Republic, and chemicals (inorganic bases and ethanol) in Jamaica have declined in relative importance, exports of assembled apparel have grown significantly. In 1989, apparel products were the top manufactured product export to the United States, accounting for 45 percent (up from 24 percent in 1983) of the Dominican Republic's, 54 percent (up from 28 percent) of Haiti's, and 52 percent (up from 9 percent) of Jamaica's manufactured goods exports to the United States. Substantial proportions of these apparel items were entered under item 807.00. Part of the recent increased importance of apparel exports may be related to the "special access" to the U.S. market that has been granted to each of these countries.

Over the 1980s, manufactured goods have become a much more important part of all merchandise exported to the United States by the nations of the Caribbean. This result is due, in part, to the rapid expansion of a rather narrow range of assembled product exports with substantial U.S.-content value. In some cases, these assembled product exports have replaced the production of other products that had yielded more local value-added and earned more net foreign exchange.

While many Caribbean nations have increased their exports to the United States, these increases have not always resulted in increased *net* foreign exchange earnings for those countries. Losses in foreign exchange earnings from declining commodity prices and reductions in U.S. sugar quotas have not been offset in most cases by earnings generated by non-traditional exports. For example, a study by the U.S. General Accounting Office notes that:

> Host-government officials said that traditional exports, such as sugar and coffee, have an estimated value-added component of 90 percent, while light manufacturing, such as in textiles, has an approximate 20-percent value-added component. Although a $1 million decline in sugar exports offset by a $1 million increase in textile exports would result in no change in reported export earnings, there would actually be a net loss of $700,000 in value-added, and an associated decline in net foreign exchange earnings. Thus a $1 million decline in sugar exports would have to be offset by a $4.5 million increase in textile exports to maintain the same level of value-added and generate the same net foreign exchange earnings.

> Using the figures of the previous example, but adding the assumption that export values have been adjusted to keep sugar and textile prices constant, and that the value-added component measures workers' wages, the employment effect can be similarly calculated for a change in real value-added. If the average agricultural wage is $750 per year as in the Dominican Republic, the $900,000 decline in value-added from sugar translates into a loss of 1,200 employee years ($900,000 divided by $750). While the $200,000 increase in value-added from textile exports translates into the generation of 200 employee years at the Dominican Republic's average textile real wage of approximately $1,000 per year, a net loss of 1,000 employee years remains. Textile exports would have to increase by $6 million to offset the employment loss from a $1 million decline in sugar exports.[60]

4.5. Trade with the United States

The use of U.S. components by offshore assembler nations has a positive effect on U.S. exports to those nations. While the duty-free portion of item 807.00 imports (U.S. components) represents an underestimate of U.S.-made merchandise contained in all U.S. imports, it can be viewed as a rough measure of U.S. exports that are generated in support of offshore assembly operations. The value of U.S. materials and components incorporated into items re-entered into the United States under the 807.00 provision (i.e., the U.S.-content value of item 807.00 imports) has risen from 3 percent of total U.S. exports in 1983 to 5 percent in 1987. For some Caribbean nations, this share is substantially higher; for example, in 1989,

34 percent of U.S. exports to Haiti were used in support of production sharing, as were 28 percent of U.S. exports to the Dominican Republic, 12 percent of U.S. exports to Jamaica, and 10 percent of U.S. exports to Belize.

5. CONCLUDING OBSERVATIONS

At a time of depressed primary commodity prices, sluggish economic growth, high unemployment, and serious balance of payments difficulties, assembly operations have provided some welcomed relief to the economies of many developing nations. These export-oriented assembly operations have generated badly-needed foreign exchange and provided expanded employment opportunities.

Some of the nations of the Caribbean are the leading assemblers of U.S. components for the U.S. market. In the 1980s, export assembly operations have been, by far, one of the most dynamic sectors of these nations. Assembled products were significant in overall exports of several countries in the region. In 1988, for example, exports of assembled goods (domestic value added only) accounted for nearly 38 percent of Haiti's total exports; for the Dominican Republic, it was over 22 percent in 1989. In some instances, assembled product exports have displaced certain traditional commodity exports as major sources of foreign exchange.

Assembly operations have been a dynamic source of employment opportunities in the Caribbean. For example, these operations have been responsible for most manufacturing jobs in the Caribbean and for creating many of the new job opportunities.

In addition to direct employment, assembly operations create jobs in supplier industries (backward linkages). Moreover, assembly operations also support jobs in the economy at large (macroeconomic effects) as assembly workers spend their income in the consumption of goods and services. However, forward linkages (e.g., jobs associated with domestic distribution of assembled products) are weak or almost non-existent in the Caribbean. This situation may improve if some assembly output were permitted to be sold in the domestic market.

Many foreign investments in assembly operations (especially in the apparel sector) have a low capital intensity per worker. Offshore assembly operations or international subcontracting arrangements in light manufacturers have been described as "footloose" since very often the factory shells are leased, secondhand machinery is used, most components are imported, and little training of the work force is required. This may result in "suitcase" industries, with no deep investment roots established in the host country, that are free to chase after lower wage locations. This situation may be changing as segments of heavier manufacturing and more capital intensive industries in developed countries move into more production-sharing arrangements with developing countries (e.g., Mexico and Korea). For some of the smaller Caribbean countries, more human-capital intensive services (e.g., data and information processing) may offer more secure roots to foreign investors.

Assembly operations in the Caribbean tend to be concentrated in a few industrial sectors. Since 1983, about 90 percent of all U.S. 807.00 imports from the Caribbean Basin have consisted of assembled apparel and electrical items. In most cases, the domestic content of these products (i.e., value-added in the host country) is very small. There is some evidence that assembly operations (especially in electrical and miscellaneous manufactured goods) have fostered some industrialization and developed sufficient backward linkages so that some products formerly imported under item 807.00 have been able to meet rule-of-origin requirements and enter the U.S. duty-free under GSP or CBI. Overall, however, assembly firms in the Caribbean have remained primarily enclave operations, and the need still exists to diversify and develop alternatives to the heavy reliance on assembly activities. But it is not clear whether some of the smaller countries in the region, with limited natural resources and factor endowments, will be able to do much to alter this situation.

In the Caribbean (as in most developing countries), workers in assembly operations are primarily women, especially young women. Often, these young women represent new entrants into the labor force. In some cases, this might offer new opportunities to supplement family income. In other cases, this might accentuate rather than ameliorate the problems of unemployment.[61] Traditionally, female labor force participation rates in Latin America and the Caribbean have been among the lowest among both developing and developed countries, but have grown rapidly since the 1960s.[62]

The proclivity to hire women may be associated with the types of assembly operations in the Caribbean (i.e., apparel and electronics) that traditionally tend to employ large numbers of women worldwide.[63] This situation may change in the future if assembly operations expand into other industries.

In the 1980s, assembly operations in some Caribbean nations have helped ease a period of economic strain. Pressure to create employment is certain to continue in the immediate future. Labor supply in the Caribbean islands, estimated at 10.8 million in 1980, is projected to reach 22.7 million by the year 2020. Only under the most optimistic growth scenarios can this expansion rate be matched by increases in labor demand.[64] Most likely, assembly operations will continue to be part of the picture, perhaps in a modified form.

NOTES

1. The views expressed here are those of the authors alone and do not necessarily reflect the positions or opinions of the U.S. Department of Labor or the U.S. government.

2. For a cost-benefit analysis of some Asian EPZs, see Peter G. Warr, "Export Processing Zones: The Economics of Enclave Manufacturing," *The World Bank Research Observer,* 4:1 (January 1989), pp. 65-88.

3. The focus of this chapter is on export assembly operations located on the Caribbean islands rather than in the more broadly defined Caribbean Basin that includes nations in Central and South America which face the Caribbean Sea. The one exception is Belize, formerly British Honduras, the smallest and only English-speaking Central American nation which is a member of the Caribbean Common Market (CARICOM).

4. For a more formal definition of EPZs see, e.g., United Nations Conference on Trade and Development, *Export processing free zones in developing countries: Implications for trade and industrialization policies* (Geneva, 1985), p. 10.

5. For more details on the institutional setting, legal and fiscal requirements and incentives, infrastructure and services, and economic significance of export-oriented operations in the Dominican Republic, Haiti, and Jamaica, see U.S. Department of Labor, *Worker Rights in Export Processing Zones,* volume 2, individual country reports (Washington, D.C.: Bureau of International Labor Affairs, August 1990).

6. See R. Cherol and S. Zalduendo, "Legal Framework for Foreign Investment in the Caribbean and Central America," *The International Lawyer,* 18:4 (Fall 1984), pp. 957-982, especially pp. 971-975.

7. See United States International Trade Commission (USITC), *The Use and Economic Impact of TSUS Items 806.30 and 807.00,* Publication 2095 (Washington, D.C.: USITC, 1988), p. 5-1.

8. See S. Rubin, *Tax-Free Exporting Zones: A User's Manual* (London: The Economist Publications Ltd., 1988), pp. 169, 188-189, 229, 236.

9. See United States International Trade Commission (USITC), *Imports Under Items 806.30 and 807.00 of the Tariff Schedules of the United States, 1984-87,* Publication 2095 (Washington, D.C.: USITC, 1988), pp. 4-3.

10. See U.S. Department of Labor, *Worker Rights in Export Processing Zones,* volume 2, Haiti, op. cit., p. 18.

11. Aruba has a free trade enclave, a free zone with no manufacturing that serves as a bonded storage area for local merchants; 65 people are employed in the zone. Curacao has a free zone, which acts as a storage and distribution point, and an industrial park where light manufacturing takes place; together, these facilities employed 700 workers in 1985 and 970 workers in 1988. See American Embassy, Curacao, unclassified telegram 0445, 14 April 1989.

12. In July 1988, the Government of Trinidad implemented legislation to establish EPZs to increase export earnings and reduce unemployment (17 percent at the time). See Canute James, "Trinidad Hopes Trade Zones Lure Investors," *Journal of Commerce,* 11 July 1988, p. 4A.

13. Investment Promotion Council of the Dominican Republic, *Investment Opportunity: Free Zones in the Dominican Republic* (Santo Domingo, 1988), p. 1.
14. See American Embassy, Santo Domingo, unclassified telegram 09186, 28 August 1989.
15. See Abreu et al, op. cit., pp. 61-69.
16. See World Bank, *World Development Report 1990* (New York: Oxford University Press, 1990), p. 122.
17. See Abreu et al., op. cit., pp. 72-75, and American Embassy, Santo Domingo, unclassified telegram 2094, 12 March 1989.
18. Leslie Delatour and Karl Voltaire, *International Sub-Contracting Activities in Haiti*, mimeographed (May 1980), p. III-3.
19. Josh DeWind and David H. Kinley III, *Aiding Migration* (Boulder: Westview, 1988), p. 110.
20. See Thomas K. Morrison, "Case Study of a 'Least Developed Country' Successfully Exporting Manufactures: Haiti," *Inter-American Economic Affairs* 29:1 (Summer 1975) and Francisco E. Thoumi, "Social and Political Obstacles to Economic Development in Haiti," in Paget Henry and Carl Stone, editors, *The Newer Caribbean: Decolonization, Democracy and Development* (Philadelphia: Institute for the Study of Human Issues, 1983).
21. John F. van Houten, "Assembly Industries in the Caribbean," *Finance and Development*, 10:2 (June 1973), p. 22.
22. Frank Long, *Employment effects of multinational enterprises in export processing zones in the Caribbean*, Multinational Enterprises Program, Working Paper Number 42 (Geneva: International Labour Office, 1986), pp. 50-51. See also, U.S. Department of Labor, Bureau of International Labor Affairs, *Worker Rights in Export Processing Zones*, vol. 2, Jamaica, op. cit.
23. Frank Long, op. cit., pp. 35-36.
24. Ibid., pp. 41-42.
25. See American Embassy, Belize, unclassified telegram 01344, 22 March 1989.
26. See American Embassy, Bridgetown, unclassified telegram 02764, 11 April 1989.
27. See American Embassy, Bridgetown, unclassified telegram 02484, 31 March 1989.
28. See American Embassy, Bridgetown, unclassified telegram 02725, 10 April 1989.
29. For more details about these provisions, see U.S. International Trade Commission, *Production Sharing: U.S. Imports Under Harmonized Tariff Schedule Subheadings 9802.0060 and 9802.0080, 1985-1988 (Formerly Imports Under Items 806.30 and 807.00 of the Tariff Schedules of the United States)*, USITC Publication 2243 (Washington: December 1989), *The Use and Economic Impact of TSUS Items 806.30 and 807.00*, USITC Publication 2053 (Washington: January 1988), and earlier reports.
30. Special tabulations of the U.S.-content value and the foreign value-added in TSUS 806.30 and 807.00 U.S. imports are made annually for the U.S. International Trade Commission by the U.S. Department of Commerce's Bureau of the Census. Analysis of item 807.00 imports presented here is based on these special tabulations.
31. The U.S. GSP program extended duty-free treatment to approximately 3,000 TSUS tariff line items, and now to about 4,150 line items under the Harmonized Tariff Schedule, that are imported directly from 140 designated beneficiary countries. Certain import-sensitive textile and apparel, leather, glass, electronic, watch, and steel products are statutorily excluded from the program. In order to receive GSP benefits, eligible items must meet rule-of-origin requirements (35 percent value-added in the beneficiary country), not exceed certain competitive-need limitations (an absolute dollar-value level or specific percentage share limit), and not be

subject to discretionary product/country exclusions. For further details, see Office of the United States Trade Representative, *A Guide to the Generalized System of Preferences (GSP),* (Washington: October 1988), and U.S. International Trade Commission, *Operation of the Trade Agreements Program, 41st Report, 1989,* USITC Publication 2317 (Washington: September 1990), pp. 148-152.

32. The Caribbean Basin Economic Recovery Act (CBERA), often referred to as the Caribbean Basin Initiative (CBI), was signed into law by the president on 5 August 1983. The centerpiece of the act was the provision for unilateral and nonreciprocal duty-free treatment for a wide range of U.S. imports from the region for 12 years, beginning 1 January 1984. Recent legislation (CBI-II), enacted 20 August 1990 as part of the Customs and Trade Act of 1990, makes the provisions of the CBERA a permanent part of U.S. trade law. At the end of 1990, 28 Caribbean Basin countries (or territories) were eligible for CBI benefits; 23 had been designated as beneficiaries. [The CBI beneficiary nations include: seven **Central and South American** republics (Belize, Costa Rica, El Salvador, Guatemala, Guyana, Honduras, and Panama (removed in 1988 and reinstated in 1990), nine small **Eastern Caribbean** island nations (Barbados, Antigua and Barbuda, British Virgin Islands, Dominica, Grenada, Montserrat, St. Kitts-Nevis, St. Lucia, and St. Vincent and the Grenadines), three moderate-sized **Central Caribbean** island nations (the Dominican Republic, Haiti, and Jamaica), and four **Oil Refining** nations (Aruba, the Bahamas, the Netherlands Antilles, and Trinidad and Tobago). Five countries eligible for CBI benefits, but never designated as beneficiaries, include: Anguilla, Cayman Islands, Nicaragua, Suriname, and Turks and Caicos Islands.] To be eligible for duty-free treatment under the CBERA, articles must meet rule-of-origin requirements (35 percent value-added in beneficiary countries, of which 15 percent can be from the United States or Puerto Rico). In addition, most textile, apparel, leather goods, and petroleum products are excluded from benefits. In many respects, the tariff preferences under the CBI program are similar to those under the GSP program. However, the CBERA provisions cover virtually all items eligible for GSP as well as many other products. The rule-of-origin is also more liberal under the CBI program than under the GSP program. Moreover, there are no provisions for country/product graduation under the CBERA; that is, under the CBERA, U.S. market access is assured. For more details, see R.C. Shelburne and C.R. Shiells, *Trade and Employment Effects of the Caribbean Economic Recovery Act, Sixth Annual Report to the Congress,* U.S. Department of Labor, Bureau of International Labor Affairs, Economic Discussion Paper 35 (Washington: November 1990) and earlier reports.

33. The United States recently negotiated special textile and apparel arrangements with a few Caribbean countries (special access program announced February 1986). These arrangements expand U.S. quotas for textile and apparel in categories that use fabric manufactured and cut in the United States; items produced under these conditions enter the United States under special provisions contained in item 807.00 (item 9802.00.8010 under the Harmonized Tariff Schedules). To date, Costa Rica, the Dominican Republic, Guatemala, Haiti, Jamaica, and Trinidad and Tobago have entered into bilateral textile agreements with the United States under the program. For more details on these agreements, see U.S. International Trade Commission, *Operation of the Trade Agreements Program, 41st Report, 1989,* USITC Publication 2317 (Washington: September 1990).

34. During 1986, Intel (Barbados) Limited and Playtex International closed large operations in Barbados, making over 1,200 persons unemployed. See Barbados Industrial Development Corporation (BIDC), *Annual Report 1986/87* (Bridgetown, Barbados: BIDC), September 1987.

35. United Nations Conference on Trade and Development, op. cit., p. 18.
36. See Barbados Industrial Development Corporation (BIDC), *Barbados: The Ideal Location for Investments* (Bridgetown, Barbados: BIDC, no date) and U.S. Department of Labor, *Worker Rights in Export Processing Zones*, volume 2, Haiti, op. cit., p. 19.
37. For a discussion of gender issues associated with assembly operations in Mexico that may apply to locations in the Caribbean, see, e.g., María Patricia Fernández-Kelly, *For We Are Sold, I and My People: Women and Industry in Mexico's Frontier* (Albany: State University of New York Press, 1983); Leslie Sklair, *Assembling for Development: The Maquila in Mexico and the United States* (Boston: Unwin Hyman, 1989), especially chapter 8; Ellwyn R. Stoddard, *Maquila: Assembly Plants in Northern Mexico* (El Paso: Texas Western Press, 1987), especially chapter 5; and Mercedes Pedrero Nieto and Norma Saavedra, *La industria maquiladora en México,* Programa de Empresas Multinacionales, Documento de Trabajo Número 49 (Ginebra: Oficina Internacional del Trabajo, 1987), pp. 42-47.
38. International Labor Organization and United Nations Centre on Transnational Corporations, *Economic and Social Effects of Multinational Enterprises in Export Processing Zones* (Geneva, 1988), p. 89.
39. The employment estimates are from the Starnberg Institute Database and refer to all activities in EPZs and other offshore manufacturing facilities and therefore may overestimate employment in assembly facilities. Considering that assembly firms tend to be predominant in EPZs and other offshore manufacturing facilities in these countries, they are used in this paper as a proxy for assembly employment. Data are not available for many Caribbean nations known to have assembly operations.
40. Monique P. Garrity, "The Assembly Industries in Haiti: Causes and Effects," *Journal of Caribbean Studies* 2:1 (Spring 1981), pp. 31-32.
41. Joseph Grunwald and Kenneth Flamm, *The Global Factory* (Washington: Brookings Institution, 1985), p. 177.
42. See American Embassy, Port-au-Prince, unclassified telegram 02776, 25 April 1989.
43. Francisco A. de Moya Espinal, *Las zonas francas industriales y las empresas multinacionales: Efectos económicos e impacto sobre el empleo en la República Dominicana,* Programa de Empresas Multinacionales, Documento de Trabjo Número 46 (Ginebra: Oficina Internacional del Trabajo, 1986), p. 23.
44. International Labour Organization and United Nations Centre on Transnational Corporations, op. cit., p. 75.
45. American Embassy, Santo Domingo, unclassified telegram 2094, op. cit.
46. Cited in Abreu et al., op. cit., p. 142.
47. Abreu et al., op. cit., p. 116; see also Moya Espinal, op. cit., p. 26, who estimates 68 percent of the free zone workers were female in 1985.
48. Long, op. cit., p. 42.
49. See American Embassy, Belize, unclassified telegram 01344, op. cit.
50. See American Embassy, Bridgetown, unclassified telegram 02764, op. cit.
51. See American Embassy, Bridgetown, unclassified telegram 02484, op. cit.
52. See American Embassy, Bridgetown, unclassified telegram 02725, op. cit.
53. See Inter-American Development Bank, *Economic and Social Progress in Latin America: 1987 Report* (Washington: 1988), p. 75.
54. Ibid, p. 56.
55. Moya Espinal, op. cit., p. 30.
56. International Labour Organization and United Nations Centre on Multinational Enterprises, op. cit., p. 77. In addition, the United States General Accounting Office (GAO) describes the expansion of the domestic services sector in response

to the growth in export assembly operations (e.g., the establishment of portable restaurant facilities outside of the free zones in the Dominican Republic and Haiti to provide inexpensive lunches for workers). See United States General Accounting Office, *Caribbean Basin Initiative: Impact on Selected Countries*, NSIAD-88-177 (Washington, D.C.: GAO), July 1988, p. 16.

57. Abreu et al., op. cit., p. 141.
58. Based on data from Banco Central de la Republica Dominicana, cited in Abreu et al., op. cit., pp. 136-137.
59. See U.S. Department of Labor, *Worker Rights in Export Processing Zones*, volume 2, Jamaica, op. cit., p. 38.
60. See U.S. General Accounting Office, op. cit., p. 18.
61. Grunwald and Flamm, op. cit., pp. 226-227.
62. Inter-American Development Bank, op. cit., p. 93.
63. International Labour Organization and United Nations Centre on Transnational Corporations, op. cit., p. 64.
64. Thomas J. Espenshade, "Growing Imbalances Between Labor Supply and Labor Demand in the Caribbean Basin," mimeographed, October 1987, pp. 7-12.

CHAPTER 8

Economic Policy, Free Zones and Export Assembly Manufacturing in the Dominican Republic[1]

Francisco E. Thoumi [2]

Export assembly in the Dominican Republic has been the most dynamic manufacturing subsector of the country during the 1970-1988 period, and it has grown at a particularly fast pace during the last few years. In spite of the recent success, the subsector's development has been limited by financial, institutional, legal and infrastructural constraints, and more generally, by a lack of an effective promotion policy of the government. Thus, it has not contributed its full potential to the country's economy. In this essay the development of export assembly operations in the Dominican Republic are analyzed, its legal and institutional frameworks are evaluated, some of the bottlenecks and factors that promote growth are identified, and a few conclusions are obtained.

1. THE LEGAL AND INSTITUTIONAL FRAMEWORKS

The assembly subsector operates under the free zone legislation (Law No. 4315 or 1955, which has been modified on several occasions) that regulates the establishment of free zones and 'special' free zones. The latter are simply manufacturing plants which are located outside the free zone areas, but which are allowed to operate as if they were in the free zones. According to the law, the authority to establish a free zone lies with the President of the Republic, who also approves the locations in which they are to be developed, and appoints their Boards' of Directors. Development of the assembly subsector has been slow. The law that authorized the establishment of free zones was approved in 1955, and during the following 14 years several were authorized but none were actually created as the necessary tariff exonerations were not granted until 1968, Law 299, after which the first free zone started operations in 1969.

Law 299 of 1968 created the Industrial Development Board (Directorio de Desarrollo Industrial) to which firms must apply for the authorization to import intermediate goods and raw materials into the free zones on a temporary basis without paying tariffs. This Board is composed of the Secretary of Industry and Commerce who presides, the Secretary of Finance, three other high level government officials and five representatives of the private sector. The Board reviews each application made by the prospective assembly operators, studies their financial solvency, the viability of the proposed business, and the "moral Standing" of the applicants. This evaluation is done to weed out undesirable businesses, although the law does not set a methodology to be followed and, the evaluation procedures applied have varied through time. The lack of specificity permits a degree of arbitrariness. After an application is approved, the interested party can then rent space in a free zone to establish the assembly plant.

The long time that elapsed between the authorization of the first free zones and their actual establishment was due not only to the lack of specific legislation for the plants to be established in the free zones, but also, and very importantly to their lack of financing, a particularly important issue for an industry in which land and buildings are a high proportion of total capital and for a country in which foreigners can own real estate only with the express authorization of the President of the country. After authorizing the establishment of the free zones the government did not create a financing mechanism for their development and furthermore, in some instances, it set totally unrealistic requirements for potential partners in the private sector. For example, the 1963 authorization to establish a free zone in Puerto Plata, required that 51 percent of the stock of the company be held by the government, while 49 percent could be held by the private sector, all of which would revert to the state after 30 years. The authorization also indicated that the government would build an airport and a port that would be paid for by the owners of the privately held stock. It is thus, not surprising that there were no interested investors in these projects.

In other cases the authorization to create a free zone has established very impractical conditions, some of which are at least partially contradictory to the goals of a free zone. For example, the authorization to establish a free zone in Barahona specifically stated that it should be devoted mainly to the development of heavy industry. In other instances the government has attempted to use the free zones to decentralize economic activity, thus, free zones have been authorized in locations which lack appropriate communications, and access to ports and airports, etc.

In 1979 the government established the National Council of Industrial Free Zones (NCIFZ) which was given the task of coordinating the administration of the different free zones and of conducting studies that would lead to the establishment of subsectoral policies. To date the Council is headed by the Secretary of Industry and Commerce, and also includes the Secretary of Finance, the President of the Central Bank, the Directors of the IFC and the Dominican Export Promotion Center (CEDOPEX) and representatives of each free zone. The latter have voice but no voting power in the Council. The Council has an executive director and a small professional staff whose main function is to negotiate textiles and apparel quotas, with the United States and to administer these quotas in the Dominican Republic. This is not an official function of the Council, but rather one it has assumed because most of the assembly plants in the free zones are in the apparel industry which exports under the quota system.

Since its creation, the Council has also played an important role in the elimination of a substantial number of "special" free zones. Law 299 of 1968 established that the free zone status could be extended to plants outside free zones whenever there were technological or other factors related to the nature of the productive process that required the plant to be located in a specific area. It was expected that many of the special free zones of the country would be established in the agroindustrial field; however, during the 1960s and 1970s the Industrial Development Board was very liberal in granting special free zone status to many plants, which did not meet the economic or technological requirements set by the law. This led to a growing suspicion that the special free zone status was used to introduce contraband into the Dominican Republic. Therefore, beginning in 1981 the NCIFZ began eliminating special free zones. In 1980 there were 31 plants with such status, a number that declined to ten in 1982. By 1987 there were only seven special free zones, four of which were agroindustries, two were making clothes and the last one was a recently established ship-building facility. By 1987 NCIFZ was requiring that the special free zones pay the cost of policing the flow of input and outputs, so that contraband could be avoided.

In several occasions the NCIFZ has elaborated studies to assess the international competitiveness of the Dominican free zones and the criteria to select the location of the free zones within the country. However, it is not clear what has been the policy impact of these studies.

Summarizing, the legislation and institutions regulating the establishment of free zones and export assembly plants have (1) placed the development of these activities under the tight control of the executive

power, reflecting the authoritarian nature of the government of the
Dominican Republic,[3] (2) have not provided a cohesive promotion program, (3) have given great discretionary power to the Industrial Development Board and the President of the country, and (4) have not been
conducive to the success of the subsector.[4]

2. EVOLUTION AND DEVELOPMENT OF THE SUBSECTOR

The first free zone was established in La Romana and was financed by
Gulf and Western, who owned the land as part of its sugar ventures, and
organized a special company to develop and administer the free zone. The
financing for the second free zone established in San Pedro de Macorís
was provided by the government through the Industrial Finance Corporation (IFC), while the third free zone in Santiago was financed by local
private sources after the president of the country appointed a commission
of local notables to be in charge of that task. Most of the free zones
developed later have been financed by private sources.

By 1983 the government had authorized the establishment of 11 free
zones but only four were in operation, one of which in Puerto Plata, was
only in its beginning stages. Indeed, between 1973 and 1983 no new free
zones were established. In 1987 there were eight free zones in operation,
two of which were undergoing important expansion processes, and another
free zone was being constructed. By then, the government had authorized
the establishment of 13 more free zones. The very fast employment growth
in the free zone subsector has induced politicians from many regions to
attempt to develop free zones as a solution to the high unemployment
facing the country, particularly, since the main traditional employer, the
sugar industry, has been in a deep recession for over a decade.

Table 8.1 summarizes the evolution of the export assembly subsector in
the Dominican Republic.[4] The number of free zone plants grew slowly
between 1969 and 1982, when there were 88 plants in operation. From that
year on the growth in the number of plants accelerated reaching 157 in
1986, a figure that was projected to reach 190 at the end of 1987. However,
the total number of plants authorized under Law 299 has been much higher
than those in a operation as some have closed down and others never
established.

Employment statistics did not followed the growth in established plants.
Indeed, employment grew until 1981, remained stagnant in 1982, increased in 1983 and 1984, fell substantially in 1985, and increased by a
dramatic 114 percent in 1986. Preliminary evidence indicates that it was
expanding very rapidly during 1987, where it was expected to have
reached 67,000 that is a 30.8 percent growth during the year.

Table 8.1. Evolution of the Export Assembly Subsector in the Dominican Republic

Year	Number of Plants in Operation[1]	Accumulated Number of Plants Authorized Under Law 299[3]	Total Number of Workers[1]	Foreign Exchange Sold to the Central Bank (millions of US$)[2]	Foreign Exchange Sold to Central Bank per Worker (US$)
1969	1	10	–	–	–
1970	2	19	126	1.36	10802
1971	5	28	362	2.85	7864
1972	10	37	1675	4.76	2844
1973	15	63	1826	5.26	2881
1974	22	93	3244	9.81	3023
1975	29	105	5072	14.73	2903
1976	33	121	6673	19.49	2921
1977	39	132	8975	26.38	2939
1978	48	149	11545	32.72	2834
1979	61	170	14160	40.02	2826
1980	71	177	16404	44.51	2713
1981	77	196	19456	57.57	2959
1982	88	203	19236	61.14	3178
1983	105	237	21387	61.85	2892
1984	123	263	25099	52.14	2072
1985	145	280	22720	43.10	1897
1986	157	308	48603	55.10	1134
1987	190*		67000*		

Source: [1]*NCIFZ,* [2]*Central Bank,* [3]*Secretariat of Industry and Commerce.*
*Projected.

According to Law 299, free zone plants must sell to the Central Bank all the foreign exchange required to cover local expenditures. The foreign exchange sold by these firms to the Central Bank increased *pari pasu* with employment in the subsector up to 1983. Between 1972 and 1983 the amounts sold to the Central Bank were between $2,800 and $3,100 per year per worker. However, beginning in 1983 the amount of foreign exchange sold to the Central Bank dropped so sharply that by 1986 while total employment in the free zones was 227.3 percent that of 1983, the Central Bank bought only 89.2 percent of the amount of foreign exchange bought in 1983. The foreign exchange per worker sold to the Central Bank in 1986 was only 39.2 percent that of 1983. Differences between the exchange rates in the official and black markets increased slowly during the 1970's up until 1981. However, this difference increased substantially since then, reaching a particularly large level in 1984, when the black market exchange rate exceeded the official one by more than 120 percent. That year coincides with both the fall in the total and per worker amounts of foreign exchange sold to the Central Bank by the free zone plants, indicating that the assembly plants were selling substantial amounts in the black market. The government unified the foreign exchange markets in 1985, however, the foreign exchange sold by the assembly operators to the Central Bank remained at low levels, due probably to the fact that the (1) Central Bank did not have any control system to verify the amounts that assembly plants should be selling; and (2) to the perception by plant managers that the exchange rate unification was only a short term phenomenon. During 1987, the government again fixed the official exchange rate and a black market developed. Assembly plants were already prepared to continue to sell foreign exchange illegally. The magnitude of illegal foreign exchange sales is believed to be very large. To give an indication of this magnitude, one could estimate how much the free zone plants should have sold in 1986 to the Central Bank if they had sold an amount, per worker, equivalent to that of 1983; using this method, it is estimated that US $140 million should have been turned in to the Central Bank instead of the US $55 million which actually was.

It is possible that the figure above is an overestimate. This is because the subsector was growing so rapidly during 1986 that many workers did not work the full year; however, the difference between what was turned in and the estimate is so large that even accounting for a possible overestimation, it could be said that a high proportion of the foreign exchange generated by the free zone has gone into the black market. One of the implications of this phenomenon is that the real cost of assembly plants in the Dominican Republic is lower than those estimated with official data since black market foreign exchange sales are a source of substantial extra profit.

Table 8.2 summarizes the most recently available desegregated information about the free zones. The subsector remains geographically concentrated in the oldest free zones: La Romana, Santiago and San Pedro de Macorís, which together in 1987 comprised 82.7 percent of the operating plants and 90.7 percent of the total free zone employment. Free zone plants are also very concentrated in a few manufacturing branches. Two-thirds of the operating plants are in the apparel branch and ten percent in shoes. The low proportion of plants in electronics and the absence of toy manufacturing is remarkable as both branches are very commonly found in export assembly operations in other countries.[6] Unfortunately, the assembly subsector is characterized by operations which require the lowest level of technology and which employ only low skill workers. Therefore, it is not likely to generate substantial external economies for the rest of the economy.

These data also show that in spite of the recent proliferation of free zones, the success of many of the new zones has been relative. The clear dependence of the assembly subsector on exports of apparel and shoes to the United States makes the subsector very vulnerable to changes in US policy.[7]

Visits to the free zones reveal that the assembly subsector employs mostly women, however, the NCIFZ does not have hard data which discriminates employment by sex. The only free zone branch in which employment is mostly masculine is shoe manufacturing. This is important since politicians frequently claim that free zone development is an alternative for the employment of the labor force displaced by the contraction of the sugar industry. It is clear that if free zones replace sugar as the main employment generator in manufacturing in the country, women will become the main source of family income in many households, while male unemployment will rise. The social implications of such drastic change has not been considered carefully by decision makers.

The export assembly subsector uses very few domestic inputs, however, there are some industries in this subsector that use mostly domestic raw materials. These plants are primarily in the food processing and cigar making branches. Production lines here offer opportunities, albeit limited, to integrate the production of the free zones with the rest of the economy. Furthermore, there is the potential to develop some backward linkages with the domestic economy in other manufacturing branches, especially the shoe sector which imports all the leather it uses. This imported leather could be substituted by domestic production.

Table 8.2. Desegregated Information About the Free Export Processing Zones in the Dominican Republic

Free Zones	Number of operating plants	Number of plants being establ.	Available Buildings	Total empl.*	Number of operating plants by product line								
					Apparel	Shoes	Other Leather Prods.	Jewelry	Electronics	Ceramics	Tobacco	Fruits & Chocolates	Other
La Romana I y II	24	4	0	10890	20	9			2		1		1
San Pedro de Macoris	61	14	0	28214	38	5		3	3	2		2	4
Santiago I y II	54	6	0	25000	36	2	4	1	2		6		1
Puerto Plata	9	1	2	1250	5						1		
Banf	3	2	2	816	3								
Itabo	3	1	0	600					3				
San Isidro	1	2	2	350	1	1							
La Vega	13	3	2	3577	11				1				
Totals	168	33	6	70697	114	17	4	4	11	2	8	2	6
Percentage Distribution					67.8	10.1	2.4	2.4	6.5	1.2	4.8	1.2	3.6

Source: NCIFZ.

*These figures were obtained by telephone from each free zone administration offices, and therefore, some of the figures could be inexact. This could explain why the total employment figures exceed that projected by the NCIFZ (see Table 8.1). All these data for August 1987.

Table 8.3. National Origin of the Firms Located in Some Free Zones (August 1987)

| Nationality | Free Zones | | | | Authorized Plants Jan-Aug 1987 |
	San Pedro Macorís	Itabo	La Romana	Baní	
Dominican Republic	7			1	12
United States	32	2	22	2	9
Puerto Rico	1				
South Korea	2				1
Hong Kong	2				3
Panama	1	1			7
Grand Cayman	1				

Source: NCIFZ.

Note: There were no data available for other free zones. The number of informants is also lower than the total of plants of some free zones.

The available data identifies the national origin of the investors in some free zones,[8] and also, that of some firms which had been authorized by the Industrial Development Board in 1987. This information is summarized in Table 8.3. The preponderance of US capital is clear, and coincides with the importance of the US market to the subsector. In La Romana, all the plants are owned by US investors. However, the national origin of the investors in plants recently authorized show a different composition from those of the established plants. It appears that the Dominican Republic is now attracting investors from other nationalities, particularly, from the Far East and Panama. This indicates that the obstacles that the US has imposed in the last few years to apparel imports from the Far East have contributed to the growth of the free zones in the Dominican Republic. The growth in Panamanian plants[9] and the one from Grand Cayman suggest that investors of undetermined origin have become interested in the assembly subsector in the Dominican Republic.

3. DEVELOPMENT POLICIES, FINANCING, COSTS AND BOTTLENECKS

As mentioned above the policies to promote development in the free zones were established by Law 299 of 1968. This law included tariff exonerations for imports and exports and income tax exonerations for the profits of foreign owned assembly plants. Tax breaks were complemented by a prohibition of organized labor unions among workers in the free zone plants. These policies leave much to be desired and have not led to the full development of the subsector. One obvious deficiency of the income tax exoneration is that in many cases it is superfluous since, on the one hand, the foreign owned plants could juggle their accounting so that profits in the official balances are not reported in the Dominican Republic, and on the other hand, in most instances, if they were to pay taxes in the Dominican Republic they would be credited against those due in the country of origin, particularly in the United States.

Furthermore, there has not been a financing policy to promote the establishment of new free zones nor to provide infrastructure to these zones. The presidential decrees which have authorized the free zones, as noted above, have not established any financing mechanism. In this subsector much of the financing needed is for building the industrial parks that make-up the free zones and the actual buildings where the plants are to be established. In the Dominican Republic, assembly plant operators have always rented buildings in the free zones; a "bad policy" given the particularly footloose nature of industries that require very little investment in machinery and equipment. In the history of the free zones, there have been very few instances where there were vacant buildings available for plant installations. Only in the very recent past and in the newer and smaller free zones have there been some empty buildings. In general, buildings are constructed only after the free zone company has signed a contract with the manufacturer. In most cases it takes about a year between the signing of the contract and when the plant is operational.

Financing for the free zones of San Pedro de Macorís and La Vega was provided by the IFC, which owns both free zones. However, these have not been managed as profit-making institutions, and have not produced enough profits to allow continuous reinvestment and expansion. In mid 1987 the IFC was charging a monthly rent of approximately 8 cents (US $0.02) per square foot to new businesses in San Pedro de Macorís and six cents (US $0.015) in La Vega.[10] However, all older established industries in San Pedro de Macorís were paying lower rents, fluctuating between three and five cents per month. When contracts were renewed, the IFC increased the rent but not to the eight cent level charged to new enterprises. IFC owned free zones are very popular because their rents are not only low, but are set in local currency at fixed rates for periods of four to eight years. In the privately owned free zones such as La Romana, the new contracts in 1987 were set in US dollars at a monthly rate of US $0.20 cents per square foot during the first four years, and 25 cents during the following four years; furthermore, the free zone required a two year rent deposit before beginning to construct the building for any new assembly plant. In view of the inflation experienced by the Dominican Republic during the recent past and the concomitant devaluation trend, the IFC system of setting rents in the free zones in local currency at fixed rates entails a growing subsidy to assembly operators.

Contraband has also been an administrative problem for free zones. Indeed, as mentioned above, the NCIFZ has attempted to control it and for this reason has closed some of the special free zones. However, smuggling from free zones continues quite freely and in fact, appears to have been tolerated by the free zone administration. For example, in 1977, the fence that surrounds the free zone in San Pedro de Macorís remained broken in several places, a situation that was condoned by the administration on the grounds that it allowed employees to take shortcuts to and from work.

The lack of financing has also resulted in deficient infrastructure in some free zones where important services such as banks, health units, street lighting, cafeterias, etc., are either lacking or are of low quality. A particularly important bottleneck to free zone growth is the increasingly erratic electricity service.[11] Interruptions in the supply of electricity have become endemic and every single free zone plant has had to install its own generator. Remarkably, efforts by the administrators of some zones to install larger, more efficient generators to serve all the plants within the free zone have been blocked by the government's legal monopoly on electrical power which outlaws the sales of electricity by the private sector except to the government's Dominican Electricity Corporation. Each free zone corporation has its own criteria for choosing and approving the firms to be installed. As noted above, in the free zones owned by the IFC this institution approves the assembly plants that operate there. However, there is no established screening process and as a result a few fly-by-nighters have established plants which were later closed down or forced into bankruptcy.[12]

Different free zones have had different goals, some of which are not conducive to maximum employment or to a large generation of foreign exchange for the country. For example, the La Romana free zone was originally designed to complement the sugar activities of Gulf and Western and to provide stable employment in an area which suffered from large seasonal variations. The original plan to establish this free zone contemplated two stages, allowing for substantial growth. By 1974 this free zone already had 17 operating plants, most of which were Gulf and Western subsidiaries. In 1982 there were only 18 plants and Gulf and Western was canceling its expansion plans for the free zone. By that time however, Gulf and Western had developed the nearby tourist compound of Casa De Campo, which was in conflict with the optimum environment for the success of the tourist compound. The large number of stable jobs in the free zone attracted a very large flow of migrants to the area resulting in an increase in the total number of unemployed, a fact looked on as detrimental to tourism development. In 1987, given the renewed growth of the subsector, La Romana resumed its expansion plans, but not in the area originally assigned for the free zone; instead it expanded away from the tourism complex at a distance of three miles from the original free zone.

The costs of assembly operations in the Dominican Republic have been declining through time, mainly because the Dominican wage rate in US dollars has fallen substantially. In 1987, total labor costs fluctuated between 40 and 65 cents per hour (in 1974 US dollars). Measuring at the official exchange rate, total labor costs were approximately 60 cents per hour. In the early 1970s, Dominican wages were substantially higher than those of other Caribbean countries such as Haiti and El Salvador. However, by 1987 they had become competitive with almost all of the other Caribbean countries. At the current wage level, further declines should not have a very strong impact on assembly costs, therefore, competition to attract assembly operators should center around other factors such as flexibility to import and export, quality of life for the mangers of the plants, adequate public utilities, political stability, etc. As mentioned, labor costs are comparable to those in most other countries in the Caribbean, the exception to this being Haiti. However, the labor force available for the free zones in the Dominican Republic is much more educated than that of Haiti, lowering the real wage differential between the two countries.

4. THE CAUSES OF RECENT GROWTH

As pointed out above, the export assembly subsector experienced very fast growth during the last three years, a period over which it has grown more than in the previous 15 years. However, this fast growth has been the result mostly of factors which have been exogenous to the government and its policies. During the fast growth period, the policies of the Dominican Republic towards the subsector have not changed, and in fact, have not been conducive to the development of the subsector. Therefore, the boom that export assembly is experiencing now can not be attributed to good government policies.

The reason for this recent growth in this subsector is that the Dominican Republic has become relatively more attractive. Particularly because political instability in Haiti, the country with the lowest wages in the Caribbean, has induced some producers to look for alternative sources; the US limits on apparel imports from the Far East; and the increase in labor costs in that area have all worked to the Dominican Republic's advantage. Furthermore, the wage costs in the Dominican Republic have fallen substantially relative to alternative Caribbean markets. All these factors have contributed to enhancing the country's comparative advantage in the subsector.

US policy towards the Caribbean has also affected the assembly subsector although this impact has not been large. The Caribbean Basin Initiative has not had a large impact on the region's exports to the US,[13] and furthermore, when it was established, it excluded textiles and garments from any benefits, the main exports of the Dominican Republic's assembly subsector. However, beginning September 1, 1986, a change in US policy extended benefits to garments assembled in the Dominican Republic as long as they are made with US made and cut material.[14] The "twin-plant" program with Puerto Rico has also had a small effect with only four assembly operators participating.

NOTES

1. Reprinted from "Economic Policy, Free Zones, and Export Assembly Manufacturing in the Dominican Republic," by F. Thoumi, pp. 167-182, in *Small Country Development and International Labor Flows: Experiences in the Caribbean*, edited by A. Maingot, 1991, by permission of Westview Press, Boulder, Colorado.

2. The essay was written while the author was a staff member of the Inter-American Development Bank, and it is based on the author's participation in Country Economic Studies in 1974, 1983, and 1987 during which data were collected, free zones were visited and assembly plant managers were interviewed. The opinions and ideas expressed here are personal and do not represent those of the Inter-American Development Bank. The author thanks Walter Cabrera, Sergio Diaz-Brisquet, Sidney Weintraub, and Maritza Bojorge for their contributions.

3. Authoritarianism in the Dominican Republic has been well documented and studied, see for example H.J. Wiarda and M.J. Kryzanek, *The Dominican Republic: A Caribbean Crucible* (Boulder: Westview Press, 1982). However, these authors praise Law 299 as a modernizing measure which promoted industrial development. While Law 299 provided a needed framework, it also was far from an optimum set-up for export assembly manufacturing.

4. Institutional and political obstacles have also limited the growth of export assembly manufacturing in other Caribbean countries, see for example F. Thoumi, "Social and Political Obstacles to Economic Development in Haiti," in P. Henry and C. Stone (eds.), *The Newer Caribbean: Decolonization, Democracy and Development* (Philadelphia: The Institute for the Study of Human Issues (ISHI), 1983), pp. 205-218.

5. The data on the export assembly operations are weak. Export assembly is treated as a service export, and thus, its data are not collected by the National Statistics Office as part of that of the manufacturing sector. Figures on the number of export assembly plants and their total employment were originally kept by the Secretariat of Industry and Commerce, however, since the NCIFZ's creation in 1979, it has collected this data. The data on authorized plants is provided by the Industrial Development Board, and data on foreign exchange sold to the Central Bank, by this institution. However, there has not been a systematic data collection system, and the time series provided by these various institutions at different times have varied. Therefore, the data of Table 8.1 do not coincide with those of other works

such as the World Bank, *Dominican Republic: An Agenda for Reform* (Washington, D.C.: World Bank, 1987), but the general trends and magnitudes are basically similar. The data in Table 8.1 represent estimates that were deemed better by the author.

6. For example, J. Grunwald and K. Flamm, *The Global Factory: Foreign Assembly in International Trade* (Washington, D.C.: The Brookings Institution, 1985), in a very complete work about export assembly manufacturing show that semiconductors are the most important branch among Japanese and US imports of this nature.

7. K. Flamm, "The Volatility of Offshore Investment," *Journal of Development Economics*, Vol 16, 1984, pp. 231-248, finds some support to the belief that export assembly operations are unstable, although the reallocation reaction to changes in labor costs is not very strong in the semiconductor industry as the large users try to spread out their sources to minimize risk and thus, are willing to tolerate some cost variation among different supply sources. However, J. Grunwald and J.J. Echevarría, "Assembly Activities in Colombia," in J. Grunwald and K. Flamm, *The Global Factory, op. cit.*, pp. 206-216, describe the Colombian case where the industry was heavily concentrated in the apparel branch and in the US market and collapsed in the late 1970s. While the situation in the Dominican Republic is significantly different from that in Colombia in the mid 1970s, the Colombian experience confirms the existence of the risks of having the assembly industry concentrated in one branch supplying one market.

8. The NCIFZ did not have this information for all free zones.

9. The 1988 suspension of Panama from the CBI and GSP benefits in US markets is likely to increase the Panamanian investment in the DR's free zones.

10. These rates are in local currency.

11. In 1987 this problem became quite grave throughout the economy, not just the free zone areas. Actually, between August 1986 and July 1987 there where 67,812 electric service outages recorded in the country (see F. Thoumi, "Some Privatization Issues in the Dominican Republic and Trinidad and Tobago," in W. Glade (ed.), *Privatization of Public Enterprises in Latin America: A Comparative survey of Strategies and Outcomes* (San Diego: Center for US-Mexican Studies, University of California, 1989).

12. By 1983 NCIFZ has compiled information that showed that until 1982, 12 of the 31 firms which had been established in La Romana had closed down, as well as 12 of 45 in San Pedro de Macorís and 11 of 48 in Santiago. NCIFZ inquired about the reasons for these closing and attributed 13 closing to incompetent management and marketing by entrepreneurs who did not have the appropriate experience. Curiously, among these, NCIFZ claimed that the reason for failure of three firms was "Dominican Entrepreneur." Other closing were attributed to the following causes: four to failure of the US partner to supply materials for processing; four to the decline of international markets; two to plants which moved to other free zones in the country; one which moved to Haiti; two were closed down by the authorities because of contraband; and in four cases the plants closed down for unknown reasons.

13. J. Pelzman and G.K. Schoepfle, "The Impact of the Caribbean Basin Recovery Act on the Caribbean Nations' Exports and Development," *Economic Development and Cultural Change*, Vol 36, No. 4, July 1988, pp. 753-796, provide data that support this statement.

14. These changes have created a communality of interest between US textile manufactures and garment cutters and the DR assembly subsector. This coalition obtained virtually unlimited market access to the US market that has eliminated the relevance of the US quotas, but which also eliminates the possibility of significant backward linkages in the DR.

PART 4

Special United States–Caribbean Economic Relations

CHAPTER 9

Special U.S.–Caribbean Economic Relations

Joseph Pelzman and *Gregory K. Schoepfle*[1]

1. INTRODUCTION

As we enter the decade of the 1990s, world events — both within the hemisphere and outside — are unfolding rapidly. Their outcome will likely have important implications for the economies of the Caribbean. Moves toward regional economic integration are underway around the globe. Within North America, the United States and Canada have entered into a broad free trade agreement, with discussions underway to include Mexico in a North American free trade agreement. President George Bush has announced his Enterprise for the Americas Initiative which has as its ultimate objective the creation of a free trade area within the entire hemisphere.

In Europe, the European Community is in the final stages of implementing a single market plan, which will permit the free flow of goods, services, capital, and people within the 12 member-states. Also, in Eastern Europe and the former Soviet Union, emerging democracies are opening their markets and seeking greater integration into the world economy that will offer new opportunities and challenges to a newly unified Europe and other Western industrial countries. In East Asia, Japan has emerged as the dominant economic player in the Pacific Rim, with South Korea, Hong Kong, Taiwan, and some of the more-recently industrializing countries in Southeast Asia (e.g., some of the ASEANs)[2] exhibiting dynamism and offering opportunities for the formation of new trading blocs within Asia. By the end of the decade, China — always a mystery and a potential economic giant — will regain its former provinces of Hong Kong and Macau, which are now open free-market economies.

175

Globalization and integration of national markets are making the conditions of trading relationships and the rules that govern them more important. A successful conclusion of the Uruguay round of multilateral trade negotiations under the auspices of the General Agreements on Tariffs and Trade (GATT) may help set the tone of trading relations in the 1990s. Such an outcome would result in further trade liberalization, extension of multilaterally-agreed rules to areas heretofore not covered (e.g., services and intellectual property), and more transparency in the application of GATT rules.

In the past, developed countries have accorded special preferences to developing countries in international trading relations. However, the rapid globalization of production, the increased interdependence of the world economies, and the trend toward more open market-oriented economies with fewer barriers to trade are likely to lead to more fierce economic competition. In this competitive global economic environment, continued unilateral developed-country special and differential treatment for developing countries may be questioned. In particular, the structure and effectiveness of continued unconditional preferential treatment of U.S. imports from less-developed countries (LDCs) may come under greater scrutiny and criticism.

Some believe that the benefits from tariff preferences provided by developed economies accrue primarily to the more-advanced developing countries (MADCs),[3] with only minor benefits flowing to the balance of developing countries (i.e, the less-advanced developing countries, LADCs). According to this view, the expected benefits to LADCs of trade preferences are likely to be minimal in the short-term, since their ability to respond to these tariff incentives is very limited in most cases (i.e., they lack the necessary infrastructure and basis for industrial production on a world-class level). However, in the longer term, LADC access to developed country markets at preferential tariff rates may act as an incentive to attract foreign investment which is necessary to generate the needed industrial base and infrastructure.

If this is true, perhaps trade preference programs should be eliminated (or at least be subject to a greater degree of reciprocity) for the MADCs, and existing trade preference programs should be drastically restructured to provide more focused preferential tariff treatment for LADC exports — thereby encouraging more rapid LADC economic growth and development.

Successive rounds of multilateral trade negotiations have led to a lower average level of tariffs (duties on imports) in most developed-country markets, thus reducing the margin of preference offered by any generalized tariff preference program. This is not to say that tariffs are now unimportant; they are, especially for many products of interest to LDCs — most of which are not eligible for special tariff preferences. In most developed countries, there are still tariff peaks (especially for labor-intensive goods such as apparel and footwear) and tariff escalation (higher duties for more highly processed goods with more value added) is common. Concurrent with the fall of tariffs in most industrial countries has been the rise in the importance of non-tariff barriers. Perhaps the most critical issue facing many LDCs (other than developing an industrial infrastructure) will be that of access to major industrial markets — access that has become more and more conditioned on LDCs opening their own economies and introducing other economic reforms.

What lessons have been learned over the past decade? For example: (1) have U.S. trade preferential programs provided economic benefits to the majority of beneficiary developing countries (BDCs) or have only a few benefitted; (2) which BDCs have received the bulk of the benefits and why; (3) what prerequisites are necessary in a developing country before trade preference programs will have an economic impact on BDCs; and (4) will exclusion ("graduation") of the MADCs from preferential trade programs create more "space" for the LADCs to increase their utilization of and the benefits derived from these programs?

In this chapter, we attempt to address some of these questions within the context of the economic relationship between the United States and the developing countries of the Caribbean. Section 2 provides an overview of two major U.S. trade preference programs available to developing countries in the Caribbean: the Generalized System of Preferences (GSP) and the Caribbean Economic Recovery Act (CBERA). In section 3, the trade performance of Caribbean countries under these programs over the 1980s is examined and contrasted with that of other LDCs. Some factors that affect BDC use of these programs are considered in section 4. Some conclusions are presented in section 5.

2. U.S. TRADE PREFERENCE PROGRAMS

The United States has two trade preference programs for LDCs: GSP and CBERA. GSP is a tariff preference program that is available to the majority of LDCs for a limited number of products. The CBERA program provides tariff preferences for a broader range of imported products from Caribbean and Central American nations.

2.1. The GSP Program

The U.S. GSP program was authorized by Title V of the Trade Act of 1974 and implemented in January 1976. It was reauthorized with several important amendments in 1984 for a period of eight and a half years, or until July 4, 1993. The GSP program consists of a system of tariff preferences granted by the United States to a group of beneficiary developing countries (BDCs). The program currently offers duty-free treatment for approximately 4,150 products,[4] subject to certain rules-of-origin, from 135 developing countries. Approximately 26 other industrial countries also have GSP programs.

From its inception, the U.S. GSP program excluded textile and apparel articles subject to international textile agreements and certain import-sensitive watches, electronic articles, steel articles, and semi-manufactured and manufactured glass products. The renewal and amendments to the GSP program in 1984 expanded the list of products that may not be designated as eligible articles under the program. These included footwear, handbags, luggage, leather flat goods, work gloves, and leather wearing apparel which were not eligible for GSP on April 1, 1984.

In order to ensure a wide distribution of GSP benefits among beneficiary countries, Section 504 of the Trade Act of 1974 established specific criteria ("graduation" criteria) under which preferential treatment for particular products from BDCs would be withdrawn. According to these criteria, exports from a specific BDC to the United States in a given category would lose preferential treatment if, in a calendar year: (1) they exceeded an absolute dollar-value limit[5] or (2) they accounted for 50 percent or more of the value of U.S. imports in a tariff schedule category. A BDC that lost preferential tariff treatment for a given product as a result of exceeding competitive-need limits in a given year could be redesignated as a beneficiary if its imports fell below the limits in a subsequent year.

The 1984 reauthorization of GSP gave the President the discretionary authority to cut competitive-need limits in half for countries determined to be "sufficiently competitive." However, the President was also given some discretion to "waive" these lower competitive-need limits under certain conditions.[6] No beneficiary countries in the Caribbean Basin have been found to be sufficiently competitive in any article; hence, all GSP beneficiaries in the Caribbean Basin are subject to the normal GSP competitive-need limits.

In 1981, the United States modified its GSP product eligibility limitations by adding a set of "discretionary" exclusions that were based on: (1) the level of BDC economic development; (2) their competitiveness in the product concerned; and (3) the overall economic interests of the United States, including the import sensitivity of the domestic industry.

In the renewal and amendments to the GSP program in 1984, a provision was included for mandatory graduation after a two-year period of any country whose per capita GNP exceeded an indexed amount that was fixed at $8,500 in 1984.[7] Also, several criteria for a *country* to be eligible for the GSP were added that were related to: (1) protection of intellectual property rights;[8] (2) reduction of trade distorting investment practices and elimination of barriers to services trade; (3) protection of worker's rights;[9] and (4) elimination of unreasonable export practices.[10] These provisions introduced the concept of *country* graduation (removal of all benefits) to the GSP program; until 1984, GSP graduation for a country had been only *product* specific.

Effective January 1, 1989, four Asian newly industrializing countries (Taiwan, South Korea, Hong Kong, and Singapore) were removed from GSP beneficiary status after a review of a broad range of economic and competitiveness indicators. It was determined that these four countries were sufficiently advanced and did not require preferential margins afforded by the GSP program. These four countries had historically accounted for about half of all the benefits under the entire GSP program. This action marked the first instance of country graduation based on a broader set of economic and competitive measures.

The modifications that have been introduced since the introduction of the GSP program have been designed to focus program benefits more sharply on the LADCs. By graduating the MADCs, it was assumed that this would alleviate problems of market access (that is, crowding-out by the MADCs). However, many LADCs are not necessarily cost-efficient producers so that graduation of the more cost-efficient MADCs may not alter the situation.

Clearly, the modifications that have been introduced to the GSP program have increased the conditionality of both product and country eligibility for this preference program, raising concerns among BDCs about their continued preferential access to the U.S. market. However, the United States, by increasing the "conditionality" of trade preferences for BDCs, is reflecting in those conditions the same principles that it strives for in its trading relationships with other developed countries. This appears to indicate a movement from special and differential treatment of developing economies toward one based on more "normal" trading relationships, based on their ability to undertake new obligations.

2.2. The Caribbean Basin Economic Recovery Act

On August 5, 1983, President Ronald Reagan signed into law a new U.S. trade initiative that was specifically directed toward developing countries in the Caribbean Basin: the Caribbean Basin Economic Recovery Act (CBERA), which is commonly referred to as the Caribbean Basin Initiative (CBI). The CBERA was designed to foster economic development in the beneficiary countries of the Caribbean Basin by encouraging greater diversification and expansion of their exports. The centerpiece of the Act was the provision for unilateral and nonreciprocal duty-free treatment for a wide range of U.S. imports from the region, beginning January 1, 1984.

The CBERA eliminated U.S. import duties for 12 years (or until September 30, 1995) on all products imported, with certain exceptions, from those Caribbean countries designated by the President as beneficiary countries. Recent legislation (known as CBI-II), enacted on August 20, 1990, as part of the Customs and Trade Act of 1990, made the provisions of the CBERA a permanent part of U.S. trade law. By the end of 1990, of the 28 Caribbean Basin countries (or territories) eligible for CBERA benefits, 24 had been designated as beneficiaries eligible to receive duty-free benefits under the provisions of the CBERA.[11]

To be eligible for duty-free treatment under the CBERA, articles must meet certain rules-of-origin requirements. In addition, some import-sensitive articles important to the economies of the Caribbean Basin have been specifically excluded from duty-free treatment under the CBERA (e.g., certain textile, apparel, leather goods, and petroleum items). Other products (primarily sugar, beef and veal, and certain textile and apparel products) may be eligible (i.e., possibly eligible) for duty-free treatment under the CBERA if certain requirements are met.[12]

In many respects, the tariff preference portion of the CBERA is similar to that under the GSP program. All CBERA-beneficiary countries also have been designated as GSP beneficiaries.[13] The CBERA provisions cover virtually all of the items covered by GSP as well as many other products. For example, in 1986 about 45 percent of the tariff schedule (TSUS) product categories were eligible for duty-free treatment under the GSP program, while about 73 percent were eligible for duty-free treatment under the CBERA. However, on the basis of goods actually traded, CBERA-eligible products accounted for 58 percent of the value of U.S. imports from all sources and 27 percent of U.S. imports from the CBERA beneficiary countries.

Most petroleum, textile, apparel, and leather products are not eligible for duty-free treatment under either GSP or CBERA. On the other hand, the CBERA rules-of-origin are more liberal than those under the GSP program.[14] One major difference between the CBERA and GSP is that there is no country/product graduation provision in the CBERA; that is, under CBERA, U.S. market access is assured.[15] In recent years, several CBERA beneficiary countries have lost their GSP duty-free treatment on several products (for example, the Bahamas for certain chemical products and the Dominican Republic for sugar and cigars).

In February 1986, President Reagan announced by Executive Order a special access program intended to expand U.S. quota limits (but not reduce import duties) for certain textile and apparel articles assembled in the Caribbean Basin. Subsequently, the United States has negotiated special textile and apparel arrangements with a few Caribbean countries under this program. These arrangements permit expanded U.S. textile and apparel quotas for assembly operations in the Caribbean that use fabric formed and cut in the United States; items produced under these conditions enter the United States under special provisions contained in the U.S. tariff schedules.[16]

Attempts to modify (either to restrict or expand) the CBERA have not met with much success. For example, efforts to expand the list of CBERA eligible products failed to get into the CBI-II legislation which extended the original program indefinitely, while prior attempts to make the program more restrictive have not been successful. Until the recent permanent extension of the CBERA, there had been uncertainty in some quarters about the continued preferential treatment of U.S. imports from the Caribbean Basin. Also, the beneficiary countries (especially the smaller nations of the Eastern Caribbean) still feel the need for broader product coverage and special incentives.

3.   BDC PERFORMANCE UNDER U.S. TRADE PREFERENCE PROGRAMS

In this section, the GSP and CBERA trade preference programs will be examined to gauge the extent to which these programs have provided trade-expanding benefits to the beneficiary developing countries.

3.1. The Benefits of the GSP Program

Table 9.1 summarizes the value of total U.S. imports, imports eligible for GSP, and the amount entered duty-free under GSP over the period 1976-1989. The period 1976-88 represents the initial phase of the GSP program before significant country graduation took place (i.e., the removal of the

Table 9.1. U.S. Imports of GSP Products, 1976-1989 (millions of dollars)

Year	U.S. Imports		U.S. Imports from GSP Beneficiaries		
	Total (1)	GSP Products (2)	Total (3)	GSP Elig. (4)	GSP Free (5)
1976	121,121.2	25,630.5	28,055.9	6,530.0	3,160.3
1977	147,141.1	30,376.6	34,661.6	7,677.6	3,878.0
1978	172,952.2	40,777.7	48,635.1	9,741.1	5,204.2
1979	205,922.7	46,598.7	59,571.9	11,725.2	6,280.0
1980	239,943.5	52,029.0	72,390.1	14,081.8	7,240.1
1981	259,012.0	60,629.3	78,851.6	16,870.4	8,395.5
1982	242,340.0	60,914.8	77,566.8	17,443.1	8,422.1
1983	256,679.5	71,231.6	88,613.5	22,583.1	10,764.4
1984	322,989.5	99,472.1	106,172.7	29,907.3	12,997.0
1985	343,553.2	101,451.2	106,741.1	29,281.9	12,165.8
1986	368,656.6	119,386.7	107,858.5	34,659.5	13,916.8
1987	400,387.8	134,231.0	126,305.3	42,738.0	16,298.4
1988	436,117.4	153,371.9	139,214.9	49,954.9	18,353.6
1989	466,379.1	172,774.8	86,085.5	24,351.6	10,015.4

U.S. Imports of GSP Products, 1976-1989 (percent)

Year	Share of Total U.S. Imports			GSP-Eligible Share		GSP Free Share of Eligible (5/4)
	GSP Products (2/1)	Imports from BDCs (3/1)	GSP Free (4/1)	All GSP Products (4/2)	All Imp fr BDCs (4/3)	
1976	21.2	25.5	5.4	25.5	23.3	48.4
1977	20.6	25.9	5.2	25.3	22.2	50.5
1978	23.6	30.9	5.6	23.9	20.0	53.4
1979	22.6	31.8	5.7	25.2	19.7	53.6
1980	21.7	33.2	5.9	27.1	19.5	51.4
1981	23.4	33.5	6.5	27.8	21.4	49.8
1982	25.1	35.2	7.2	28.6	22.5	48.3
1983	27.8	38.0	8.8	31.7	25.5	47.7
1984	30.8	36.2	9.3	30.1	28.2	43.5
1985	29.5	34.2	8.5	28.9	27.4	41.5
1986	32.4	32.2	9.4	29.0	32.1	40.2
1987	33.5	34.7	10.7	31.8	33.8	38.1
1988	35.2	35.1	11.5	32.6	35.9	36.7
1989	37.0	20.3	5.2	14.1	28.3	41.1

Source: Compiled from official statistics of the U.S. Department of Commerce and the Office of the U.S. Trade Representative.

four Asian tigers: Taiwan, Hong Kong, South Korea, and Singapore). In this discussion, 1986 is used as a reference year for this initial period.

U.S. Imports of GSP Products

It is clear from Table 9.1 that U.S. imports of GSP products (from both BDCs and non-BDCs) have increased substantially over this period. The GSP-eligible share of total U.S. imports from the BDCs increased from 23 percent in 1976 to 36 percent in 1988, but fell to 28 percent in 1989 after Hong Kong, Singapore, South Korea, and Taiwan were graduated from the program. The share of GSP-eligible imports from the BDCs in total U.S. imports from all countries increased from 5.4 percent in 1976 to 11.5 percent in 1988, before falling to 5.2 percent in 1989. The importance of the GSP program to the beneficiary countries is highlighted by noting that the share of GSP-eligible BDC exports to the United States relative to similar products from all countries increased from 25 percent in 1976 to 33 percent in 1988, before dropping to 14 percent in 1989.[17]

The effects of increased application of product/country graduation from the U.S. GSP program can be seen from the decline in GSP-free imports as a share of total GSP-eligible imports from all BDCs (see Table 9.1). This share declined from 48 percent in 1976 to 37 percent in 1988. With the graduation of the four East Asian newly industrializing countries (NICs), which had accounted for a substantial portion of the product graduations, the share rose to 41 percent in 1989.

BDC Exports of GSP-Eligible Products to the United States

Table 9.2 presents the 83 leading beneficiary developing country suppliers of GSP-eligible products (each with over $1 million in 1986) to the U.S. market by share of their total exports to the United States in 1978 and 1986. For many of these countries, the share of GSP-eligible exports to the United States has increased substantially.

Fourteen countries, for which GSP-eligible products represented over 50 percent of their exports to the United States in 1986, accounted for slightly less than a third of all GSP-eligible imports from the BDCs, with Taiwan accounting for 98 percent of these. Except for Taiwan, these countries were mainly small countries with a low volume of trade. GSP eligible products comprised between 25 and 50 percent of total exports to the United States for 24 BDCs in 1986. Countries in this group accounted for nearly 60 percent of all GSP-eligible products imported from BDCs in 1986 and were some of the major beneficiaries of the U.S. GSP program (i.e., those

Table 9.2. Leading Beneficiary Country Suppliers of U.S. Imports of GSP-Eligible Products by 1986 Share of Total Exports to the United States (value in millions of dollars; share in percent)

Beneficiary Developing Country	Value of GSP-Eligible U.S. Imports		Share of Total Country Exports to the U.S.		Value of GSP Duty-Free U.S. Imports		Share of GSP Eligible Entered Free	
	1978	1986	1978	1986	1978	1986	1978	1986
Over 50% Exports Eligible for GSP								
Taiwan**	1,998.1	10,854.0	38.7	54.9	1,433.4	3,761.9	71.7	34.7
Haiti	76.9	188.8	39.8	51.3	22.8	44.6	29.7	23.6
Zambia	86.8	40.4	79.0	64.1	0.0	0.3	0.0	0.8
Bahrain*	0.0	39.4	0.3	50.8	0.0	38.0	25.0	96.6
Malta & Gozo	3.3	21.4	60.6	62.2	3.0	19.0	91.8	88.8
Lebanon	0.6	15.5	13.0	67.1	0.4	12.5	64.9	80.5
Swaziland	14.2	15.4	99.5	82.0	7.7	12.7	54.2	82.5
Mozambique	2.6	9.6	6.8	51.9	1.6	8.8	59.5	91.6
Fiji	5.1	6.5	49.6	55.5	1.4	6.2	26.7	96.5
St. Vincent & Grenadines	0.0	5.4	7.5	69.2	0.0	0.1	0.0	1.9
French Polynesia	1.7	2.8	94.5	50.5	1.5	2.3	86.1	80.9
Montserrat	0.5	2.3	89.9	65.1	0.1	0.3	19.0	13.2
Grenada	0.0	1.5	6.7	50.6	0.0	0.0	11.4	0.0
Yemen (Sana)	0.0	1.0	1.0	84.5	0.0	0.5	0.0	51.9
25-50% Exports Eligible for GSP								
Mexico	1,575.9	6,504.9	26.2	37.9	458.3	1,301.3	29.1	20.0
South Korea**	1,089.4	4,683.5	28.8	36.9	647.6	2,220.4	59.4	47.4
Hong Kong**	1,324.9	3,557.2	38.7	40.5	537.5	1,423.8	40.6	40.0
Brazil	682.1	1,901.6	24.5	28.5	468.1	1,108.8	68.6	58.3
Singapore**	281.7	1,444.7	25.3	30.7	153.2	730.2	54.4	50.5
Israel	205.1	866.0	28.7	35.9	192.0	421.4	93.6	48.7
Dominican Republic	159.1	317.7	29.8	30.0	24.2	117.5	15.2	37.0
Chile****	271.4	316.4	71.5	38.6	87.0	59.4	32.1	18.8

(Continued)

Beneficiary Developing Country	Value of GSP-Eligible U.S. Imports		Share of Total Country Exports to the U.S.		Value of GSP Duty-Free U.S. Imports		Share of GSP Eligible Entered Free	
	1978	1986	1978	1986	1978	1986	1978	1986
Argentina	195.0	301.2	34.8	35.8	148.0	164.6	75.9	54.6
Yugoslavia	173.9	292.7	42.8	45.2	152.3	281.3	87.6	96.1
Bahamas	17.1	154.1	1.7	34.9	5.9	86.2	34.6	55.9
Macau	3.6	154.0	6.0	37.4	3.4	138.6	94.4	90.0
Morocco	6.4	17.4	14.9	40.2	6.1	15.8	95.7	90.9
Belize	16.9	15.3	58.4	30.5	14.8	4.4	87.5	28.9
St. Kitts-Nevis-Anguilla	5.7	9.3	84.4	42.2	5.5	2.9	95.7	31.4
Paraguay***	8.0	7.7	15.7	25.2	7.3	7.6	91.0	99.3
Dominica	0.2	7.1	91.4	46.9	0.2	0.5	96.5	6.9
Niger	0.0	4.9	0.3	41.9	0.0	0.0	50.0	0.7
Antigua & Barbuda	0.1	4.5	11.7	38.0	0.1	1.2	88.6	26.5
Tunisia	2.6	4.1	12.3	38.8	2.6	3.0	99.7	74.0
Jordan	0.0	3.9	5.0	38.2	0.0	0.2	0.0	4.1
Mali	0.1	2.8	33.8	33.9	0.1	0.7	39.3	25.7
Senegal	0.1	2.5	7.1	38.1	0.1	1.6	52.7	63.1
Seychelles	0.0	2.0	0.0	26.4	0.0	0.7	0.0	36.0
Less than 25% Exports Eligible for GSP								
Malaysia	114.0	402.3	7.5	16.7	42.4	188.6	37.2	46.9
Thailand	82.7	394.9	19.2	22.5	37.6	351.1	45.5	88.9
Philippines	276.6	394.8	23.4	20.0	71.0	229.5	25.7	58.1
India	143.8	250.2	14.8	11.0	120.1	218.9	83.5	87.5
Venezuela+	22.5	208.0	0.7	4.2	0.0	130.8	0.0	62.9
Colombia	46.4	201.8	4.4	10.8	33.7	94.8	72.6	47.0
Peru	189.3	187.1	29.1	24.6	78.8	121.4	41.6	64.9
Costa Rica	33.7	98.3	11.3	15.2	24.4	57.4	72.4	58.4
Guatemala	37.1	85.2	10.9	13.9	11.1	43.6	29.9	51.1
Romania***	55.5	67.8	16.1	9.0	50.3	62.9	90.5	92.7
Zaire	4.9	53.7	2.2	24.3	0.6	41.1	11.6	76.4
Turkey	12.3	52.6	6.8	8.5	6.8	39.4	55.4	74.9
Honduras	35.4	49.5	10.5	11.5	31.3	18.2	88.5	36.8
Pakistan	12.2	41.5	14.9	12.9	11.6	39.3	94.8	94.6
Indonesia+	16.2	37.3	0.5	1.1	0.0	34.5	0.0	92.5
Uruguay	55.0	35.6	45.0	7.5	53.9	34.1	98.0	95.9
Panama	34.9	35.4	22.4	10.1	6.0	19.4	17.1	54.8
Jamaica	12.5	34.8	3.3	11.7	7.5	11.9	60.1	34.1

(Continued)

Beneficiary Developing Country	Value of GSP-Eligible U.S. Imports		Share of Total Country Exports to the U.S.		Value of GSP Duty-Free U.S. Imports		Share of GSP Eligible Entered Free	
	1978	1986	1978	1986	1978	1986	1978	1986
Ivory Coast	74.1	27.5	17.8	6.6	42.0	25.1	56.7	91.5
Mauritius	18.1	24.1	76.4	20.7	13.0	18.6	71.9	77.3
El Salvador	52.5	23.4	18.0	6.3	9.4	19.2	17.9	82.3
Ecuador+	26.4	22.8	3.6	1.6	0.0	19.1	0.0	83.7
Trinidad & Tobago	20.1	21.5	1.4	2.7	19.0	9.9	94.6	46.3
Kenya	2.9	14.0	5.8	10.0	2.4	7.8	84.2	55.9
Barbados	16.8	13.6	42.3	12.5	8.4	3.4	50.1	24.8
Sri Lanka	5.7	13.0	9.5	3.9	3.5	11.7	61.1	89.7
Guyana	7.4	10.0	12.2	15.8	1.8	9.8	24.0	98.0
Zimbabwe (Rhodesia)+	0.0	10.0	0.0	14.7	0.0	9.0	0.0	89.7
Congo (Brazzaville)	0.5	8.2	0.6	2.3	0.4	8.2	72.7	99.0
Bolivia	15.2	7.7	9.0	6.3	14.9	5.9	98.4	76.4
Cameroon	3.0	5.5	3.9	1.8	2.7	3.2	91.8	58.4
Madagascar (Malagasy)	4.2	5.2	3.9	8.3	2.7	4.9	65.7	94.1
Papua New Guinea	0.2	4.3	0.3	9.5	0.1	4.2	42.9	97.9
Netherlands Antilles-Aruba	6.4	3.0	0.5	1.3	3.6	0.9	56.7	28.5
Bangladesh	3.7	2.9	4.7	1.2	1.8	2.7	48.9	94.2
Egypt	4.5	2.8	4.9	2.7	4.0	2.2	89.3	79.7
Suriname	0.5	2.0	0.4	5.1	0.0	0.4	8.3	20.6
Tanzania	5.5	1.8	6.8	15.1	0.2	1.1	4.3	60.9
Cayman Islands	2.3	1.8	76.5	12.0	2.1	1.3	93.3	73.6
Cyprus	1.1	1.8	15.8	18.0	0.4	1.5	40.2	81.2
Kiribati (Gilbert Islands)#	0.0	1.8	0.0	14.7	0.0	0.9	0.0	50.5
Burma (Myanmar)+	0.4	1.6	12.0	11.5	0.1	1.5	29.9	89.2
Syria	0.3	1.5	0.8	17.5	0.3	1.3	82.4	85.9
Nepal	0.2	1.3	5.2	4.1	0.2	0.5	90.4	34.8
New Caldonia	0.0	1.2	0.0	13.5	0.0	0.2	0.0	18.9

Note: Beneficiary Developing Country suppliers with over $1 million in GSP-eligible products in 1986 are included. ****Removed from GSP in December 1987. ***Removed from GSP in March 1987. **Removed from GSP in January 1989. *Removed from GSP in July 1989. +Eligible for GSP beginning March 1980. #Removed from GSP in July 1988. #Removed from GSP in

Source: Compiled from official statistics of the U.S. of Department of Commerce.

with a large value entered GSP duty-free). For the bulk of the other major BDC suppliers (45 countries), GSP-eligible products accounted for less than a quarter of their exports to the United States in 1986. As a group, these countries supplied only about 8 percent of all GSP-eligible products. While not a significant part of their total exports to the United States, a substantial portion of these GSP-eligible products entered duty-free.

Table 9.2 shows the importance of the GSP program (in terms of the value entered GSP-free) to many of the more-advanced developing countries in the Americas (e.g., Brazil and Mexico). For some less-advanced developing countries (e.g., St. Vincent and the Grenadines, Montserrat, and Grenada), a majority of their exports to the United States were eligible for GSP, but few qualified for duty-free entry. However, there were a number of the less-advanced developing countries, including some in the Caribbean, where GSP-eligible exports accounted for less than 10 percent of their exports to the United States, but most qualified for duty-free entry.

In Central America and the Caribbean, countries such as the Bahamas, Haiti, St. Vincent, Grenada, and Antigua have substantially increased their share of GSP-eligible exports to the United States; in other countries (such as Belize, St. Kitts-Nevis, Dominica, Barbados, El Salvador, and Panama), the share has declined.

Major GSP Beneficiaries by Region and Country

In 1986, the Asian GSP beneficiaries provided 67 percent of all GSP-eligible products to the U.S. market and accounted for 71 percent of all GSP duty-free entries. The BDCs in the Americas (Central America, the Caribbean, and South America) accounted for most of the balance; the BDCs in Oceania and Africa, each as a group, provided less than one percent of the total of either the GSP-eligible products or duty-free GSP entries.

Within each world region (based on 1986 data), only a few countries were major users of the U.S. GSP program. In Central America and the Caribbean, Mexico accounted for 86 percent of the region's GSP-eligible products and 75 percent of its GSP duty-free value. Second to Mexico was the Dominican Republic with less than 10 percent of Mexico's GSP-free exports to the United States. In South America, the leading GSP beneficiary was Brazil, which accounted for 59 percent of the region's GSP eligible goods and 63 percent of the GSP duty-free entries; a not so close second was Argentina. In Europe, Yugoslavia supplied 67 percent of the region's GSP eligible products and 70 percent of its GSP free entries; the other major GSP beneficiary was Romania, but to a much lesser extent.

In Asia, the major GSP beneficiaries were Taiwan (which accounted for 47 percent of the region's GSP eligible and 38 percent of its GSP free), South Korea, Hong Kong, Singapore, and Israel prior to 1989; in 1989, Malaysia, Thailand, the Philippines, and India replaced the four graduated East Asian NICs. Although the Oceania and African regions have been minor users of the GSP program, the primary beneficiary countries in each respective region were Fiji and Zaire.

On the basis of the value of GSP duty-free imports, the country distribution of major GSP beneficiaries has not changed a great deal.[18] However, for many less-advanced BDCs, GSP-free trade has become more important. As noted earlier, the high proportion of GSP-eligible exports that enter the United States (in some cases, with a substantial portion duty-free) demonstrates that many less-advanced developing countries have the greatest stake in the GSP program.

Overall, the preferential treatment of GSP-eligible products has provided a small number of more-advanced BDCs, primarily in Asia, with the economic advantages associated with that program. The skewed country distribution of the GSP beneficiaries raises a fundamental question: Does the commodity/industry structure of products eligible for duty-free treatment under the GSP program present an obstacle to the majority of beneficiaries? As noted earlier, the U.S. GSP program covered approximately 45 percent of the tariff line items over the 1976-86 period. While the commodity coverage has changed over time, its basic structure has remained unchanged.

Industrial Structure of GSP-Eligible Products

Table 9.3 presents the share of GSP-eligible products in total BDC exports to the United States and the BDC share of all U.S. imports in 1986 by two-digit Standard Industrial Classification (SIC). The leading industrial sectors where GSP-eligible exports constituted a significant share of all BDC exports to the United States (over 75 percent) were: furniture and fixtures (SIC 25); tobacco manufactures (SIC 21); rubber and plastics (SIC 30); paper and allied products (SIC 26); fabricated metal products (SIC 34); and non-electrical machinery (SIC 35). However, BDCs supplied less than one-third of all U.S. imports of paper products (SIC 26) and non-electrical machinery (SIC 35). At the other extreme, BDCs supplied over half of all U.S. imports of tobacco manufactures (SIC 21).

Table 9.3 also reveals several import product groups — such as apparel (SIC 23), leather products (SIC 31), and crude and refined petroleum products (SIC 13 and SIC 29) — in which BDCs accounted for a large share of total U.S. imports, but only a small portion of their exports were

Table 9.3. GSP-Eligible U.S. Imports by 2-Digit SIC Product Group, 1986 (percent)

SIC Code and Description	GSP Beneficiary Countries Share of Total U.S. Imports	GSP-Eligible Product Share of Total Imports, GSP Beneficiary Countries
01 Agricultural Products	86.2	8.7
02 Livestock & Livestock Products	31.3	3.2
08 Forestry Products	87.9	0.0
09 Fishery Products	47.2	4.2
10 Metallic Ores	31.9	4.7
12 Coal	25.6	0.0
13 Crude Petroleum & Natural Gas	50.7	0.0
14 Nonmetallic Minerals	36.7	4.9
20 Food	33.2	33.7
21 Tobacco	53.2	88.6
22 Textiles	38.0	7.9
23 Apparel	86.1	3.6
24 Wood	25.4	57.1
25 Furniture & Fixtures	41.2	100.0
26 Paper	6.5	78.9
27 Printing & Publishing	16.5	40.1
28 Chemicals	12.4	58.9
29 Refined Petroleum Products	42.7	0.0
30 Rubber & Plastics Products	36.2	83.2
31 Leather & Leather Products	70.9	7.9
32 Stone, Clay, Glass Products	24.5	63.6
33 Primary Metal Products	20.1	28.8
34 Fabricated Metal Products	33.1	77.6
35 Machinery, Except Electrical	14.2	75.3
36 Electrical Machinery	43.3	51.5
37 Transportation Equipment	5.7	42.4
38 Scientific Instruments	16.7	65.2
39 Miscellaneous Manufactured Products	55.5	65.9
99 Other	20.8	2.4
Total	29.3	32.1

Source: Compiled from official statistics of the U.S. Department of Commerce and the Office of the U.S. Trade Representative.

eligible for GSP duty-free entry as reflected in the program's product exclusions.[19]

Given the fact that the major beneficiaries of the U.S. GSP program consist of a small group of more-advanced developing countries and are available only for a limited set of products, can elements of the GSP program be targeted towards the less-developed countries in the Caribbean? The Caribbean Basin Economic Recovery Act represents such an attempt. We now turn to a discussion of beneficiary country performance under this program.

3.2. The Benefits of the CBERA Program

After seven years of operation, the CBERA program has produced some mixed results — disappointment for some who had higher expectations and the realization of new hopes for others. Many of the short-term effects of the tariff preference program probably have been felt already as some beneficiary countries have begun restructuring their export mix to the United States to better utilize available preferences.[20] However, the long-run effects of the program will depend, to a large part, on the ability of each of the beneficiary countries to attract new investment and induce major structural changes in their export and export-related sectors.

Total U.S. Imports from the Caribbean Basin

Over the period 1983-89, the value of U.S. imports from the CBERA-eligible nations has declined at an annual average rate of 4.1 percent, while U.S. imports from developed nations have increased at an annual rate of 11.2 percent and those from other developing nations have increased at an annual rate of 9.2 percent; overall U.S. imports from all sources have increased at an annual rate of 10.5 percent a year over the same period.

CBERA beneficiary nations' exports to the U.S. market were dominated by high-value petroleum products in 1983. However, by 1986, U.S. imports from the region of agricultural products exceeded those of crude and refined petroleum. And, by 1989, U.S. imports of apparel had become the major item imported from the region, accounting for 25 percent of all U.S. imports from the region.

While there have been changes in the overall CBERA beneficiary export commodity structure, it is enlightening to note the regional differences which exist.

- The **Central American** beneficiaries (Costa Rica, Guatemala, Honduras, El Salvador, Panama, and Belize) primarily export to the United States unprocessed agricultural products, followed by food products, fishery products, and apparel.

- The larger **Central Caribbean** island nations (Dominican Republic, Haiti, and Jamaica) export a broader and more diversified range of products to the United States, lead by apparel and followed by food, agricultural, primary metal, miscellaneous manufactures, and electrical machinery products.

- The small island nations of the **Eastern Caribbean** (Barbados, Antigua and Barbuda, British Virgin Islands, Dominica, Grenada, Montserrat, St. Kitts-Nevis, St. Lucia, St. Vincent and the Grenadines) predominately export electrical machinery products (followed by apparel and food products) to the United States.

- Crude and refined petroleum products (followed by chemical products) dominate the exports to the United States of the **Oil Refining** nations (Bahamas, Netherlands Antilles-Aruba, and Trinidad and Tobago), though the prominence of these exports has declined dramatically in recent years.

Table 9.4 presents the customs value, share subject to duty, dutiable value, calculated duty, and average rate of duty for U.S. imports from the CBERA-beneficiary countries by regional group over the period 1983-89. While U.S. imports from the CBERA beneficiaries have declined from $8.8 billion in 1983 to $6.1 billion in 1986 before rising to $6.8 billion in 1989, the value of this trade that was subject to duty (i.e., not most-favored-nation (MFN) free) has fallen also from $6.9 billion in 1983 to $3.7 billion in 1986 before rising to $4.9 billion in 1989, reflecting an increase in the share of MFN duty-free imports from 21.7 percent in 1983 to 38.6 percent in 1986 before the decline to 29.0 percent in 1989.

On a regional basis, about one-half to two-thirds of U.S. imports from the Central American beneficiaries entered the United States MFN duty-free; for the Central Caribbean beneficiaries, less than one-quarter entered MFN duty-free. By 1989, less than 10 percent of U.S. imports from the Eastern Caribbean and the Oil Refining beneficiaries entered the United States MFN duty-free.

The product composition of CBERA exports to the United States has a tremendous bearing on the ability of beneficiary countries to take advantage of the tariff preferences under the CBERA. For example, most petroleum and apparel products are excluded from duty-free treatment under the CBERA; the former have declined as rapidly as the latter have expanded in terms of recent CBERA exports to the U.S. market. On the other hand, many primary mineral (e.g., bauxite) and agricultural product

Table 9.4. U.S. Imports from the CBERA Beneficiary Countries: Total, Subject to Duty, Dutiable Value, and Duties Paid, 1983–89 (value in millions of dollars; share and tariff rate in percent)

County	Value of Total U.S. Imports			Share of Total U.S. Imports Subject to Duty			Dutiable Value of U.S. Imports			Value of Import Duties Paid			Average Tariff Rate (duties/dut.val.)		
	1983	1986	1989	1983	1986	1989	1983	1986	1989	1983	1986	1989	1983	1986	1989
Central America, total	1,848.3	2,466.3	2,578.3	41.0	33.9	53.9	358.6	238.6	515.0	20.8	30.1	78.8	5.8	12.6	15.3
Belize	27.3	50.2	43.1	73.7	83.6	79.3	5.9	7.2	5.2	0.3	1.1	0.9	5.7	15.0	18.1
Costa Rica	386.5	646.5	967.9	47.7	55.6	69.3	71.8	93.7	200.4	6.5	13.8	34.3	9.1	14.7	17.1
El Salvador	358.9	371.8	243.9	37.7	20.5	46.3	52.0	25.6	42.6	3.6	2.8	5.8	6.9	10.8	13.6
Guatemala	374.7	614.7	608.3	44.6	25.1	51.7	92.0	44.2	135.4	3.2	2.8	18.0	3.5	6.3	13.3
Honduras	364.7	430.9	456.8	39.1	28.5	38.9	75.5	25.2	54.9	4.4	3.7	9.7	5.9	14.7	17.7
Panama	336.1	352.2	258.3	32.2	23.0	31.2	61.3	42.6	76.4	2.7	6.0	10.1	4.5	14.1	13.2
Central Caribbean, total	1,406.4	1,725.2	2,535.5	59.2	71.6	77.5	363.3	298.5	565.0	27.9	47.3	96.6	7.7	15.9	17.1
Dominican Republic	806.5	1,058.9	1,636.9	59.1	66.7	80.2	259.1	142.0	349.9	14.8	24.3	60.1	5.7	17.1	17.2
Haiti	337.5	368.4	371.9	86.7	93.2	93.7	85.2	86.7	96.0	10.2	12.3	14.4	11.9	14.2	15.0
Jamaica	262.4	297.9	526.7	24.4	62.4	57.7	19.1	69.7	119.1	2.9	10.7	22.1	15.4	15.4	18.6
Oil Refining Cntry, total	5,268.4	1,682.5	1,601.5	95.6	91.5	86.8	4,884.4	1,309.7	1,059.7	19.9	8.3	10.0	0.4	0.6	1.0
Bahamas	1,676.4	441.0	460.7	97.2	93.3	89.7	1,562.0	259.1	138.3	6.7	2.3	2.3	0.4	0.9	1.7
Netherlands Antilles–Aruba	2,274.5	455.1	375.5	96.4	90.3	88.4	2,117.6	373.1	321.7	8.3	2.0	3.9	0.4	0.5	1.2
Trinidad and Tobago	1,317.5	786.4	765.3	92.0	91.3	84.2	1,204.8	677.5	590.6	5.0	4.1	3.8	0.4	0.6	0.6

(Continued)

County	Value of Total U.S. Imports			Share of Total U.S. Imports Subject to Duty			Dutiable Value of U.S. Imports			Value of Import Duties Paid			Average Tariff Rate (duties/dut.val.)		
	1983	1986	1989	1983	1986	1989	1983	1986	1989	1983	1986	1989	1983	1986	1989
Eastern Caribbean, total	240.8	190.9	124.9	96.8	59.5	90.2	68.6	43.0	42.2	6.9	5.4	4.6	10.0	12.6	11.0
Antigua and Barbuda	8.8	11.8	12.3	93.0	85.5	87.7	3.4	4.9	8.1	0.4	0.7	0.1	11.2	13.6	0.9
Barbados	202.0	109.0	38.7	97.6	37.2	87.0	50.1	14.2	9.2	5.4	2.4	0.9	10.8	17.0	9.8
British Virgin Islands	0.9	5.9	1.1	64.9	95.4	42.3	0.4	0.0	0.2	0.0	0.0	0.0	3.9	7.9	2.0
Dominica	0.2	15.2	7.7	91.3	82.4	86.7	0.0	6.8	5.1	0.0	0.3	0.6	24.0	4.7	12.1
Grenada	0.2	3.0	7.9	5.7	64.5	77.0	0.0	1.7	1.8	0.0	0.1	0.2	12.9	5.1	10.9
Montserrat	0.9	3.5	2.3	90.8	75.9	96.1	0.3	0.5	1.6	0.0	0.0	0.1	9.4	9.1	4.0
St. Kitts-Nevis-Anguilla	18.8	22.4	21.8	94.0	97.5	94.1	10.6	6.8	2.7	0.4	0.8	0.3	3.5	11.6	12.6
St. Lucia	4.7	12.3	24.0	94.4	87.3	97.6	1.9	3.8	11.9	0.3	0.7	2.2	15.6	18.6	18.6
St. Vincent & Grenadines	4.3	7.8	9.2	93.5	96.5	96.9	1.8	4.2	1.8	0.3	0.4	0.2	19.4	8.8	12.5
CBERA Beneficiary total	8,763.9	6,064.8	6,840.2	78.3	61.4	71.0	5,674.8	1,889.8	2,172.8	75.5	91.2	190.0	1.3	4.8	8.7
Addendum: Other CBERA-eligible countries not included above (date designated as a beneficiary)															
Cayman Islands (n. d.)	8.6	14.6	48.0	23.5	13.4	3.9	1.6	0.6	1.7	0.0	0.0	0.1	0.4	4.3	4.0
Turks and Caicos (n. d.)	4.0	4.8	2.5	1.9	1.7	1.6	0.1	0.1	0.0	0.0	0.0	0.0	19.6	9.1	0.3
Nicaragua (Nov. 1990)	99.0	1.1	0.0	60.4	85.4	32.8	37.8	0.8	0.0	0.9	0.1	0.0	2.3	7.9	6.0
Guyana (Nov. 1988)	67.3	62.9	55.9	27.9	18.1	10.1	2.1	1.1	1.2	0.6	0.1	0.2	28.8	13.1	13.1
Suriname (n. d.)	63.1	38.6	73.9	0.7	14.1	22.2	0.3	5.0	0.8	0.0	0.4	0.1	10.2	8.4	7.8

Note: n.d. = never designated; Panama lost its beneficiary status over the period April 9, 1988 to March 17, 1990. Data for St. Kitts-Nevis includes the non-beneficiary country Anguilla.

Source: Compiled from official statistics of the U.S. Department of Commerce.

(e.g., coffee, bananas, shellfish, cocoa beans) exports from the region enter the U.S. MFN duty-free.

These overall results affect the CBERA regions in different ways. Apparel products now account for about three-quarters of the duties paid (at an average rate of over 20-percent ad valorem) on U.S. imports from the CBERA beneficiaries (the same could be said for the beneficiaries of the Central and Eastern Caribbean and Central America). On the other hand, crude and refined petroleum products account for over three-quarters of the duties paid (at an average rate of under 1-percent ad valorem) on U.S. imports from the Oil Refining nations. We now turn to a closer examination of the effects of the CBERA on the beneficiary countries.

U.S. Imports of CBERA-Eligible Products

Table 9.5 presents the value of CBERA-eligible U.S. imports from the CBERA beneficiaries over the 1983-89 period by region and country. Data for 1983 are included as a point of reference, since it represents the last year before the CBERA tariff preference benefits took effect; however, GSP benefits were (and still are) available to the CBERA beneficiaries. In this table, U.S. imports which are not MFN-free or are not specifically excluded from CBERA duty-free treatment are considered to be "CBERA eligible" (i.e., they include the eligible and possibly eligible groups referred to above).

Over the 1983-89 period, the value of CBERA beneficiary imports which were eligible for CBERA duty-free treatment has fluctuated in a small range between $1.6 and $2.1 billion; however, the share of these imports as a percent of those subject to duty nearly doubled from 23 percent in 1983 to 44 percent in 1986 (and 1989). On a regional basis, CBERA-eligible exports to the United States from the Central Caribbean beneficiaries increased steadily from $625.2 million in 1983 to $766.1 million in 1986 to $944.7 million in 1989; those from the Oil Refining beneficiaries also increased dramatically over this period from $114.5 million to $218.3 million to $365.3 million. On the other hand, CBERA-eligible exports from the Central American beneficiaries[21] fell from $602.3 million in 1983 to $563.5 million in 1986 before rising to $742.9 million in 1989; those from the Eastern Caribbean beneficiaries[22] plummeted over this period from $215.7 million to $89.4 million to $77.1 million.

Products Assembled of U.S. Materials

Table 9.5 also presents the value of CBERA-eligible imports from the CBERA beneficiaries that were entered under U.S. tariff provisions 806.30 and 807.00.[23] These two provisions extend special duty treatment to U.S. imports from any country that contain U.S.-made components. These items are subject to duty only on the foreign value-added to the product. While these provisions do not eliminate duties, they do offer the opportunity for duty reductions on CBERA-eligible items that do not meet the rules-of-origin requirements.

In 1983, nearly a third of the CBERA-eligible products from the Caribbean entered the United States under the 806/807 provisions; 70 percent of the value of these items consisted of U.S.-made materials or components. By 1986, slightly less than a fifth of the CBERA-eligible products were entered under these provisions and their U.S. content had risen to 75 percent. These trends suggest that certain assembly operations which incorporate U.S.-made materials or components were moving toward more local value added, sufficient to switch from 806/807 provisions to the duty-free provisions of the CBERA. It should be noted, however, that the use of 806/807 provisions for the entry of CBERA-eligible products has been used extensively only by the beneficiaries of the Central and Eastern Caribbean. While the 806/807 provisions have been used by the Central Caribbean beneficiaries (with increasing U.S. content) for about 30 percent of the CBERA-eligible products over the 1983-89 period, the share for the Eastern Caribbean beneficiaries (with declining U.S. content) has fallen from 75 percent to 28 percent over this period.

Utilization of Tariff Preference Programs

With an increasing share of many beneficiary exports becoming eligible for duty-free treatment under the CBERA, how effective have the developing countries in the Caribbean been in utilizing these benefits?

As noted earlier, the scope of products eligible for duty-free treatment under the CBERA is broader than that under GSP (i.e., virtually every GSP-eligible product is also CBERA-eligible, but the converse is not true). In 1983, 36 percent of the CBERA-eligible imports from the beneficiaries (that is, products which would have been eligible if the CBERA program had been in effect) entered GSP duty-free. In 1984, this fell to 32 percent as the CBERA began its first year of operation with 31 percent of the CBERA-eligible products entering duty-free under the CBERA. The combined use of CBERA and GSP duty-free benefits accounts for over 60

Table 9.5. U.S. Imports of CBERA-Eligible Products from Beneficiary Caribbean Basin Countries, 1983-89 (value in millions of dollars; share in percent)

Beneficiary Developing Country	Value of CBERA-Eligible U.S. Imports			CBERA-Eligible Share of Total Imports Subject to Duty			Share of CBERA-Elig Entered Duty Free Under CBERA or GSP			Share of CBERA-Elig Entered Under Tariff Items 806/7		
	1983	1986	1989	1983	1986	1989	1983	1986	1989	1983	1986	1989
Central America, total	602.3	563.5	742.9	79.5	67.5	53.4	44.0	77.0	74.1	22.1	11.5	14.2
Belize	13.7	28.0	20.2	67.9	66.7	59.2	70.0	88.4	99.2	0.0	0.0	0.0
Costa Rica	140.7	226.6	378.3	76.3	63.1	56.4	36.3	76.0	74.1	31.1	15.3	13.4
El Salvador	122.2	51.5	55.3	90.3	67.5	49.0	31.2	62.1	73.4	61.3	29.5	23.3
Guatemala	115.9	112.5	155.1	69.4	73.0	49.4	63.1	87.7	87.7	0.0	1.4	1.2
Honduras	128.9	95.9	104.3	90.4	78.2	58.7	37.9	75.3	70.0	9.7	11.5	17.3
Panama	81.0	49.0	29.7	74.9	60.5	36.8	54.9	69.2	0.0	2.3	5.5	5.8
Central Caribbean, total	625.2	766.1	944.7	75.1	62.0	48.1	31.4	64.1	69.1	31.8	28.9	27.3
Dominican Republic	358.8	445.7	675.5	75.3	63.1	51.4	27.2	71.5	72.3	15.3	21.2	24.4
Haiti	217.0	233.4	178.5	74.2	68.0	51.2	29.2	62.8	54.4	62.8	46.8	41.6
Jamaica	49.3	86.9	90.7	77.1	46.8	29.8	72.0	73.0	74.6	15.5	20.1	20.5
Oil Refining Cntry, total	114.5	218.8	365.3	2.3	14.2	26.3	59.0	87.4	18.5	2.2	0.3	0.7
Bahamas	81.7	169.6	301.1	5.0	41.2	72.8	73.6	87.9	3.3	0.3	0.1	0.1
Netherlands Antilles-Aruba	12.1	8.4	7.1	0.6	2.0	2.1	26.9	66.9	66.2	18.9	6.0	4.2
Trinidad and Tobago	20.7	40.8	57.1	1.7	5.7	8.9	20.5	89.5	92.6	0.2	0.0	0.0

(Continued)

Beneficiary Developing Country	Value of CBERA-Eligible U.S. Imports			CBERA-Eligible Share of Total Imports Subject to Duty			Share of CBERA-Elig Entered Duty Free Under CBERA or GSP			Share of CBERA-Elig Entered Under Tariff Items 806/7		
	1983	1986	1989	1983	1986	1989	1983	1986	1989	1983	1986	1989
Eastern Caribbean, total	215.7	89.4	77.1	92.6	78.8	68.5	16.9	34.2	60.6	75.2	34.1	27.7
Antigua and Barbuda	5.4	9.1	2.9	66.0	89.9	26.6	0.1	19.1	92.9	96.7	44.3	0.0
Barbados	186.4	33.9	30.1	94.5	83.4	89.4	18.8	40.2	55.8	77.4	49.3	34.5
British Virgin Islands	0.6	0.4	0.3	99.8	7.3	59.0	0.0	0.0	49.6	0.5	0.0	0.0
Dominica	0.1	12.2	3.2	22.6	97.9	48.7	84.0	10.4	30.6	0.0	0.2	0.7
Grenada	0.0	1.7	3.4	83.3	87.1	55.8	0.0	2.3	66.7	40.0	0.0	28.2
Montserrat	0.8	2.5	2.0	93.2	96.3	92.6	1.0	11.8	7.9	97.6	78.7	28.0
St. Kitts-Nevis-Anguilla	16.0	16.7	17.6	90.8	76.7	85.9	5.3	54.5	81.4	43.4	23.3	15.8
St. Lucia	4.0	7.0	10.4	90.1	65.7	44.7	0.7	32.6	33.8	78.3	50.2	52.6
St. Vincent & Grenadines	2.5	5.8	7.1	62.2	76.8	79.5	20.0	37.8	82.0	79.9	3.9	15.9
CBERA Beneficiary total	1,557.7	1,637.9	2,130.1	22.7	44.0	43.8	36.3	70.0	61.8	31.9	19.4	18.2

Note: In 1989, $264.6 million of U.S. imports of aromatic drugs (HTS 2918.90.30) from the Bahamas entered duty-free under a special duty-rate suspension in effect for that year; normally, these products (eligible for both GSP and CBERA duty-free benefits) would have entered duty-free under GSP or CBERA.

Source: Compiled from official statistics of the U.S. Department of Commerce.

percent of all CBERA-eligible products (63 percent in 1984, 70 percent in 1986, and 62 percent in 1989).

On a regional basis, 44 percent of the Central American beneficiaries', 31 percent of the Central Caribbean beneficiaries', 59 percent of Oil Refining beneficiaries', and 17 percent of the Eastern Caribbean beneficiaries' exports of CBERA-eligible products entered the United States duty-free under GSP in 1983. By 1989, the combined use of CBERA and GSP for duty-free entry into the U.S. market had risen to 74 percent for the Central American beneficiaries, 69 percent for the Central Caribbean beneficiaries, 87 percent for the Oil Refining beneficiaries,[24] and 61 percent for the Eastern Caribbean beneficiaries.

The short-term impact of the CBERA on beneficiary country exports of eligible products has been dramatic. However, the benefits of the CBERA have been concentrated in a few countries. By 1989, nearly 80 percent of the CBERA-eligible products were imported from five beneficiary countries (the Dominican Republic, Haiti, Costa Rica, Bahamas, and Guatemala); these same countries also accounted for nearly 80 percent of the CBERA-free and GSP-free entries from the CBERA beneficiary nations.

Products Eligible for CBERA But Not GSP

To determine the marginal benefit of the CBERA, we next look at the benefits that the CBERA provides beyond those available under the GSP duty-free provisions (i.e., for those products eligible for CBERA duty-free benefits, but not for GSP duty-free benefits).

Table 9.6 presents summary statistics on the value and share of U.S. imports from CBERA beneficiary countries by regional group of products eligible for CBERA but not GSP for the period 1983-89. U.S. imports of products eligible for CBERA but not GSP have constituted a rather small but increasing share of imports subject to duty from the CBERA beneficiaries, rising from 8 percent of imports subject to duty in 1983 to 12 percent in 1989. By 1986, over a half of these items entered duty-free under the CBERA and about a third (down from almost two-thirds in 1983) entered under the 806/807 provisions with nearly three-quarters U.S. content.

On a regional basis, items eligible for CBERA but not GSP have constituted about a third to a quarter of the Central American beneficiaries' exports to the United States subject to duty (with nearly two-thirds of these entering duty-free under CBERA), about one-sixth to one-tenth of those from the Central Caribbean (with two-fifths of these entering CBERA free), and less than 2 percent of those from the Oil Refining beneficiaries (with CBERA-free entries rising from 12 percent in 1984 to 79 percent in 1989). In 1983, CBERA eligible but not GSP products accounted for about 60 percent of Eastern Caribbean beneficiaries' exports subject to duty; by 1989, this share had fallen to 22 percent (with nearly 50 percent entering CBERA free), reflecting the fact that certain semiconductors became MFN duty-free in 1985.

The short-term impact of the CBERA on products eligible for CBERA but not GSP has been limited and has benefitted primarily the beneficiaries of Central America and the Central Caribbean whose current export structure favors these products. By 1989, six beneficiary nations (Costa Rica, Dominican Republic, Jamaica, Guatemala, Honduras, and Haiti) accounted for 84 percent of the CBERA-eligible but not GSP U.S. imports from the CBERA beneficiaries and nearly 83 percent of the CBERA-free entries of these items.

Table 9.7 presents 3-digit SIC-based import categories with CBERA duty-free value of one-million dollars or more in 1989. Categories marked with an asterisk indicate categories with CBERA-free entries over one-million dollars of products eligible for CBERA but not GSP. These products, which represent some of the primary exports of the Central American and Central Caribbean beneficiaries, include: meat and meat packing products; vegetables and melons; sugar and confectionery products; electronic components and accessories; industrial organic chemicals; prepared fruits and vegetables; field crops; toys and sporting goods; steel mill products; cigars and cheroots; fresh fruits; and beverages.

In summary, the major CBERA program users (in value terms) have been the larger and more economically diversified nations in Central America (especially Costa Rica, Guatemala, and Honduras) and the Central Caribbean (especially the Dominican Republic and Haiti). While most of the exports from the smaller Eastern Caribbean island nations to the United States consist of products eligible for CBERA duty-free treatment, only a few nations (Barbados and to a lesser extent St. Kitts-Nevis, St. Lucia, and St. Vincent and the Grenadines) have posted over a million dollars in CBERA duty-free trade. In contrast, most of the exports of the Oil Refining nations to the United States consist of products not eligible for CBERA duty-free treatment; however, as petroleum products are becoming less important in their export mix, the level of CBERA duty-free entries (especially the Bahamas and Trinidad and Tobago) and program utilization has been increasing steadily. Similar patterns of CBERA program utilization by region and country (though at greatly reduced levels) emerge if the marginal benefits of CBERA over GSP (i.e., those products eligible for CBERA but not GSP) are considered.

Table 9.6. U.S. Imports of Products Eligible for CBERA but not GSP from Beneficiary Caribbean Basin Countries, 1983-89 (value in millions of dollars; share in percent)

Beneficiary Developing Country	Value of U.S. Imports Eligible for CBERA But Not GSP			CBERA-Eligible not GSP Share of Total Imports Subject to Duty			Share of CBERA-Elig not GSP Entered CBERA Duty-Free			Share of CBERA-Elig not GSP Entered under Items 806 and 807		
	1983	1986	1989	1983	1986	1989	1983	1986	1989	1983	1986	1989
Central America, total	268.9	246.7	339.1	35.5	29.5	24.4	0.0	64.3	66.4	45.5	22.8	25.1
Belize	0.1	11.3	12.0	0.7	27.0	35.2	0.0	85.4	99.2	0.0	0.0	0.0
Costa Rica	78.5	125.8	167.4	42.6	35.0	25.0	0.0	67.0	63.0	49.8	23.7	30.2
El Salvador	82.1	28.1	31.4	60.6	36.8	27.8	0.0	34.2	54.0	91.1	54.2	41.0
Guatemala	34.0	26.2	71.7	20.4	17.0	22.8	0.0	77.2	89.2	0.0	6.0	2.5
Honduras	63.8	44.0	50.5	44.7	35.9	28.4	0.0	69.2	53.7	10.5	15.6	35.6
Panama	10.3	11.3	6.0	9.5	13.9	7.5	0.0	38.3	0.0	17.9	23.4	28.7
Central Caribbean, total	120.5	198.9	202.4	14.5	16.1	10.4	0.0	43.1	40.9	66.1	44.4	52.9
Dominican Republic	69.6	109.6	126.6	14.6	15.5	9.6	0.0	44.8	41.8	59.2	41.1	51.3
Haiti	39.4	38.8	33.5	13.5	11.3	9.6	0.0	14.8	15.2	80.7	70.2	77.7
Jamaica	11.5	50.5	44.3	18.0	27.2	14.6	0.0	61.0	57.9	57.8	31.8	38.7
Oil Refining Cntry, total	19.3	24.4	18.8	0.4	1.6	1.4	0.0	72.1	78.9	1.9	0.1	0.0
Bahamas	1.1	5.0	3.1	0.1	1.2	0.8	0.0	39.2	92.3	0.0	0.0	0.0
Netherlands Antilles-Aruba	2.5	0.3	0.2	0.1	0.1	0.1	0.0	33.7	22.4	13.1	6.8	0.0
Trinidad and Tobago	15.7	19.1	15.5	1.3	2.7	2.4	0.0	81.4	77.0	0.3	0.0	0.0

(Continued)

Beneficiary Developing Country	Value of U.S. Imports Eligible for CBERA But Not GSP			CBERA-Eligible not GSP Share of Total Imports Subject to Duty			Share of CBERA-Elig not GSP Entered CBERA Duty-Free			Share of CBERA-Elig not GSP Entered under Items 806 and 807		
	1983	1986	1989	1983	1986	1989	1983	1986	1989	1983	1986	1989
Eastern Caribbean, total	141.3	43.8	24.2	60.6	38.6	21.5	0.0	22.6	49.9	97.5	55.7	40.2
Antigua and Barbuda	5.3	4.6	0.0	64.2	44.9	0.1	0.0	2.1	60.9	99.5	85.3	0.0
Barbados	127.1	20.1	11.3	64.5	49.5	33.5	0.0	29.7	68.9	98.3	67.4	25.4
British Virgin Islands	0.5	0.3	0.2	85.5	5.3	42.6	0.0	5.4	61.5	0.6	0.0	0.0
Dominica	0.0	4.7	0.1	0.9	37.6	1.7	0.0	3.8	13.5	0.0	0.5	19.7
Grenada	0.0	0.0	0.3	41.7	2.1	4.4	0.0	0.0	31.0	0.0	0.0	7.8
Montserrat	0.0	0.3	0.3	0.4	10.7	12.1	0.0	0.0	3.3	33.3	66.0	93.4
St. Kitts-Nevis-Anguilla	3.4	7.3	4.2	19.3	33.6	20.3	0.0	21.7	36.8	100.0	47.9	62.2
St. Lucia	3.5	6.3	7.8	78.0	58.9	32.5	0.0	31.7	32.4	76.5	51.2	50.8
St. Vincent & Grenadines	1.5	0.2	0.1	38.8	2.2	1.1	0.0	26.8	0.0	100.0	6.5	13.0
CBERA Beneficiary total	549.9	513.8	586.6	8.0	13.8	12.1	0.0	52.9	57.3	61.9	32.9	34.6

Source: Compiled from official statistics of the U.S. Department of Commerce.

Table 9.7. 3-Digit SIC-Based Import Categories with CBERA Duty-Free Value of One Million Dollars or More in 1989 (millions of dollars)

		All Imports from CBERA Nations		CBERA Duty-Free	
	SIC-Based Product Group	1986	1989	1986	1989
*201	Meat & meat packing products	129.3	140.1	121.1	132.6
*206	Sugar & confectionery products	248.8	224.7	126.7	124.5
*203	Prepared fruits & vegetables	46.2	564.7	26.6	89.9
*367	Electronic components	163.5	89.8	33.5	57.4
*286	Industrial organic chemicals	55.3	103.1	29.4	47.5
*013	Field crops, except cash grains	37.4	54.6	25.3	41.1
*394	Toys & sporting goods	62.8	55.1	26.2	40.9
391	Jewelry & silverware	81.6	133.2	15.8	39.4
364	Electric lighting & wiring equip	32.7	72.4	19.3	35.0
*016	Vegetables & melons	43.8	47.5	34.0	34.9
384	Medical & dental instruments	5.7	70.4	1.4	31.9
*212	Cigars & cheroots	35.7	35.9	21.8	29.0
*208	Beverages & flavoring extracts	22.9	23.3	13.9	15.3
*331	Blast furnace, steel products	50.6	78.4	23.7	13.7
313	Leather cut to shapes for shoes	38.8	102.5	4.0	13.7
*018	Horticultural specialties	31.1	31.5	3.8	13.0
091	Fish, fresh, chilled, or frozen	200.0	214.4	6.5	12.9
237	Fur wearing apparel	7.7	13.7	1.6	12.8
259	Furniture & fixtures, nspf	12.7	30.3	1.3	10.1
267	Converted paper & paperboard product	–	41.3	–	9.8
*017	Fresh fruits	1,393.0	453.5	21.2	8.1
362	Electrical industrial apparatus	5.8	13.4	3.8	7.7
308	Miscellaneous plastics products	–	17.7	–	6.8
361	Electric distribution equipment	4.8	28.0	2.1	6.3
349	Fabricated metal products, nspf	9.9	11.5	1.3	5.4

(Continued)

4. FACTORS AFFECTING BDC PERFORMANCE

From the evidence presented above, it is clear that both the GSP and CBERA programs have expanded trade opportunities and resulted in substantial duty-free exports from many of the larger and more-advanced developing countries in the Caribbean and Central America. For many of

		All Imports from CBERA Nations		CBERA Duty-Free	
	SIC-Based Product Group	1986	1989	1986	1989
335	Nonferrous rolled, drawn products	17.4	22.3	2.6	5.1
204	Grain mill products	4.5	9.2	0.3	5.0
*283	Drugs	142.6	285.1	50.8	4.6
369	Electrical machinery & equipment	13.0	17.7	1.3	4.5
249	Miscellaneous wood products	15.9	16.5	6.8	4.1
284	Soaps, detergents, & cleaners	6.8	7.6	2.6	3.1
243	Millwork, plywood, veneer	4.7	9.4	1.3	3.0
399	Miscellaneous manufactures	6.8	11.5	0.1	2.8
207	Food preparations	0.8	3.4	0.6	2.6
*366	Communications equipment, nspf	7.7	4.9	2.6	2.5
373	Yachts or pleasure boats	2.4	2.6	1.1	2.2
396	Costume jewelry & notions	3.9	5.0	1.0	2.2
209	Miscellaneous food preparations	28.5	16.8	5.2	2.2
356	General industrial machinery & equip	3.5	3.9	(z)	2.1
239	Fabricated textile articles	20.3	26.3	(z)	2.0
306	Druggist & medical supplies	–	4.6	–	1.8
238	Wearing apparel & accessories	21.5	60.4	0.1	1.5
371	Motor vehicles, & parts, nspf	4.9	1.6	0.6	1.0
	Total, selected items	3,025.1	3,159.7	641.2	891.8
	Total, all items	5,775.6	6,637.8	656.9	905.8

Note: "(z)" denotes less than $50 thousand and "–" denotes not available. "*" indicates items with more than $1 million in CBERA duty-free entries in items eligible or possibly eligible for CBERA, but not eligible for duty-free entry under GSP. Data include U.S. imports from the CBERA beneficiary countries in 1989 (i.e., data for Panama are excluded and data for Guyana are included).

Source: U.S. Department of Labor, Trade and Employment Effects of the Caribbean Basin Economic Recovery Act, *Sixth Annual Report to the Congress, 1990 (Washington, D.C.: Bureau of International Labor Affairs), pp. 77-78.*

the smaller and less-advanced developing economies in the region, the dollar value of their GSP and CBERA duty-free exports to the United States has been much lower, but their utilization of these programs (duty-free as a percent of eligible) has been, in some cases, quite high. In other cases, a number of Caribbean countries seldom utilize these trade preferences. Two major reasons for this, as already noted, may be the commodity structure of the programs and the strong competition from other more-developed BDCs.[25] While these reasons may explain a significant portion of the problem, they cannot fully account for the inability of the less-advanced LDCs in the Caribbean to increase the dollar value of duty-free trade under the GSP or the CBERA programs. Other factors may account for this, namely, the structure of BDC domestic production and trade, existing economic and trade policies, investment climate, infrastructure, and resource endowment. Further, the presence of transnational corporations and the declining margin of preference accorded by the preference programs play a role.

4.1. Structure of Production and Trade

The utilization of the GSP and CBERA programs depends, in large part, on the stage of development of a beneficiary's economy. Overall, the economic growth experience of the major BDCs in the Caribbean and the Americas has been far below the overall developing country norm, based on data from the World Bank.[26] During the 1980-85 period, most developing economies in the Caribbean and the Americas experienced negative rates of growth in GDP and in manufacturing output. Given these negative growth rates, it should not be surprising that these economies would lag behind other BDCs in their utilization of available U.S. trade preference programs.

Overall, manufacturing has been the most dynamic sector in the majority of all LDCs; however, this has not been generally the case for the beneficiary economies in the Caribbean and the Americas. In contrast to the MADCs in Asia, over 25 percent of manufacturing value-added in the economies of the Caribbean and the Americas is concentrated in the food sector and less than 25 percent is devoted to textiles, clothing, and machinery.

Overall, the structure of manufacturing in the Caribbean and the American BDCs is sufficiently different from the MADC economies in Asia to help explain a major source of divergence in the level of utilization of benefits under the U.S. GSP program. This conclusion is reinforced by noting that even in Mexico (the major beneficiary of the GSP program within the Americas), manufacturing value-added is concentrated in the food and other (residual manufactures) sectors.

For all LDCs as a group, machinery, transport equipment, and other manufactures represent just over 40 percent of their total exports. For the LDCs in the Americas and the Caribbean, these commodities represent, in general, 20 to 30 percent of their total exports. While primary-product, fuel, and mineral exports have declined in importance in most of these economies since 1965, they still represent key export categories. Further-more, while some would argue that non-tariff barriers in textiles and ap-parel are limiting the exports of the less-advanced BDCs in the Americas, these products represent on average less than 5 percent of these countries' manufactured exports (e.g., Mexico). However, textile and apparel products now account for 25 percent of all Central American and Carib-bean country exports to the United States. For some of these countries (e.g., Haiti and St. Lucia), textile and apparel items account for over half of the country's total exports to the United States, and for some others (e.g., Belize, Costa Rica, Dominica, Dominican Republic, and Jamaica) over a third of their total exports to the United States.

In 1985, approximately 65 percent of all LDC imports consisted of machinery, transport, and other manufactures, while primary products, fuels, and food represented the balance. In the case of the Americas and the Caribbean economies, an even larger share of their imports consisted of machinery, transport equipment, and other manufactures. However, given the current debt position of many of these economies, they greatly reduced the level of their imports and this has resulted in a more limited supply of inputs needed to support export-oriented industries.

Overall, exports from the less-advanced BDCs in the Americas have been concentrated in a narrower set of products than the average for all LDCs. From this, one might conclude that any advantages afforded by the preference margins contained in the GSP and CBERA programs have not substantially improved the trade or development prospects for many of the developing countries in the Americas and the Caribbean. Furthermore, in many cases, their domestic infrastructure and structure of domestic output and trade have not been sufficiently developed and diversified to attract foreign direct investment, which has flowed to the more-advanced LDCs in Asia.

4.2. Labor Force

A key to the development of a competitive export production base and the ability to attract investment is the availability of an industrial labor force. The proportion of the labor force in industry remains below 25 percent in most LDCs in the Americas and the Caribbean. The exceptions are Brazil, Mexico, and Argentina. For the other economies in the region, their labor force is engaged primarily in agriculture or services (nontradeables such as domestic commerce, tourism, banking, etc.). For the very-small economies where tourism is a major employer, utilization of the current GSP and CBERA programs is negligible.

While there is an abundant supply of workers in most LDCs in the Caribbean and the Americas, the quality and skill level varies widely. Some of the larger Caribbean countries (e.g., Haiti and the Dominican Republic) have an ample supply of unskilled, low-wage workers. However, in some of the Eastern Caribbean countries (e.g., Barbados, Trinidad, and St. Lucia), the supply of such workers is much more limited and wage levels tend to be higher than in other countries in the region.

4.3. Existing Economic and Trade Policies

For years, many of the developing economies in the Caribbean and Latin America have pursued a policy of import substitution by protecting and subsidizing inefficient local industry, sometimes through state ownership or through high external tariff and non-tariff barriers. In many cases, there has been little desire by local producers to export, especially given their captive and protected domestic market. Restrictive policies on ownership and access to market were often not conducive to foreign investors. In cases where foreign investment occurred, there were restrictions on repatriation of earnings and availability of foreign exchange.

Faced with high rates of inflation and accumulation of substantial debt burden, alternative policies were sought out. The success of the East Asian NICs and pressures from international lending institutions for structural adjustment have led some countries in the Caribbean to a new orientation toward a policy of export promotion. In particular, industrial free zones or export processing zones have sprung up all around the Caribbean. By opening their markets to foreign competition and privatizing and deregulating protected local industries, more competitive industries may develop with a capability to export.

4.4. Investment Climate

Many factors affect the investment climate in a country: political and social stability, local controls (licenses and customs procedures) on imports and exports, foreign exchange controls, availability of hard currency for imports, size of the domestic market, efficiency of bureaucracies, availability of managerial talent or skilled technical labor, supply of unskilled low-wage labor for agriculture and assembly operations, presence of supporting or supplier industries, infrastructure, and transportation costs (and timeliness) in getting final products to market.

Faced with difficulties in many of these areas, most LDCs have developed a variety of incentives to help attract investments: tax holidays and other fiscal incentives, increased access to foreign exchange, development of industrial estates or export processing zones with subsidized utilities and services, and improved telecommunications and transportation networks.

With an increasing number of LDCs pursuing an export-led growth strategy, the competition is very keen for the available investment funds. This competition will require LDCs to exploit their comparative advantage — whether it be specialization, relative labor costs, or productivity — to remain competitive vis-a-vis other countries in their region and at their stage of development.

4.5. Role of Transnational Corporations

With the globalization of production and national markets, transnational corporations are playing a much more important role in the development of LDCs, especially through provision of employment, labor force training, and technology transfer.

Given the relatively small size of the local markets in the Caribbean, most multinational investment has been geared toward facilities for the export of goods and services and not production to serve the local market. These export platforms for multinational corporations have sprung up all around the Caribbean. Most are located in industrial estates or export processing zones and enjoy special benefits and privileges.[27] However, for the most part, these industrial enclaves remain isolated from domestic markets and are primarily engaged in light assembly operations. In most cases, a multinational's investment is not deeply rooted, and the technology transferred is minimal. Employment and foreign exchange earnings are the main benefits provided to the host country. In some cases, subcontracting arrangements can provide marketing experience for local entrepreneurs. In most cases, it is unlikely that there will be an evolution from light manufacturing and assembly into more substantial and deeply rooted manufacturing with more locally-sourced value-added.

4.6. Declining Margin of Preference

As the result of agreements made in the Tokyo Round of multilateral trade negotiations (MTN) which concluded in 1975, reductions in U.S. (and other GATT signatories) MFN tariff rates have been phased-in; the final staged rates will take effect in 1992. As a result, the margin of preference for eligible products under CBERA and GSP has declined since the inception of these programs. By 1992, the average MFN rate of U.S. duty will be about 5 percent; however, rates of duty for certain sensitive products (e.g., footwear, textiles, and apparel — the main products excluded from U.S. preferential tariff programs) will remain substantially higher (see Table 9.8). In the past, MTN duty reductions have preserved the structure of U.S. tariffs.[28] The conclusion of the most recent Uruguay Round of MTN may trigger a new round of tariff reductions over the next 10 years.

The United States has negotiated a free trade agreement (FTA) with Canada and is in the process of negotiating one with Mexico. Under broad FTAs that are more comprehensive than other special unilateral trade preference programs, the potential exists for trade diversion, especially vis-a-vis Mexico and the Caribbean Basin. Mexico, with its 2,000 mile land border with the United States and greater proximity to the U.S. market, developed transportation links to the United States, and large low-wage labor pool, may be more attractive to investors than alternative sites in the Caribbean.

4.7. Program Modification

Special and differential treatment of BDCs under the U.S. GSP program is scheduled to expire in 1993, while the CBERA will continue to extend duty-free benefits indefinitely to the beneficiary nations in the Caribbean Basin. Undoubtedly, pressures will mount to amend and modify these programs. The strongest argument for developed countries to modify their existing trade preference programs for LDCs is the "crowding out" phenomenon (i.e., lack of room for new entrants). Factor market advantages, combined with trade preferences, provide the more-advanced developing countries with a sufficient differential incentive to attract foreign investment away from the less-advanced developing countries. Without such investment, the less-advanced economies will be less able to move up the industrialization path. Continued differential treatment of most-advanced developing country[29] exports by the United States will perpetuate differential investment incentives to these countries that will continue to generate a crowding out effect.

The establishment of an efficient world-competitive manufacturing base and the rapid growth of manufactured exports from the most-advanced LDCs has been both a confirmation of the positive impact of export-led growth and a cause of concern for many in the Americas and the Caribbean because, as new suppliers, they may face increased difficulties in entering established markets. In retrospect, it appears that the paradigm offered by Singer, Prebisch, and others (and granted official respectability by UN-CTAD) that condemned the LDCs to a vicious circle of poverty was incorrect. Yet, it is this rapid industrialization and associated expansion in

Table 9.8. 3-Digit SIC-Based Import Categories with Dutiable Value and Ad Valorem Tariff Rates (AVEs) of 10 Percent or More, Based on 1985 U.S. Imports from the World and 1992 Rates of Duty (value in millions of dollars)

SIC-Based Product Group	Customs Value	Duty	AVE
302 Footwear, rubber or plastic	260.3	102.3	39.3
223 Wool broad woven fabrics	178.8	51.2	28.6
211 Cigarettes	11.7	3.0	26.0
232 M-B shirts, trousers, nightwear	3,661.4	907.8	24.8
234 W-G-I undergarments & nightwear	425.7	86.6	20.4
325 Structural clay products	279.8	52.6	18.8
236 Outerwear, of textile materials	4,049.1	753.1	18.6
233 W-G-I dresses, blouses, coats	4,247.0	769.2	18.1
203 Prepared fruits, vegetables, soups	1,738.3	301.0	17.3
316 Luggage of leather, textile materials	523.7	85.6	16.4
231 M-B suits & coats	732.8	117.2	16.0
225 Knit fabrics & hosiery	81.2	13.0	16.0
222 Silk & MMF broad woven fabrics	977.1	138.8	14.2
315 Gloves, leather	147.3	20.9	14.2
317 Handbags	956.1	124.9	13.1
322 Glass & glassware	709.3	81.0	11.4
286 Industrial organic chemicals	3,642.8	411.8	11.3
016 Vegetables & melons	592.8	61.9	10.4
990 Miscellaneous commodities, nspf	2,158.9	218.6	10.1
Total	25,374.3	4,300.5	16.9

Note: These 19 3-digit SIC-based import groups accounted for 10.3 percent of the total value of U.S. imports from the world in 1985 that would be subject to duty in 1992. The calculated duties for these 19 groups represent 34.4 percent of total duties at 1992 rates. MFN duty free imports have been excluded. Duty was calculated on the 1985 customs value for each 5-digit TSUS item, using 1992 AVEs based on tariff rates from the U.S. International Trade Commission. SIC-based codes for each 5-digit TSUS item are based on the Census Bureau SIC code assignment for the 7-digit TSUSA item within a 5-digit TSUS with the largest value of U.S. imports from the world in 1985.

Source: Compiled from official statistics of the U.S. Department of Commerce and the U.S. International Trade Commission.

manufactured exports — as well as the formation of regional trading blocs — that are now creating new concerns in the less-advanced developing countries. As Isaiah Frank has noted,[30] the most important issue facing the developing countries is to maintain "access to markets." Thus, the success of most-advanced developing country exports places in jeopardy the effectiveness of differential treatment of the less-advanced developing countries in the Americas and the Caribbean.

In the current environment of more and more negotiated market access, it is in the interest of the less-advanced economies of the Americas and the Caribbean to encourage the gradual elimination of preferences for the most-advanced LDCs. Indeed, the United States has moved in that direction by graduating the four East Asian NICs from GSP beneficiary status beginning in 1989.

Given the small size of most Caribbean economies and the low volume of trade now transacted by any single Caribbean country (especially those in the Eastern Caribbean), there will be a need to strengthen existing regional associations (e.g., Central American Common Market (CACM) and Caribbean Common Market (CARICOM)) and explore new associations. Consolidation of economic power and market size will help attract more investments and increase international bargaining power. Also, there will be a need in the near future for the more-advanced LDCs in the Caribbean Basin and the Americas (e.g., Mexico, Brazil, and Venezuela) to integrate the less-advanced economies of the region into their own development programs.

In many cases, basic domestic infrastructure may be missing in many countries in the Americas and the Caribbean. For GSP and CBERA to be effective development programs, they must be viewed as long-term programs with marginal effects in the short-run. With tariff levels already quite low in most industrial countries, the price effects of tariff preferences for developing country exports will be less important. Instead, LDCs will need to focus on internal reforms which will help attract new foreign investment. Continued differential treatment of most-advanced developing country exports by the United States will maintain differential investment incentives to those countries that will perpetuate a crowding out effect. However, graduating the most-advanced BDCs in the relevant competing sectors would create additional marginal benefits to attract investment into the Americas.

5. CONCLUSIONS

The decade of the 1980s was not particularly kind to the economies of Latin American and the Caribbean. Citizens in most countries in that region faced a sharp decline in real income and a high rate of inflation as their countries suffered under an increasing international debt burden. With many of the economies in the region dependent on the export of primary agricultural and mineral products, fluctuating world commodities prices (and uncertainty of future markets) have led to reduced export earnings.

However, the decade of the 1990s may offer some new opportunities which may help alleviate some of the problems of the past decade.

5.1. Elements of Change

Domestic Economic Reform

In response to the bleak circumstances of the 1980s, many countries in Latin American and the Caribbean have begun to adopt economic and structural reforms, often at the prodding of international lending institutions. By opening their economies to international trade and competition (e.g., removing protection for non-competitive industries and shedding parastatals), it is hoped that new investment will be attracted which will provide the industrial infrastructure needed for export-led growth.

LADCs have faced severe competition from the MADCs. Recently, the United States has begun to graduate some of the more advanced LDCs from its GSP program. However, the graduation of the (low-cost and efficient) more-advanced developing countries from trade preference programs — usually on the basis of demonstrated world competitiveness — is likely to place even more pressures on the other LDC to become more competitive.

Global Change

Just as economic reforms were slowly beginning to be instituted in Latin America and the Caribbean, other more dramatic changes in Europe were unfolding even more quickly and capturing the world's attention: the European Communities' formation of a single market, the unification of Germany and the emergence of nascent democracies in Eastern Europe and the former Soviet Union. These events have captured the attention of the world — in short, the birth of new competition for the LDCs in Latin America and the Caribbean (that is, the diversion of U.S. interest and attention from Latin America to "bigger" events in Europe).

However, the easing of relations between the United States and the former Soviet Union is likely to have overtones for the Americas. U.S. policies toward countries in Latin America and the Caribbean are likely to have more economic (rather than political or ideological) imperatives. Especially in Central America, former military aid can now be transformed into truly economic assistance.

5.2. New Initiatives for the Hemisphere

The 1990s may be marked by a period of more inward reflection — with a trend toward the formation, building, and strengthening of regional economic alliances. The United States has announced several.

Andean Trade Initiative

In September 1990, the U.S. government proposed the Andean Trade Preference Act (ATPA) which is a trade preference program (a mirror image of the CBERA) directed toward Bolivia, Colombia, Ecuador, and Peru for a 10-year period. With the U.S. Congress's cooperation, the Act became law in December 1991.

Enterprise for the Americas Initiative

On June 27, 1990, President Bush announced his Enterprise for the Americas, a proposal that would eventually lead to the economic integration of the Americas. The initiative is three-pronged: debt relief linked to economic reform; trade liberalization through free trade agreements with Latin American and Caribbean countries; and promotion of investment through a $300 million investment fund (with equal contributions from the United States, Japan, and the European Community) to be administered by the Inter-American Development Bank in conjunction with an investment loan program. The objective of the initiative is to encourage movement from the statist policies of the past toward ones based on free markets; an incentive to reinforce free market reform. U.S. economic interaction with the region is to be focused on a new economic partnership — based on trade, not aid. Due to budget limitations as well as global forces that are moving in that direction, direct economic aid (except for the most needy) is unlikely to grow.

It is unlikely that the United States will negotiate a free trade agreement with each nation in the hemisphere. The United States has already negotiated a free trade agreement with its neighbor to the north and has indicated that it intends to do the same with its neighbor to the south, its two largest trading partners in the hemisphere. Likely candidates for accession to this North American free trade arrangement might include some of the following regional associations of countries in Latin America and the Caribbean: Chile; Argentina, Brazil, Uruguay, and Paraguay (ABUP); Andean Group; Central American Common Market (CACM); Caribbean Common Market (CARICOM). Thus, U.S.-Caribbean economic relations in the 1990s may portend a period of reform, integration, and mutual partnership, and not one of aid or other unilateral benefits given by the United States. Rather, the opportunity exists for a deepening of bilateral and multilateral relations within the hemisphere.

NOTES

1. Joseph Pelzman is a professor of economics at the George Washington University, Washington, D.C.; Gregory K. Schoepfle is an international economist with the Bureau of International Labor Affairs, U.S. Department of Labor, Washington, D.C. The authors would like to thank Jorge F. Pérez-López for extremely helpful comments. The views expressed here are solely those of the authors and do not necessarily reflect the positions or opinions of their respective institutions.

2. The ASEAN (Association of Southeast Asian Nations) consist of Indonesia, Malaysia, the Philippines, Singapore, Thailand, and Brunei Darussalam.

3. For example, Brazil, Mexico, Hong Kong, South Korea, Singapore, Taiwan, and Yugoslavia.

4. Under the Harmonized Tariff Schedule (HTS) introduced on January 1, 1989. Approximately 3,000 products were eligible under the Tariff Schedules of the United States (TSUS), the U.S. tariff classification that was in place before 1989.

5. The absolute dollar limit is indexed each year (by indexing the original limit by the ratio of current GNP to 1974 GNP) to account for inflation and real growth in the U.S. economy after 1974. With a base value limit of $25.0 million for 1974, the dollar-value competitive-need limit was $26.6 million for 1976; by 1989, it had risen to $88.9 million. Section 1111 of the Trade Agreements Act of 1979 amended the statute to waive the 50 percent competitive-need rule for categories in which U.S. imports were valued at less than a 1979 base level of $1 million (this was increased to $5 million when the GSP program was renewed in 1984). This absolute *de minimis* level is also adjusted annually to reflect the growth in GNP. For 1989, the *de minimis* level was set at $10.4 million. The 1984 GSP renewal also waived the competitive-need limitations for least developed developing countries (LDDCs).

6. These circumstances permit the United States to negotiate with beneficiary countries to obtain important benefits in return for use of waiver authority. In deciding on waiver, the President must consider, among other things, assurances of equitable and reasonable market-access and protection of intellectual property rights. For example, as the result of the General GSP Review (announced in April 1987), the President reduced the competitive-need limits on 290 products involving nine countries (Argentina, Brazil, Colombia, Hong Kong, South Korea, Mexico, Singapore, Taiwan, and Yugoslavia). Of the $3.8 billion competitive-need exclusions announced, $2.5 billion were the result of the reduced competitive-need limits.

7. Under this provision, four beneficiary countries (Bahrain, Bermuda, Brunei Darussalam, and Nauru) were dropped from beneficiary status in July 1988.

8. A 1987/88 review of Thailand's practices with regard to intellectual property rights led to a denial in 1989 of competitive-need waivers and the application of lower competitive-need limits on some GSP-eligible products imported from Thailand.

9. As of 1990, six countries (Central African Republic, Chile, Myanmar [Burma], Nicaragua, Paraguay, and Romania) had either been removed or suspended from GSP beneficiary status on the basis of their practices as they relate to internationally recognized worker rights.

10. It is worth noting that these four criteria also were reflected in the CBERA enacted in 1983 as well as in the overall goals and objectives of the United States in the most recent round (known as the Uruguay Round) of multilateral trade negotiation held under the auspices of the GATT.

11. By the end of 1983, the President had designated the following 20 countries as beneficiaries to start receiving benefits on January 1, 1984: Antigua and Barbuda, Barbados, Belize, British Virgin Islands, Costa Rica, Dominica, Dominican Republic, El Salvador, Grenada, Guatemala, Haiti, Honduras, Jamaica, Montserrat, Netherlands Antilles, Panama (removed in 1988, reinstated in 1990), St. Kitts-Nevis, St. Lucia, St. Vincent and the Grenadines, and Trinidad and Tobago. Subsequently, the President designated the following as beneficiary countries: Bahamas (1985), Aruba (1986), Guyana (1988), and Nicaragua (1990). Countries eligible for CBERA, but never designated, include: Anguilla, Cayman Islands, Suriname, and Turks and Caicos Islands.

12. For example, filing of a food production plan, quota limits are not filled, or, for textile and apparel items, items which are handloom folklore products or which fail to meet certain fiber-type content by weight or value specifications in the CBERA product exclusions.

13. When the President designated Nicaragua as a CBERA beneficiary in November 1990, he did not grant GSP beneficiary status to that country, however.

14. The rules-of-origin under GSP differ from those under the CBERA in two ways: (1) GSP rules stipulate that 35 percent of the value-added must be made in the beneficiary country (or a recognized association of countries), while the CBERA rules provide that the 35 percent value-added requirement can be met through processes that take place in several CBERA beneficiary countries; (2) in computing the 35 percent value-added under the CBERA, up to 15 percent may be accounted for by U.S.-made components with the remaining 20 percent by CBERA beneficiary countries; the value of items produced in Puerto Rico and the U.S. Virgin Islands may be counted as CBERA nations' value.

15. However, section 1909 of the Omnibus Trade and Competitiveness Act of 1988 (PL 100-418) broadens the President's authority to withdraw, suspend, or limit the application of duty-free entry for a particular product from a CBERA beneficiary (in lieu of removing the country entirely from the program) if that country is no longer in compliance with the program's criteria for designation. Panama (designated in 1983, removed in 1988, and reinstated in 1990) is the only beneficiary country that lost all CBERA benefits for failing to be in compliance with one of the criteria for designation (narcotics cooperation certification criteria).

16. Item 9802.00.8010 of the Harmonized Tariff Schedule (formerly under special provisions contained in item 807.00 of the TSUS, also known as 807A or "super 807") which assesses U.S. import duties only on the foreign value-added in the assembly of U.S. sourced materials and components. By the end of 1990, Costa Rica, the Dominican Republic, Guatemala, Haiti, Jamaica, and Trinidad and Tobago had entered into bilateral textile agreements with the United States under the program.

17. In 1986, a lower bound estimate of the dollar value of the GSP program — equal to the value of the tariff foregone — was $728 million. This duty equivalent is equal to actual 1986 GSP-free trade evaluated at the 1992 duty rates. Thus, it is an understatement of the duties that would have been paid in 1986 if these goods were not subject to GSP duty-free entry. Further, it represents an understatement of the value of the GSP program since a nominal duty rate was used instead of the effective rate.

18. The top-five beneficiaries in 1986 (Taiwan, Korea, Hong Kong, Mexico, and Brazil) were the same as those in 1976. In 1986, they accounted for slightly less than 80 percent of GSP-eligible imports and 70 percent of GSP-free imports (up from slightly less than 60 percent in 1976).

19. GSP beneficiary countries supplied a substantial portion of total U.S. imports of forestry products (SIC 08); however, most of these products were eligible for most-favored-nation (MFN) duty-free entry.

20. It has been estimated that if CBERA program had been introduced in 1983 with no product exclusions and CBERA beneficiaries were unable to expand their capacity or shift their exports from other markets, then CBERA exporters would have benefitted to the tune of $75.3 million — just 4.5 percent of the total U.S. foreign aid to the region. If the CBERA product exclusions are taken into account and only those goods eligible for CBERA but not GSP are considered and it were assumed that CBERA countries were able to expand their exports, then the estimated benefits would range from $25 million to $267 million, with the upper-bound representing about a 3 percent increase in CBERA exports. See J. Pelzman and G.K. Schoepfle, "The Impact of the Caribbean Economic Recovery Act on Caribbean Nations' Exports and Development," *Economic Development and Cultural Change*, 36:4 (July 1988), pp. 753-796.

21. Costa Rica was the only Central American beneficiary to show a sustained increase in CBERA-eligible exports over this period.

22. Some smaller Eastern Caribbean beneficiaries (St. Lucia and St. Vincent and the Grenadines) have posted significant increases in the value of CBERA-eligible exports to the United States over this period.

23. Now items 9802.0060 and 9802.0080 in the new Harmonized Tariff Schedule of the United States which was introduced on January 1, 1989.

24. The actual overall share for the Oil Refining beneficiaries in 1989 was 19 percent. This regional average was skewed by the fact that certain analgesics and aromatic drugs were temporarily accorded duty free entry in 1989. Previously, substantial amounts of these CBERA-eligible items from the Bahamas had entered duty-free under GSP.

25. This is not to say that there is unshakable proof that eliminating this competition would result in trade diversion in favor of these less-advanced LDCs. With the graduation of the four East Asian NICs from the GSP program in 1989, it is still too early to tell whether this change will matter.

26. The following discussion is based on data from the World Bank, *World Development Report, 1987* (New York: Oxford University Press), 1987.

27. For a description of export processing zones in Mexico and the Caribbean, see G.K. Schoepfle and J. F. Pérez-López, "Export Assembly Operations in Mexico and the Caribbean," *Journal of Interamerican Studies and World Affairs*, 31:4 (Winter 1989), pp. 131-161.

28. Based on 1985 U.S. imports from the world and final (1992) MTN staged tariff rates, 30 3-digit SIC-based import groups (each with duties of $100 million or more) accounted for about 75 percent of the value of imports subject to duty and 75 percent of the calculated duty with an average tariff rate of 5.1 percent. Ten 3-digit SIC-based import groups (each with import value of $5 billion or more) accounted for slightly over half (56.8 percent) of the value of U.S. imports subject to duty and about a third (32.7 percent) of total duties with an average tariff rate of 2.9 percent.

29. By most-advanced developing countries, we refer to the NICs.

30. Isaiah Frank, "The 'Graduation' Issue in Trade Policy Toward LDCs," *World Bank Staff Working Paper*, No. 334 (1979), Washington, D.C.

PART 5

Conclusions

CHAPTER 10

Challenges and Opportunities for Trade in the Caribbean

Irma T. de Alonso

The findings of this publication have substantiated three salient characteristics of the multilateral trade patterns found in the Caribbean. First, a
large portion of Caribbean trade occurs with those developed countries of
North America and Europe, in which the Caribbean simultaneously exports
mainly primary goods, while importing manufactured goods. Second,
intra-regional trade is very limited, as it is with other developing nations,
particularly those in Latin America. Third, trade has been dependent on
incentives offered by the advanced economies outside the region.

The Caribbean faces new challenges and competition with the many
transformations occurring in the world economy. The year 1992 will bring
structural changes within the European Economic Community. The
preferential treatment under the Lomé Convention, offered by the United
Kingdom to its previous colonies in the Caribbean will most probably be
subject to revision. Concurrently, challenges will arise for the region via
the Enterprise for the Americas Initiative, presented by the Bush Administration, whereas other nations of the Western Hemisphere, Mexico in
particular, will be competing with the Caribbean to enter the free market
agreement between the U.S. and Canada. Additional contention is being
created by the countries of the Pacific Rim, with Japan as the main trade
partner in that area.

What can Caribbean countries formulate to answer the current dynamics
faced in relation to emerging world trade patterns? With developed
countries facing a sluggish domestic markets, part of the trade with the
Caribbean islands can be expected to decline. What can be predicted? As
expressed by Lewis,[1] and as recommended by a study prepared for the
Caribbean Community Secretariat with support from the Commonwealth
Secretariat,[2] there is a need for South-South trade. The Caribbean nations

would have to integrate their markets with other developing countries, which are more advanced and are in close proximity to exploit opportunities of common borders. This has to be accomplished without abandoning current trade agreements with developed nations.

In order to expand trade the Caribbean economies must join together and seek solutions to the following problems: better means of transportation, financing of investment, improvement of marketing techniques, cooperative efforts in matter of trade and finance, aid coordination, development of human resources, technology transfer, and the development of a system of payments, just to name a few. The recommendations to be presented in these concluding remarks can be divided into aspects dealing with the modifications of incentives, the need to preserve the agricultural sector in the Caribbean countries, the expansion of intra-regional and extra-regional markets, improvements of the infrastructure, and the importance of trade of services, among other general considerations.

1. MODIFICATION OF INCENTIVES

The incentives offered by the developed countries to the Caribbean region are varied, but they can be classified according to the offering of tariffs exemptions, as is in the case of the Caribbean Basin Initiative, and/or as guaranteed markets, as is in the case of sugar quotas.

Caribbean trade with the U.S. and Europe has been basically in sugar, guaranteed by the establishment of quotas. Because of protectionist measures, among other factors, the sugar quotas have been significantly reduced. Given the importance of sugar in the context of these economies, the decline in sugar production brought to the Caribbean countries the troublesome situation of increased unemployment, with corresponding decreases in output and income, not to mention the further deterioration of their fiscal and trade deficits. Supply side shocks, aggravated by the volatile oil price, added to the high inflationary pressures.

As an alternative to sugar, and in order to advance their industrialization efforts, the policy strategy of import substitution was replaced by that of export promotion. Non-traditional exports were explored, and in this respect export processing zones (EPZs) were instituted. This shift brought the difficulty that, contrary to the case of sugar production, the local value added by the EPZs has been cut significantly.

The main challenge faced by the Caribbean countries is that of increasing local value added. This could be accomplished by modifying the backward and forward linkages of the assembly operations. The EPZs are governed by special local laws, which restricts their operation so as to limit linkages to other sectors of the economy. It would be advisable that the EPZs statutes be modified allowing for some output to be made available in the local markets, thereby creating forward linkages affecting direct and indirect employment. It is equally advantageous that additional changes be made in these laws requiring the use of local inputs, in addition to the labor services of the primarily low-skill female labor force.

There is likewise the opportunity of some technological transfer related to these EPZs. Up to now these operations have been characterized as "footloose" or "suitcase" operations, in the sense that they are not related to the economic activity of the host country. A case in point is that of Haiti as compared to the Dominican Republic. The findings reveal that Haiti has been able to attain and increase its local value added because their assembly operations are characterized by a significant management component of local origin, local capital, and the use of some local inputs. However, in the case of the Dominican Republic, the activities of the EPZs are so unconnected to the local economy, that they are not even included in the national accounts [Chapter 4].

On the part of the developed nations, it will be necessary to modify the existing incentives. Most of the manufacturing activity, e.g. apparel products, taking place in the Caribbean is excluded from duty free entry. It has been concluded as well that most of the benefits are received by the most advanced countries in the region. If the benefits are going to be extensive to the less advanced nations, some changes are needed either in terms of excluding to some extent the more advanced countries from the preferential treatment or in providing incentives to change the production structure of the less advanced countries. Investment opportunities, in addition to trade opportunities, are needed by the developing countries in order for them to be able to compete favorably with the more advanced countries.

2. AGRICULTURE

The structural transformation with respect to manufacturing activities has been accomplished at the expense of a decline in agriculture. However, this should not be so. The weather, soil, and geographical characteristics are excellent for the diversification of agricultural production to include the growing and harvesting of other crops, in addition to the traditional sugar, coffee, and banana crops. There are other non-traditional crops, in particular, winter vegetables which can be available all year around. Various fruits, like citrus, and melons, offer excellent cultivation opportunities. Another possibility could be the growing of flowers and production of seeds. In this aspect the countries of Central America have instituted this strategy and have been successful in promoting and intensifying their exports[3] and it is certain that the same degree of success could be witnessed in the Caribbean islands.

Agricultural production offers increased possibilities to advance the manufacturing base in the form of food processing. In addition to sugar, there are many other viable alternatives, for example, canned or frozen processed fruits and vegetables. The Caribbean should not overlook these important sources of foreign exchange.

Another industry to be stressed is that of fishing. It is perplexing that the Caribbean islands have not capitalized on the bounty of the Caribbean and this important opportunity given that they are totally surrounded by water. In this endeavor, the countries of Central America have not been dormant and have successfully created a fishing industry, comprised of fish and shellfish, that are processed in a fresh and/or frozen form.[4]

3. INTRA-REGIONAL TRADE

The third recommendation deals with the expansion of local markets. Integration has been attempted by CARICOM, but this experience has been limited to the English-speaking Caribbean. Recently it has been expanded to grant observer status to other countries in the region, for instance the Dominican Republic and Haiti. Caribbean integration can be expanded to include many other Caribbean nations as well. In this way local markets can be enlarged and economies of scale can be achieved.

Lewis[5] identified that trade among developing countries could concentrate on five major groups: food, fertilizers, steel, cement, and machinery. Concurrently, he mentioned the heavy trade dependence of manufacturing goods. In his opinion some progress could be expedited with trade of the first four groups, and of some light manufacturing, while machinery would require a much longer time horizon to be fulfilled. It is possible for the Caribbean nations to trade some of the above mentioned items among themselves, but some coordination is required. Food can conceivably be produced by all, but if they want to trade there have to be some degree of diversification and complementarity. Fertilizers and cement cannot be produced by all, but it can be produced by some areas with a comparative advantage so that trade can be stimulated. Steel, and machinery can be best left for trade with other developed nations, but there is certainly some room for trade of light manufacturing intra-regionally.

A case in point is the trade experience of Puerto Rico with the rest of the Caribbean which was found to contribute to more employment creation than with trade with the U.S., given the different nature of goods traded [Chapter 6]. Their trade with the U.S. is characterized by high technological items, while trade with other Caribbean islands is in light manufacturing, requiring more local labor. This experience can also be imitated by other nations in the region. Equally, twin-plant operation open new dimensions to trade intra-regionally, providing at the same time the additional advantage to some goods to enter the U.S. market without tariff restrictions.

Mainland Latin America represents another important market for the Caribbean countries. In particular, it is imperative that trade with the other countries in the Caribbean Basin be intensified. Mexico, Colombia, and Venezuela, the closest neighbors in Latin America, represent excellent markets for selected Caribbean products. Mexico and Venezuela have some trade cooperation in terms of providing oil in concessionary terms to some Caribbean Basin countries, through the San Jose Agreement. Studies have identified various products which can be mutually advantageous in terms of trade between these nations and the other Caribbean Basin countries.[6] Similarly, Mexico, Colombia, and Venezuela have provided for some partial trade agreements to offer duty free entry to some lists of products specified. It is astonishing that when trade between them is studied, no appreciable correspondence is attained between the list of products included in the agreements and the goods actually traded.[7]

Planning and policy coordination are needed if indeed intra-regional trade is going to be broadened. The coordination of economic plans will have to rely on the nations which have had some experience already with economic integration, and the institution of the Caribbean Community Secretariat and the Caribbean Development Bank could certainly assume leading roles in this endeavor.

4. INFRASTRUCTURE

In the fourth place, trade depends on better transportation and communication facilities. There is no other way to exchange goods and services without the necessary infrastructure. In this aspect some countries have some comparative advantage compared to others. The case of Puerto Rico can be mentioned because it has the best facilities in the area, and naturally has become the hub for transportation and communications in the Caribbean. Infrastructure improvements have also occurred in the other more advanced nations, but it is a major problem for the least developed nations of the region. More trade will certainly require that shipping services be provided. As found in the studies dealing with variables determining trade, distance is a main obstacle to trade [Chapter 3].

The Government Development Bank of Puerto Rico has an important role to play in this attempt. The GDB has investment funds, the so-called

936 funds, that can be made readily available to finance projects in the region, whether they are for public infrastructure or for specific private manufacturing projects. Other sources of investment funds will be forthcoming with the establishment of the integrated Caribbean Stock Exchange.

5. SERVICES

Not all countries will equally share the benefits from trading in the light manufacturing goods sector, but space is left open for other types of trade in the service sector. The Caribbean is an ideal location for tourism to flourish, so that those countries that are unable to successfully trade manufacturing goods, may as well capitalize on tourism. This sector can be made locally oriented, so that it does not further deteriorate the balance of payments if all goods to be used in the sector have to be imported, as is happening at present.

Other services that can be provided include information systems, like data processing, and other telecommunication facilities. Other possibilities include financial services, such as banking and insurance. Some countries have already delved into these activities and have found them rewarding. This same experience can be received by others and applied to the remaining countries.

6. OTHER CONSIDERATIONS

In order to continue trading with the developed nations and to face the new challenges offered by the new trading arrangements, all of the countries in the Caribbean will have to improve their marketing techniques. This aspect is not limited only to packaging and labeling. In order to trade effectively with other nations, attention should be given to standards and quality controls as well. Special consideration will have to be given to the reliability of exports and to on time deliveries.

Other aspects that cannot be overlooked are the political stability in the region, and the control of input costs of operations so as to compete favorably with other possible locations in the world. Similarly, the development of human resources is a basic element in the attainment of these goals.

It has been found both that not all the nations in the Caribbean are receiving the benefits of the incentives being offered, while at the same time, the incentives offered have not been sufficient to promote investment

and trade in the region. The expectation is that the recommendations offered here will contribute to the solution of these two problems.

NOTES

1. W. Arthur Lewis, "The Slowing Down of the Engine of Growth," *American Economic Review*, Vol. 70, No. 4 (1980), pp. 555-564.
2. C. Bourne, et al., *Caribbean Development to the Year 2000* (London and Georgetown: Commonwealth Secretariat and Caribbean Community Secretariat, June 1988).
3. Eva Paus (editor), *Struggle Against Dependence: Export Growth in Central America and the Caribbean* (Boulder and London: Westview Press, 1988).
4. Eva Paus (editor), *Struggle Against Dependence, op. cit.*
5. W. Arthur Lewis, "The Slowing Down of the Engine of Growth," *op. cit.*
6. Rafael Trejos, Manuel Gollás, et al., *Industrialization and Trade in the Caribbean Basin* (San Jose, Costa Rica: IESCARIBE, 1988).
7. Manuel Gollás, "El Comercio de Mexico con Centro America" (mimeo), El Colegio de Mexico, 1989.

Index